MW00903429

Steadfast Charity

Sisters of Charity of Saint Vincent de Paul, Halifax
1972–2002

Mary Sweeney, SC
Martha Westwater, SC
Elaine Nolan, SC
Julia Heslin, SC

Photographs are from the Sisters of Charity, Halifax Congregational Archives.

Archway Publishing books may be ordered through booksellers or by contacting:

Archway Publishing
1663 Liberty Drive
Bloomington, IN 47403
www.archwaypublishing.com
1 (888) 242-5904

ISBN: 978-1-4808-7049-9 (sc)
ISBN: 978-1-4808-7050-5 (hc)
ISBN: 978-1-4808-7048-2 (e)

Library of Congress Control Number: 2018912688

Print information available on the last page.

Archway Publishing rev. date: 01/07/2019

This book is dedicated,

with love and gratitude,

to the Sisters of Charity

who have gone before us.

Contents

Introduction

Heidi MacDonald

Founded more than 160 years ago, the Sisters of Charity, Halifax[1] developed into the largest English-speaking congregation of women religious (commonly called nuns) in Canada. In 2008, Canada's Minister of the Environment recognized the congregation's accomplishments, including educating close to a million students in five countries, by designating the Order's foundation a National Historic Event.

The Sisters of Charity, New York were invited to Halifax in 1849 to staff the city's only parochial school, St. Mary's. At the time, Halifax was a century old and had a population of less than 20,000; approximately 40 percent were Catholic, most of them Irish. Four sisters arrived in May of that year, and by the end of their first year in Halifax enrolment at St. Mary's had doubled from 200 to 400, and the convent had become home to 20 orphaned children. A few years later, a new and independent congregation, the Sisters of Charity, Halifax, was formed as an offshoot of the New York group. This rapid growth foretold the pattern of the

[1] The organization's canonical name is the Sisters of Charity of Saint Vincent de Paul and its legal name is simply the Sisters of Charity. For clarity, the independent congregation formed in Halifax is frequently referred to as Sisters of Charity, Halifax to distinguish it from the several other branches of Elizabeth Seton's daughters referred to as Sisters of Charity throughout the US and Canada. In this manuscript, "Sister of Charity, Halifax" and "Sisters of Charity" both refer to the congregation formed in Halifax, although the sisters live and work throughout North America and the world.

next century: the period from 1849 until the 1960s was characterized by increasing membership, drawn primarily from Canada and the United States, and insatiable requests from all over the world for the sisters' skills as teachers, healthcare professionals, and social welfare workers. Each decade brought challenges and accomplishments which have been well documented in Sister Maura Power's book, *The Sisters of Charity, Halifax* (1956) and Sister Mary Olga McKenna's book, *Charity Alive: Sisters of Charity of Saint Vincent de Paul, Halifax, 1950–1980* (1998).

This book, the third in a series on the comprehensive history of the Sisters of Charity, Halifax, begins in the midst of the congregation's most complex decade, 1965–1975. In 1962, Pope John XXIII had called the Second Vatican Council (known as Vatican II) to address the Church's role in the modern world. Secularism, feminism, consumerism, the sexual revolution, state-controlled social welfare policies, and a more influential media were pressing upon the Church as never before. During the Council's meetings over the next three years, one word was used repeatedly: *aggiornamento*, meaning bringing up to date. This mandate acknowledged that aspects of the Church had fallen behind the times. Reactions to Vatican II varied according to the listener's perspective; some Catholics believed it had gone too far in accommodating the modern world, while others thought it did not go far enough.

The majority of the Sisters of Charity, Halifax were among the North American women religious who welcomed the chance to realign their goals with the needs of the modern world and to enjoy more central roles in their Church. The sisters followed closely the news of the Council and the release of each of the sixteen Council documents. Although most of the Vatican II documents related to the sisters in some way, *Perfectae Caritatis* [Decree on the Adaptation and Renewal of Religious Life], promulgated on October 28, 1965, affected them most directly, shaking the congregation and many individual sisters to the very core.

Perfectae Caritatis applied the themes of Vatican II to religious institutes by requiring them to "return to the sources of all Christian life and to the original spirit of the institutes and their adaptation to the changed conditions of our time" (Art. 2). For the Sisters of Charity, this meant a serious re-examination of the charism of their founder, Elizabeth Seton, and a thorough reconsideration of the needs of contemporary society. Just as significant for the future of the congregation as *Perfectae Caritatis*' call for renewal, however, was its mandate that *all* sisters were to contribute to this transformation. In the words of the decree, "An effective renewal and adaptation demands the cooperation of all the members of the institute" (Art. 4). A subsequent document, *Ecclesiae Sanctae* [Governing of the Holy Church], explained that adaptation and renewal should be negotiated within each congregation's general chapters, the wide-ranging meetings of elected delegates that were usually held every four to six years (depending on the individual congregation's constitutions) to address congregational governance and mission. While in session, a general chapter represents the highest authority of the congregation, superseding mother superiors and other members of the governing councils.

The special general chapters of renewal that *Perfectae Caritatis* set in motion were far more comprehensive than the regular general chapters. In the fall of 1966, each member of the Sisters of Charity received an "Explorations for Renewal" package, consisting of 10 pages of worksheets exploring potential agenda items for the upcoming chapter, leading questions, and a space for suggestions.[2] Five salient topics raised in the initial questionnaire, all inspired by *Perfectae Caritatis*, became the focus of discussion and research: spiritual life; government and organization; community life; apostolic works; and formation. Instructions for the follow-up questionnaire in 1967 stated, "Each sister is encouraged to express herself as fully as she wishes. The more spontaneous and complete the answer, the more helpful it will be ... [As] our aim is to ascertain the sisters' uninhibited thinking, the questionnaires need not be signed." During the extensive consultation and preparation for the Chapter of Renewal, the 1,629 members of the Sisters of Charity submitted over 1,000 proposals, the majority from provincial and regional chapters, but

---

[2] Unpublished materials discussed in this chapter are from the Sisters of Charity, Halifax Congregational Archives or from interviews conducted by the author. For more detailed information see the Selected Sources.

200 from individual sisters. An election was held for the 54 Chapter delegates who, along with 12 ex-officio members, would begin the long process of considering and voting on these proposals. They met for eight to ten hours a day, six days a week, for six weeks in the summers of both 1967 and 1968.

The Vatican greatly underestimated the impact of *Perfectae Caritatis* and even seemed surprised that North American and Western European congregations, long overdue for real discussions about religious life, not only accepted the request for renewal but often exceeded its intentions. As the Sisters of Charity (and hundreds of other congregations of women religious) engaged in the renewal process, studying such Vatican II documents as *Lumen Gentium* [Dogmatic Constitution of the Church] and *Gaudium et Spes* [Pastoral Constitution on the Church in the Modern World] and participating in dozens of self-reflective workshops, many were energized to deeply question how to best live their vocations for the remainder of their lives.

Before Vatican II, sisters received their assignments annually. The needs of the Church and the congregation were the foremost consideration, and the individual sisters were not usually consulted. After Vatican II, sisters were asked to reflect on their own gifts and consider how best to contribute. With so many sisters in such a large congregation simultaneously engaged in profound self-reflection, community life became invigorating but chaotic. Sisters of Charity historian Mary Olga McKenna explained this turning point as follows, "Until the time of Vatican II, women religious were perhaps the most dependable but at the same time most expendable resources in the Church on the congregational, parochial, diocesan, and even global level" (1998, 194). After Vatican II, many sisters asserted their views with a frankness for which most people outside the convent – and some inside it – were unprepared.

The Sisters of Charity, Halifax may have been more disoriented by these changes than many other North American congregations because the congregational leader in the 12 years leading up to Vatican II, Mother Stella Maria Reiser, had discouraged any changes to religious life and was loyal to the horarium and the concept of obedience. In contrast, Mother Maria Gertrude (Sister Irene Farmer), who was elected in 1962 at the age of 49, strove for the openness that Vatican II encouraged. Thus, the differences in the congregation "before" and "after" Vatican II were particularly stark for the Sisters of Charity, Halifax, adding extra tumult to the already unstable times.

The consequences of Vatican II are ultimately what this book is about. Some changes happened almost immediately: habits were modified, the horarium became much less rigid, and far fewer permissions were required. Sisters were encouraged to be more autonomous, and some started living outside convents in smaller groups; apostolates shifted away from schools and hospitals to work more directly with the poor and in ways that fit with individual sister's interests. Between the Chapter of Renewal in 1968 and the Twelfth General Chapter in 1972, 138 Sisters sought dispensations from their vows for a variety of reasons, including the belief they could live out their vocations equally well outside the congregation. The impact of Vatican II initiatives and related changes are still being felt today, more than 50 years after the Council's closing session. The congregation continues to recalibrate its mission to meet the needs of the modern world in the spirit of the congregation's founder and tradition, and within the capacity of the collective talents and skills of the sisters, who are now much diminished in numbers and affected by a rising average age.

The falling membership, common to all active North American congregations of women religious in the post-Vatican II era, has been extremely difficult for the Sisters of Charity to negotiate. For at least two decades following Vatican II, most sisters hoped that entrance rates would rise again, if not to the high level of the 1950s, at least to a level that would sustain some demographic balance in the congregation. By 1985, however, the flow of entrants had dried up, with a few notable exceptions. The increasing number of departures (laicizations) and the deaths of elderly members also contributed to falling membership. In the decade following Vatican II, the Sisters of Charity lost one quarter of their members and the total number of women religious in Canada fell 32 percent from approximately 66,000 to 44,127. This was a proportionally greater decline than in the United States, where the number of women religious dropped from 179,954 to 139,225, or 25 percent over the same period. Some congregations lost over 50 percent of their members and only a small minority were unscathed. These numbers have continued to decline, so that there are fewer than 300 Sisters of Charity, Halifax, today. There are only 13,000 women religious in Canada, and 48,500 in the United States.

If there was one symbol of the challenges facing the Sisters of Charity after Vatican II, it was the Mount Saint Vincent Motherhouse. Built in the mid-1950s to replace their former Motherhouse, which had burned to the ground a few years earlier, the new Motherhouse was built at a cost of $7 million and, at 350,000 square feet, was at the time the largest building east of Montreal. It was an imposing structure built at the top of a three-level landscaped hill, part of the original farm purchased in Rockingham in the late nineteenth century. By the end of September 1959, five main groups were settled into the new Mount Saint Vincent Motherhouse: the postulants and novices in the back southwest and northwest corners; the academy students in the front northeast part of the building; the generalate (congregational headquarters) in the front southeast corner; the retired sisters in the back of the Motherhouse below the novitiate and postulate; and the newly professed sisters who shared the back of the buildings with the retired sisters. Eighty percent of the 900 available beds were occupied soon after the building opened and full capacity was expected within a couple of years.

No one could have anticipated that within a decade of its opening, the stately Motherhouse would become an albatross. With the more than 90 percent drop in entrance rates and the departure of several hundred members in the decade after Vatican II, not only did the congregation not need such a large Motherhouse, it also did not have the revenue to maintain its $1-million-a-year expenses, including its $32,000 annual tax assessment. By the early 1970s, the congregation owed close to $15 million on various buildings in the United States and Canada. No buyer could be found for the Motherhouse, and several other buildings were sold well below their value. Concurrently, the congregation's main income source – the collective salaries of public school teachers – decreased 25 percent. A financial crisis was averted through a rigorous program of divestment of properties, including several convents and two hospitals. Again, the Sisters of Charity were far from alone among North American women's religious congregations; many had instigated optimistic building projects in the 1950s.

After attempts in the 1970s and early 1980s to sell the building – first to an extended care corporation and then to Mount Saint Vincent University – half of the basement level was rented out as university residence accommodation. This is where my story intersects with the Sisters of Charity. As a first-year Mount Saint Vincent University student in 1986, I was assigned Room 1256 in Vincent Hall.

I applied to Mount Saint Vincent from my rural PEI home because of its well-known Public Relations program, but after taking a couple of history courses, my passion for Canadian women's history was too strong to consider anything else. And as a young Protestant woman, I could not have been more intrigued by living in a Motherhouse. I discussed with my residence friends from the "1200 Wing" what it might have been like to be a sister. For some reason, we had it in our heads that there was a morgue at the end of our wing, on the other side of the door that said "Sisters Only." This was never confirmed. I regret that I did not speak with a sister that year, even though I lived in a functioning Motherhouse. I did, however, think often about how different life in the building would have been when most of the rooms were filled with postulants, novices, and Academy students, instead of first-year undergraduates like me. I wondered what the future would hold for the Motherhouse. I enjoyed walking up and down the hill to and from the Seton Academic Centre where I attended classes, the library in Evaristus, and the cafeteria in Rosaria. The image of the Motherhouse as I climbed the hill is forever etched in my mind, at least three versions of it, one for each of the three seasons I lived on campus.

In my last year, I participated in an oral history project on the Sisters of Charity. A history professor, whose own research was on a completely different time period and topic, applied for a student summer grant in order to preserve some oral histories for the use of future researchers. This was 1990, two years after the congregation had transferred ownership of Mount Saint Vincent University to its Board of Governors, for a cost of one dollar. My professor had heard that the congregation was trying to sell the Motherhouse and we both became obsessed with the need to preserve the Sisters' history. As outsiders, we did not realize that the Sisters of Charity had done a good job of preserving their own history. We must have come across as rather overwrought neophytes. Our research project did not go smoothly. We were not able to get the sisters' permission to do as many interviews as we wanted and the congregation would not let us choose the sisters we interviewed. Nevertheless, this project was a real turning point in my life. Interviewing those 10 sisters in the summer of 1990 was the start of a career studying women religious. As the congregation got to know me over the years, I have been granted broad access to their records and have become attached to individual sisters as well as to the whole congregation. Thirty years after I first walked up the hill to the Motherhouse, I cannot believe it is not there anymore. In some way, the chapters of this book are what is left of the Motherhouse.

One cannot understand the history of Halifax, the history of education, the history of health care, the history of feminism, or the history of religion without understanding the history of women religious, especially before the relatively recent development of the social welfare state. This book brings the history of the Halifax Sisters of Charity up to 2002. The book's chapters are organized around "Chapters" – that is a joke that only sisters will get – usually from the perspective of the congregational leadership teams, which were led by Sisters Katherine O'Toole (1972–1980), Paule Cantin (1980–1988), Louise Bray (1988–1996), and Mary Louise Brink (1996–2002). It should be noted that the decade preceding the period covered in this book (1962–1972), when Sister Irene Farmer was the congregation's leader, is covered in a biography by Sister Geraldine Anthony, *Rebel, Reformer, Religious Extraordinaire: The Life of Sister Irene Farmer* (1997).

As previously discussed, Vatican II (1962–1965) was a turning point for the Catholic Church and for the Sisters of Charity. This book is largely about the consequences of that important Council, as individual sisters and the congregation as a whole re-evaluated its mission in light of the needs of the modern world, the spirit of its founder, and its resources. Each chapter gives an overview of world events during the period it covers, and places the congregation's history within this larger history.

Chapter 1, by Sister Mary Sweeney, "Maintaining Essentials, Adapting to Change: 1972–1980," describes the era of Sister Katherine O'Toole's leadership. O'Toole, who was only 37 when she became congregational leader, embraced the Vatican II renewal begun under Sister Irene Farmer's leadership. This renewal was challenging, given the congregation's state of flux, which was caused in part by the ongoing departure of sisters as well as by many sisters discerning a change in their apostolate (work). Still, the congregation moved forward in several key areas, including establishing long-term Latin American missions, completing a draft of their revised Constitutions, and withdrawing from most of their large institutions in favor of working more directly with the economically poor.

Chapter 2, by Sister Martha Westwater, "Moving Toward the People of God, Accepting the Call to Continuing Conversion: 1980–1988," examines the congregation during Sister Paule Cantin's leadership, a time that continued to experience the aftershocks of the "explosive" changes of Vatican II. Westwater emphasizes the congregation's deepening appreciation of feminism and globalization, as well as the challenge of embracing solidarity with the economically poor. She marks the relinquishing of Mount Saint Vincent University to a lay Board of Governors as a particularly tough moment for the congregation.

Chapter 3, by Sister Elaine Nolan, "Refounding the Congregation, Creating New Structures: 1988–1996," considers the "reforming" of the congregation. Whereas previous leaders encouraged adaptation and change, Sister Louise Bray and others on the leadership team called for the congregation to "start anew." They did this using the latest sociological and psychological approaches, including the theology of "The New Story," and this reform lead to the dissolving of the eight provinces. Many Vatican II-related initiatives also continued, including concerted lobbying of large companies on social justice issues and a focus on more care and consideration for the elderly and retired members of the congregation.

Chapter 4, by Sisters Julia Heslin and Mary Sweeney, "Living into New Structures, Moving into a New Millennium: 1996–2002," examines the intensification of several issues raised in earlier chapters. It highlights the impact of the dissolution of the provinces on regional governance and identity, the closing of Mother Berchmans Centre, which resulted in the relocation of 68 infirm Sisters to Parkstone (a lay-administered complex for assisted living with full nursing care), and the reorganization of social justice lobbying through the Global Concerns Resource Team.

July 2018 is the 50th anniversary of the opening of the Halifax Sisters of Charity's Chapter of Renewal. Members of the congregation approached the special Chapter with a variety of emotions, including excitement, hope, trepidation, and dread. No one could have imagined how much of a turning point the two-year Chapter would be in the history of the congregation. The Vatican II decree *Perfectae Caritatis* prompted a thorough reassessment of the congregation's purpose and individual sister's vocations. The reassessment is still playing out today, as the congregation regularly recalibrates its mission to serve the needs of the modern world within the spirit of the Gospel, the intentions of their founder, and the realities of their resources. It is this ongoing dynamism that defines the history of the Sisters of Charity, Halifax.

Selected Sources

Primary Documents

Paul VI. 21 November 1964. *Lumen Gentium* [Dogmatic Constitution of the Church]. Vatican.va Available at http://www.vatican.va/holy_father/paul_vi/motu_proprio/documents/hf_p-vi_motu-proprio_19660806_ecclesiae-sanctae_en.html.

Paul VI. 28 October 1965. *Perfectae Caritatis* [Decree on the Adaptation and Renewal of Religious Life]. Vatican.va. Available at http://www.vatican.va/archive/hist_councils/ii_vatican_council/documents/vat-ii_decree_19651028_perfectae-caritatis_en.html.

Paul VI. 7 December 1965. *Gaudium et Spes* [Pastoral Constitution on the Church in the Modern World]. Vatican.va. Available at http://www.vatican.va/archive/hist_councils/ii_vatican_council/documents/vat-ii_const_19651207_gaudium-et-spes_en.html.

Paul VI. 6 August 1966. *Ecclesiae Sanctae II*, #1– 3, Vatican.va Available at http://www.vatican.va/holy_father/paul_vi/motu_proprio/documents/hf_p-vi_motu-proprio_19660806_ecclesiae-sanctae_en.html.

Sisters of Charity, Halifax, Congregational Archives. Office of the Congregational Secretary Fonds, 11th General Chapter, 1967–1969.

Published Sources

Anthony, Geraldine. 1997. *Rebel, Reformer, Religious Extraordinaire: The Life of Sister Irene Farmer, SC.* Calgary, AB: University of Calgary Press.

Canadian Religious Conference (CRC). 1973–2004. *Statistics on Religious Life in Canada,* [Reports published biennially from 1973-2004]. Ottawa: Canadian Religious Conference.

Canadian Religion Conference (CRC) (15 February 2010) *CRC Statistics 2009 - 2010* [Press Release] Available at: http://www.crc-canada.org/wp-content/uploads/2017/02/Stats-2011-2012.pdf

Ebaugh, Helen Rose Fuchs. 1993. *Women in the Vanishing Cloister: Organizational Decline in Catholic Religious Orders*. New Brunswick: Rutgers University Press.

Lessard, Marc A., and Jean Paul Montminy. 1965. *The Census of Religious Sisters in Canada*. Ottawa: Canadian Religious Conference.

McKenna, Mary Olga. 1998. *Charity Alive: Sisters of Charity of Saint Vincent de Paul, Halifax, 1950-1980*. Lanham, MD: University Press of America.

Power, Maura. 1956. *The Sisters of Charity, Halifax*. Toronto: Ryerson.

1

Maintaining Essentials, Adapting to Change: 1972–1980

Mary Sweeney, SC

The history of the Congregation of the Sisters of Charity between 1972 and 1980 is a microcosm of the changes that were afoot in the Church, in Canadian and American societies, and in the world. Widespread liberation movements and developments in science, psychology, philosophy, and theology fuelled the desire for change – but even when they are welcomed, these upheavals rarely come without a loss of equilibrium, some confusion, and efforts to seek the old balance.

In both Canada and the United States, 1972 to 1980 was a tumultuous period. The liberation movements that began in the 1960s were growing and maturing, and new leadership was taking societies in new directions. Canada's growing sense of identity manifested itself in 1976 with the creation of the Canadian Radio-Television and Telecommunications Commission (CRTC). The goal of this commission, which strengthened and broadened an earlier law known as CanCon, was to promote Canadian culture by creating a quota for Canadian content and participation in broadcasts. The Commission gave Canadians the opportunity to spotlight and to support their own artists and their own national voice. While this national identity was being solidified, biculturalism was being discussed at the provincial level. In May of 1974, New Brunswick became the first province to declare both French and English as official languages; in July of that same year, Quebec made French the official language of government and business, a stand that was strengthened in 1977 with the Charter of the French Language. In 1976, Quebec's Parti Quebecois urged a radical move toward separatism. At the same time, the First Nations were beginning to assert their claims and identity.

The United States, after years of painful national division over its involvement in Vietnam, was moving toward withdrawal and slow healing. The presidential campaign of 1972 had sown the seeds of Watergate, deceit, and a prolonged investigation of the White House. The resulting resignation of Richard Nixon in 1974 gave evidence of the power of the law and the stability of the federal government. Efforts to improve race relations, which had generated both positive change as well as resentment, continued to stir up tensions in some areas. When a judge in Boston determined that schools should be racially balanced, students were bused in from other neighbourhoods. The enmity that some felt was captured by cameras and served as a reminder of just how far the ideal of racial equality was from the reality.

The impact of international economic realities registered in both countries. When OPEC raised prices on crude oil, people in the United States and some parts of Canada were forced to deal with gas shortages and long lines at the pumps. At the same time, the growing environmental movement made people in both countries aware of the damage that our energy consumption was doing to the planet. Internationally, oil became central to economic and political crises, and political tensions were growing in the Middle East, with some groups choosing kidnapping as a means of gaining publicity, meaning innocent citizens of other nations were held captive for years. Within the Western Hemisphere, Central America was experiencing great suffering, as *campesinos*, held in place for centuries by wealthy landowners, began to call for justice, oftentimes with the help of the Church.

Scientific advances moved ahead at an amazing speed. New

knowledge, new products, and new procedures flourished and made new choices possible. In 1978, the world was awed by the birth of Baby Louise, the first test-tube baby. Developing technology made communication easier, and people grew accustomed to making long distance phone calls. Increased mobility facilitated economic migration and led, in too many instances, to the erosion of close-knit communities that had held people together for generations.

Society was changing. The divorce rate rose, new lifestyles demanded acceptance, and issues such as feminism, abortion, and sexual identity reshaped traditional views. The Church was no stranger to these changes and the related tensions. Under the leadership of Pope John XXIII, the Second Vatican Council (1962–1965) had convened bishops from around the world in an attempt to reorient the thinking and practices of the church on a host of issues and to create an atmosphere that encouraged engagement with the world in positive ways. When Pope Paul VI closed the Council in 1965, the bishops had produced sixteen documents that would have an extraordinary impact on every facet of church life.

By the 1970s, most Roman Catholic parishes had incorporated into their liturgies the changes mandated by Vatican II. The increasingly active role of the laity, while less immediately obvious, was also having a profound effect. As more laity recognized the universal call to holiness, it seemed to elevate them, reminding them that they had a rightful place in the Church, gifts to offer, and a right to be treated with dignity. Active participation, not only in the liturgy but in a host of different arenas, created energy and a sense of ownership. While such changes inevitably lead to some tensions, many parishes moved into the 1970s with renewed enthusiasm.

Within the papacy itself, there was extraordinary change as three men occupied the Chair of Peter in rapid succession, Following the death of Pope Paul VI on August 6, 1978, Pope John Paul I was elected. His sudden death on September 28, thirty-three days after his election that same year, shocked the world. He was succeeded by Pope John Paul II.

Like the rest of society religious life was also undergoing enormous change. The following pages attempt to show how the changes shaped one organization: the Sisters of Charity, Halifax. Between 1972 and 1980, the chapter mandates, the developments within community living, and the influences of a changing society challenged this congregation of women to adapt to changing times while retaining what was essential to their lives as vowed religious.

With the hindsight of nearly four decades and the experience of eight general chapters, the Sisters of Charity of the early twenty-first century may look back on the Twelfth General Chapter of 1972 and marvel at the ways that congregational governance has changed. The Chapter of 1972 opened on July 16 and concluded on August 17. The theme was "Call – Response – Mission," concepts that invited reflection, trust, and generosity. Of the fifty-seven delegates, forty-four were elected from the congregation's seven provinces, and thirteen were *ex officio* members who were either members of the general council or provincial superiors. The delegates met at Mount Saint Vincent Motherhouse, and the enactments, written in parliamentary language, flowed from seven committees: Spirit and Mission; Authority and Government; Commitment, Membership, Extended Community; Finance; Retirement; Formation; and Foreign Missions.

On the second ballot, Sister Katherine O'Toole, formerly Sister Vincent Francis, was elected General Superior. In keeping with the version of Canon Law that was then in effect, the local ordinary, Archbishop James M. Hayes of Halifax, confirmed the election. Following Sister Katherine's election, Sister Rita C. MacDonald was elected First Assistant and Vicar General; Sister Elizabeth Hayes, Second Assistant and Canadian liaison; and Sister Francis Fay, Third Assistant and American liaison. In addition, Sister Anne Casey was appointed Secretary General, and Sister Mary Moore was reappointed Treasurer General. All of these women would give generously of their gifts and energy for the life of the congregation. Years later, Sister Elizabeth Hayes recalled a private conversation with Sister Katherine that followed the election. Recognizing how much would be asked of her in her new position, and how it would transform her, Sister Katherine spoke of the line from the Fourth Eucharistic Prayer: "that we might live no longer for ourselves but for him." In her eight years as superior general, Katherine, assisted by the members of the Governing Board, would face the responsibilities of administration and the challenges of renewal.

These five women, along with the provincial superiors, constituted the Governing Board, the body responsible for overseeing the ongoing life of the congregation between chapters. In keeping with the mandate of the Chapter of Renewal of 1968–1969, the new administration was elected for four years. The term of office for the provincials was six years, but not all provincials were elected the same year. As a result, over one term of a general administration, a province might be represented by two provincials. During Katherine's first four-year term, the sisters who served as provincials were Doris McKenna succeeded by Genevieve Morrissey for Antigonish; Grace Bransfield succeeded by Catherine Hanlon for Boston; Frances McLaughlin succeeded by Paule Cantin for the Central Province; Elizabeth Adams succeeded by Maria F. Sutherland for the Halifax Province; Mary McGowan for the New York Province; Bernadette McCarvill succeeded by Mary Therese Gavin for the Western Province; and for the Vice Provinces, Margaret Guthrie from Halifax and Louise Kenney from Wellesley. These last two positions were created at the Twelfth Chapter.

Although many religious congregations of women consider their chapters of renewal in the late 1960s as pivotal moments of change, several of the most significant developments had begun in the 1950s. First, Pope Pius XII had stressed the need to improve the professional competence of religious. In the United States, the Holy See convoked the first national congress of major superiors in 1952. It was clear that sisters needed better preparation to carry on their missions effectively. In 1954, the Canadian Religious Conference met for the first time to address the need for updating religious life.

Of major significance to religious throughout North America was the founding of the Sister Formation Conference in 1957, which brought together leading women religious to discuss these issues and to make recommendations. As a result of this collaboration, religious congregations began updating their approaches to the formation of new members, specifically by recommending that religious complete bachelor's degrees before being missioned. More broadly, they began to consider how their daily practices might be altered to incorporate new insights from psychology and theology and the changing demands of life in the twentieth century.

The Church-wide movement for renewal took root in Vatican II. Moved by the desire for a "New Pentecost," Pope John XXIII opened the first session in 1962, and Pope Paul VI drew the final session to a close in 1965. While the Council Fathers stressed "the call of the whole Church to holiness,"[3] (*Lumen Gentium* [Dogmatic Constitution on the Church], Chapt. V), they also recognized the unique call to vowed religious life. For vowed religious, the most significant document was *Perfectae Caritatis* [Decree on the Adaptation and Renewal of Religious Life], promulgated in October 1965.

The first constitution of the Council, *Sacrosanctum Concilium* [Constitution on the Sacred Liturgy], promulgated in December 1963, called for the renewal of the liturgy and asked for "full, conscious, and active participation" (#14). With hindsight, these words might also have been applied to the way members of religious congregations would be asked to renew their lives. Something new was being born in the Church and in religious life, and it would ask for great dedication, great energy, and great trust.

By 1972, a number of changes had already taken place in the congregation of the Sisters of Charity, Halifax. These changes had a significant impact on the life of each individual sister. The idea of a universal schedule for the entire congregation was long gone; the form, time, and place for personal prayer and spiritual reading were no longer mandated. Gone, too, were the long dinner tables where sisters sat according to priority. Furthermore, sisters were receiving a modest monthly stipend to spend as they wished on a variety of incidentals,

---

[3] All of the quotations from Vatican documents in this chapter are from *The Documents of Vatican II*. Walter M. Abbott, SJ Editor. New York: Guild Press, 1966.

such as personal items, telephone calls, and entertainment. Most visibly perhaps, the religious habit, which had gone through various adaptations and experiments, had become optional in 1969. Although this issue would present itself in proposals at subsequent chapters, in general the congregation had made peace with the decision, as it had with the return to baptismal and family names.

The congratulatory messages Katherine received when she was elected reveal something of the tenor of the times. Several well-wishers wrote of her job as challenging and difficult. And while one expressed enthusiasm for the "wonderful days of the Church,"[4] another expressed hope that Katherine would lead the congregation to a return to its past. Fully aware of the challenges and tensions, Katherine wrote to the sisters on August 22, "It is only with faith in God and confidence in the power of the Spirit that one could accept such a responsibility." She looked to the congregation to be "strengthened by a realization of unity of purpose and cooperation toward common goals on the part of all sisters."

As the newly elected Superior General, Sister Katherine O'Toole (1935–1990) brought an array of personal and intellectual gifts to her role. After her profession in 1955, the native of Dorchester, Massachusetts had served as a teacher and principal in schools in the New York Province. In 1969, in preparation for assuming responsibility for formation in the congregation, she pursued studies at Duquesne University's Institute of Formative Spirituality in Pittsburgh. Her thesis, "Personal Responsibility in Human Living and Its Implications for Religious Life," provided her with the opportunity to explore themes and issues that were of significant value in those days of renewal. At the age of 37, Katherine (often called Katie by her family and friends) was the youngest Superior General ever elected in the congregation and represented a new perspective; but as a woman of vibrant faith and deep love for the congregation, she also stood for enduring values. Although she came to the office with little congregation-wide experience, her Duquesne experience proved to be

[4] Unpublished materials discussed in this chapter are from the Sisters of Charity, Halifax Congregational Archives or from interviews conducted by the author. For more detailed information see the Selected Sources.

excellent preparation and, coupled with her other gifts of intelligence, wit, and charm, made her an extraordinary leader at this challenging time in religious life.

The enactments of the Twelfth General Chapter, which were to set the congregation's direction for the next four years, were presented in a booklet that was itself a statement: its collages of newspaper headlines, varied font types and sizes, and graphics revealed that something new was happening, even as something traditional remained in the enactments' language. As Marshall McLuhan might have remarked, the medium was indeed the message.

The theme of the publication was stated succinctly: "Jesus is Lord. We as Sisters of Charity have a radical obligation to measure our lives against this claim." As Sister Mary McGowan recalled, it was Sister Katherine O'Toole who spoke the first part of the statement, a quotation from St. Paul (Phil. 2:11), in a chapter session.

Among the agenda items of the Twelfth Chapter, some of which arose from the Church's call for a renewal within religious life and some from the specific lives of Sisters of Charity, was a major item drawn directly from the *Perfectae Caritatis*. In that document, the Council Fathers had written, "The appropriate renewal of religious life involves ... a continuous return to the ... original inspiration behind a given community" (Art. 2). This was reenforced less than three years later when Pope Paul VI, in the document *Evangelica Testificatio* [Apostolic Exhortation on the Renewal of Religious Life according to the Teachings of the Second Vatican Council], wrote that the Council "rightly insists on the obligation of religious to be faithful to the spirit of their founders, to their evangelical intentions and to the example of their sanctity"(#10).

Although the Twelfth Chapter took up the concept of returning to the spirit that gave birth to the congregation as a response to the Vatican II Decree and the document issued by Pope Paul VI, the Chapter delegates also recognized that turning to Elizabeth Seton as a model for their common life and spirit would help to draw the congregation together in these turbulent times. Some sisters had begun to feel that the congregation's cohesiveness was threatened as the provinces grew in different directions. The introduction to the enactment, the first of the Chapter, states, "The provinces are gradually assuming different characters and there is need for a unifying factor binding the congregation as a whole, and it seems that the original inspiration of the congregation should be a source of that unity."

The sisters were invited to come to a deeper knowledge of and devotion to the spirit that Elizabeth had bequeathed to those who followed her. In its enactment, the Chapter called on the congregation "to examine how our corporate vision reflects this spirit" and to "discern prayerfully how in truth, simplicity, and love we can incarnate for our times the spirit of Elizabeth Seton."

Central to this pursuit was the research, writing, and speaking of Sister Francis Fay. Prior to the Chapter, Sister Francis had responded to the Council's directive and had begun to research the life of Elizabeth and to share her insights. It was no surprise, then, that when the Chapter asked the Governing Board to make this enactment a focus, it was Sister Francis Fay whose name came to the fore. Perhaps it was in part because Francis, a native of Brooklyn, saw Elizabeth Seton as a fellow native New Yorker as well as a holy woman that she committed herself to the work with such great joy. Francis relished the opportunity to share stories and to convey Elizabeth's journey. She shared her own reflections and questions in the booklet *Hazard It Forward*. (The title of the booklet was based on a misunderstanding of a quotation from Elizabeth. In time, the phrase came to be known as "Hazard Yet Forward," the motto of William Seton's family.)

In keeping with the enactment that the Spirit and Mission Committee had shepherded through the Chapter, each province was to name a representative as well as a core group of sisters "with the function of assisting the local houses to make this search a lived experience" (IA2). Individually and in communities, sisters pursued a deeper knowledge of Elizabeth and her spirit, and several provinces invited biographers of Elizabeth to share their insights. Annabelle Melville, author of *Elizabeth Bayley Seton, 1774-1821*, and Joseph Dirvin, CM, author of *Mrs. Seton,*

Foundress of the American Sisters of Charity, fleshed out her story for attentive audiences.

In June 1973, the representatives from the provinces joined the Governing Board at Seton Lodge in Falmouth, Massachusetts to report on the progress of the enactment. These reports, in which sisters related the insights culled from their immersion into Elizabeth's life and spirit, also contain glimpses of many of the issues that the congregation faced during those years. Some comments focused on God's call, on response, and on community. Others spoke of ministry and service to the poor and deepening familiarity with Scripture consistent with Elizabeth's spirituality. One province cautioned against "losing our focus to the current trends such as group dynamics." Consistent with Elizabeth's spirit, one report highlighted the need for prayer to balance those moments when "we sometimes experience chaos within the community," an experience that challenged some sisters sorely in those years. Many reports echoed the lines from Vincent's rule that Elizabeth had adapted for her fledgling community, urging sisters to care for those "who through shame would conceal their necessity." Other voices spoke of a concern for simplicity, in imitation of Elizabeth, a concern that Sister Katherine O'Toole would also take up in her time as Superior General.

The result of the June meeting was a statement naming the common spirit of the congregation and its affiliated characteristics and relating them to the heritage of Elizabeth. The statement ended with the familiar exhortation, "Be children of the Church." The committee, after sharing the insights from the provinces, determined that mission would be the focus for the following year.

This focus on Elizabeth also served to prepare the sisters for the celebration of the bicentennial of Elizabeth Seton's birth, which occurred in 1974. In that bicentennial year, Pope Paul VI announced that in 1975 he would canonize Elizabeth Seton as the first American saint. With the various congregations that made up the Federation of Elizabeth Seton enthusiastically reaffirming their roots in her life and holiness, a solid foundation was growing for strong collaboration to mark the canonization.

The study of Elizabeth nourished the congregation, but the Church had issued an additional call during these years. Of increasing importance, not only to religious congregations but to the Church, was the call to social justice. While the Gospel parable of Matthew 25 ("whatsoever you do …") taught care for the poor in a concrete way, the Church, since the 1891 publication of the encyclical *Rerum Novarum* [Of New Things], had looked to the needs of the poor by reflecting on the rights of individuals and on the institutions and practices that seemed to hinder their growth. As Church writings developed, the concept of social justice grew; specifically, the idea that, as David Hollenbach writes, "Human dignity is a social rather than a purely private affair. Human dignity makes a genuine moral demand upon the organizational patterns by which public life is structured" (1979, 55).

The differences between rich and poor were familiar, but after World War II, the growing wealth of some nations and the relentless poverty of others created extremes. During the papacies of John XXIII and Paul VI, the Church began to look at social justice in a more specific way. With Vatican II's statement on the dignity of the human person, found in *Gaudium et Spes* [Pastoral Constitution on the Church in the Modern World], human dignity and human development and their relationship to social institutions became major considerations, with the popes issuing related encyclicals, and national episcopal conferences publishing their own statements on these issues.

Concern for the poor had always been part of the Vincentian tradition, and the new impetus provided by the Church reenergized the congregation. In the Chapter of Renewal (1968–1969), the issue of social justice had remained at the margins of the conversation; the more urgent need at that time was to address the congregation's internal renewal at the local, provincial, and general levels. In 1972, it was time to take up social justice.

The world was growing smaller, with easy access to news from around the world vividly portraying the many faces of poverty. As delegates reflected on the gospel call and the reality of so much suffering, the statement that they issued inspired the congregation to look more carefully at the needs of the world and to consider ways to respond:

> The Chapter calls on each sister personally and corporately
> to develop a sensitivity to those whom the world oppresses,
> to right in great ways and small the injustices we see around us,
> to heal the wounds of the embittered,
> to speak peace to the troubled,
> to urge the mighty to right wrongs in order that we, the one and the many,
> may be a visible means of healing in the time in which God has placed us.

As if to awaken the congregation with visual prods, fragments of headlines and contemporary concerns were scattered around a quotation from Pope Paul VI, with the chapter statement, given above, positioned on the facing page. The phrases of the statement became familiar to the sisters as they read it together at prayer and at meetings. There was a new energy to look more carefully at the world's pain and to consider ways of responding.

Over the course of the next four years, the congregation reviewed its investment portfolio with an eye toward social justice and, although its own fiscal health warranted care, the congregation made donations to the poor of the world, particularly to Central America, and marked the canonization of Elizabeth Seton in 1975 with a major donation to the poor.

As individual sisters were assuming more responsibility for their lives and ministries, they responded to the statement in a variety of ways, many making changes in their lives that they felt more consistent with the spirit of the statement. Such personal commitments were essential to the work of renewal. The concern for social justice led to new, sometimes difficult, questions: Where should the Sisters of Charity be ministering? Is it appropriate to serve in wealthy parishes and communities? How does this statement alter what the Sisters of Charity are doing now? Do the suburbs have to lose to the inner city? Are there other kinds of poverty in addition to economic poverty? Should sisters live and/or minister in high-crime areas? Does Liberation Theology have an impact on places of ministry outside of Latin America?

A woman of her times, Sister Katherine O'Toole knew first-hand the growth as well as the difficulties that renewal spawned in religious communities. Speaking at St. Paul Convent, Herring Cove, NS ten months before she was elected, Katherine shared the fruits of the work she had done at Duquesne. She addressed the topic of personal responsibility in religious life by identifying the mix of idealism and practical realities in community life in those years. Speaking rhetorically as the ideal Sister of Charity, Katherine reflected, "I am called by life to bring myself to the highest possible human fulfillment of which I am capable ... I must face the consequences of my decisions and actions and must be ready to stand answerable to others and ultimately to God as a person, as a Christian, as a religious." Lofty ideals, but Katherine also knew well the mundane issues that created tensions at the local level. Moving into the new era, sisters were living with less structure and more autonomy, and local coordinators wielded less authority than local superiors had – the new difficulties were predictable. In her straightforward way, Katherine listed some of the questions raised in local community meetings: "What about people who never take a share in the house work ... who never contribute to house forums?"

Most religious congregations had lived by constitutions that had changed little over the decades. Now, as part of the renewal and the updating of their constitutions, these same groups were invited to a period of experimentation. The Twelfth Chapter had formulated two statements on local government: "That the experiment in co-responsible local government continue, subject to review by the Governing Board." (#12) and "That every local community evaluate itself annually" (#13). The former statement, terming co-responsible government an "experiment," is revelatory of a stage of growth and change. The interim constitutions, *Covenant of Renewal* (1969), had named collegiality/co-responsibility as one of the five basic principles of religious life. As renewal took hold, individuals were growing into new ways of relating to their local communities and of sharing responsibility and accountability for decision-making. This was especially true as smaller communities multiplied.

This approach to community living called for an investment of care and time at house meetings where issues were discussed and difficulties resolved. Various sisters chaired the meetings and usually any sister could add an item to the agenda and speak her concerns or suggestions. For some, this approach to local governance was welcomed, but others resented the investment of time or found it taxing to discuss all of the issues ranging from spiritual practices to basic practicalities, even though all these things hold local religious communities together. Some personalities found this approach challenging, particularly introverts and those who favoured resolution more than process, but it was meant to recognize the gifts and insights of all members. Sister Katherine knew that such meetings could be sources of tension as well as expressions of it. In her letter promulgating the enactments of the chapter, Katherine had urged all sisters: "Be willing to share your word of truth with others that together we may find the Truth which alone give [sic] meaning to life."

Again, as part of the renewal of government at the local level, sisters had been asked to take time at the beginning of a new community year to formulate goals for the community. Now, the 1972 Chapter mandated that each house evaluate annually how those goals were realized. This was meant to provide members with an experience of accountability – they had to consider, explicitly consider, how intentionally they had kept the common goals before their eyes and worked on them. In some communities, monthly meetings included the reading of the goals as a means of reminding the sisters of their common vision.

But the issues of local governance were only a small portion of the enactments concerning government of the congregation. Of the sixteen other recommendations for government, some dealt with government at the generalate level: "[T]he superior general is the canonical head of the congregation and as such has those rights which are given to her by the Church" (#2); "That the secretary general and the treasurer general be voting members of the Governing Board; that the secretary general and treasurer general be appointed for a stated term of not less than two nor more than five years. They may be reappointed; they may not serve for more than eight consecutive years."(#6).

Other enactments dealt with the Governing Board, placing on that body the responsibility of formulating a policy for interprovincial transfers. In an effort to protect the rights of individual sisters as well as those of the congregation, the Governing Board also took on the task of determining the composition, procedures, and responsibility for a board of appeals at the congregational level. (During the two terms of Katherine's leadership, no need existed to gather such a board.) The Governing Board was also asked to coordinate a study of government, initiate a study of general chapters, and implement any changes. This would have major implications for future general chapters. By the following June, the Governing Board had endorsed the idea of a chapter of total involvement, though how this phrase would be realized was not yet clear.

Connecting the two levels of general and provincial structures, the Governing Board's Executive Committee had the responsibility of approving nominations and ratifying the elections of provincial superiors. There were other enactments on the government structure that had an impact at the provincial level. Although the first resolution stated that "no major change be made in the government structure at this time," (#1) there were two statements that had specific reference to the Rockingham Province (B.3.a.b.). The Rockingham Province had been created in 1968. Its purpose was to link the sisters in western Nova Scotia with those sisters who lived in the motherhouse but whose ministry was outside its confines. The resolution from the Chapter dissolved the province. The sisters would become part of the Halifax Province. The delegates to the Rockingham Provincial Chapter would reconvene to implement the directives of the General Chapter. In addition, the Chapter stated "that the experiment in interprovincial community at Mount Saint Vincent University not be continued," (#8) and that those sisters become members of the Halifax Province.

Another change in the structure made by the Twelfth General

Chapter was the establishment, on an experimental basis, of a vice province for retired sisters. This was an attempt to respond to the needs of the aging population. In some areas of the congregation, sisters retired from their salaried positions at the same age as their lay colleagues because of contractual agreements. In other areas, sisters continued to work full-time in their ministries beyond the normal retirement age. While the needs varied from province to province, the need for congregational planning was clear. The new vice province would consist of the two regions of Mount Saint Vincent, Halifax and Mount Saint Vincent, Wellesley. These regions would be the residence of both retired and infirm sisters who qualified. The Chapter recognized that it might eventually include members who lived outside the two buildings.

In the ensuing years, the structure for the retirement centres would undergo various revisions. Initially, each region was represented on the board of the new vice province, with a full board meeting twice a year. Each region had its own superior, through whom local administrators and coordinators would relate their concerns to the provincial of the vice province. The first vice provincial was Sister Ann Gill; the regional superiors were Sister Margaret Guthrie (Halifax) and Sister Louise Kenney (Wellesley). The structure proved cumbersome for both the leaders and members (160 sisters in Halifax and 111 sisters in Wellesley), and in 1975 each region became a vice province. The experimental basis on which these changes rested reveals again the fluidity of structures at this time in the congregation's history.

The enactments at this Chapter empowered provincial boards to make decisions and to create policy at the provincial level. This approach was built on the principles of subsidiarity and collegiality that had been stated in the *Covenant of Renewal*. With consensus as the mode of decision-making, there was a strong sense that all voices should be heard and respected.

The Chapter also passed several proposals that were juridical in tone and related to the individual sister. The fact that all of these enactments were related to sisters who were living away from congregational convents indicates the increased mobility of sisters during this period and the effort being made to keep sisters connected to the congregation when they were living in atypical circumstances, whether due to ministry, or to study or family needs.

In these enactments, there is an attempt at both continuity and change. There are familiar structures, yet there are "experiments" and efforts to incorporate the principles stated in the *Covenant of Renewal* and to accommodate new realities. In 1972, the congregation had only had the *Covenant* for three years. One senses in the recommendations developed by the Chapter that year an attempt to tidy up loose strands so as to prevent the basic structure from being undone. In the recommendation "that a study of government be made throughout the congregation; that each province undertake research, evaluation and education of government at all levels: that the result of this study be shared by all provinces and coordinated at the general Governing Board level" (B.12a.b.c.), it is possible to see the outline of a very different form of congregational government emerging from this period of experimentation. Each of these enactments and recommendations came to the Chapter with its own history and its own potential to change the congregation.

Like other Chapter committees, the Commitment/Membership/Extended Community Committee dealt with continuity. The chapter statement reminded the congregation, "A Sister of Charity expresses her total commitment in a faith response to the ongoing personal call of the Lord Jesus. Through the power of His Spirit, she responds by ever deepening her relationship with God and by ministering to the People of God through community" (C.1). But the Committee also looked at newer issues and possibilities. Because there had been a growing call for all members to participate in the life of the congregation, the chapter delegates voted that "Sisters in temporary commitment be given the right of passive voice" (C.2.b.), thus allowing them to be elected to some positions within the congregation. This decision also signalled the congregation's willingness to be open to the influence of younger sisters.

In addition, the subsequent chapter gave the Governing Board the responsibility of discerning the request of the Boston and New York non-canonical novices for active and passive voices in chapters. The origins of this request dated back to the 1969 Chapter of Renewal in which the congregation's formation program had been discontinued. As a result, the postulants who had entered at Mount Saint Vincent, Wellesley in 1968 became members of local communities in the New York and Boston Provinces, finishing their degrees at various schools. Their canonical novitiate and profession were delayed. The six young women who persevered through those unusual circumstances were actively involved in the life of the congregation, and in order to participate officially in the chapter process, they had requested both active and passive voices. Following the chapter, this request was taken up by the Governing Board at their meetings over the next several years. After calling upon canonical consultants for insights, the request was finally sent to Rome. In June 1973, the Sacred Congregation for Religious refused the request, citing the lack of profession as the reason. That same year, the sisters made their novitiate at St. Nicholas of Tolentine under the direction of Sister Margaret Bickar, and made their first profession in 1974, nearly six years after their entrance, instead of the usual three years.

As religious life was changing, new forms seemed to be emerging in some areas, forms that saw vowed religious join to create communities with those who were not vowed religious. The final recommendation from the Commitment/Membership/Extended Community committee dealt with this concept of extended community. The Chapter assigned to the Governing Board the responsibility to "initiate research and permit experimentation if feasible in collaboration with provinces" (C.3). In keeping with this recommendation, the Governing Board appointed Sister Francis Fay to oversee this project. During the next four years, the Governing Board heard about the interest of a few people, primarily former members, in forming an extended community, but no formal communities developed, although variations did evolve. At Mary House in Quincy, Massachusetts, sisters offered to make their home the centre, but not the residence, of a prayer community for neighbours and parishioners at St. Boniface Church.

Finance had been of major concern in the life of the congregation since the Chapter of Renewal. The cost of living was rising, members were retiring, and medical expenses were increasing. In one effort to offset this difficulty, some sisters, with the permission of provincial superiors, sought outside employment where they earned salaries, instead of stipends. The utility companies, the medical field, business and government offices were some of the new sites of work. Some non-canonical novices were also part of this new "work force" during summer months. An additional concern was the fact that a number of the wage-earning sisters had begun to leave the congregation. Their departure also raised the question: What did the congregation owe them for the years they had served? What was a just allotment? What about social security and pension contributions? This topic would demand a great deal of attention and careful planning over the next four years, much of it done under the wise direction and foresight of Sister Mary Moore, who had been reappointed Treasurer General from the last administration.

At the Chapter, three basic statements indicated the congregation's positions on these financial issues.

1. The Governing Board is to continue to exercise control of the finances of the congregation.
2. The provinces will move toward an equal "per capita" congregational tax basis over the next four years.
3. The congregational pension program is to become effective as soon as possible. (D.1.,2.,3.)

These statements, joined to the work done on finances since the Chapter of Renewal in which the delegates had agreed to dispose of property and institutions, were significant decisions and helped to lay the foundation for a better financial footing for the congregation.

The loss of institutions caused much reflection. For decades, the Sisters of Charity had given of their lives and resources to maintain these institutions as part of their Gospel outreach, tending the sick, teaching children, and supporting those in need. It was not surprising that withdrawal would evoke sadness and raise questions about how the congregation would be perceived and where the sisters would minister. The decisions were not always simple, nor were they met with easy assent. Sisters were required to consider their attachments and the comfort of living and working in the familiar. Over the years, the wisdom of this financial planning and the difficult decisions it required came to be seen as a blessing.

As larger numbers of members approached retirement, not only were there financial issues, there were also questions about the quality of their lives and their expectations of retirement. With this in mind, the Retirement Committee sponsored the following recommendation, which the Chapter endorsed: "The establishment of pre-retirement programs is to be given high priority in each province" (E.). This recommendation would prove to be of great value in an aging congregation and would evoke creative responses over the years of Katherine's administration.

In addition to this concern about senior members, there was also concern about new members. Congregational formation had been in uncharted waters since the previous chapter. After the 1969 dissolution of the formation program, four Canadian non-canonical novices began their canonical year in 1970 in Ottawa under the direction of Sister Anne Harvey. One sister was professed; then, due to lack of candidates, the novitiate closed. Although no official postulate existed, a small number of young women continued to express interest in the congregation. The Chapter stated, "Phase I of the formation program is to be considered an unofficial and informal state of initial formation." (F.2.). Since 1969, those women had been invited to meet with sisters and to participate informally in the life of the local communities as affiliates. If these women continued to feel called and the congregation agreed, they would then move into a local house and participate more intentionally in the life of the community. During this phase, they were called associates, a title that would take on a different meaning decades later. They would continue to earn and to keep their salaries, but begin to live more in keeping with the spirit of poverty and with the intention of entering one of the novitiates that would eventually be established in Hempstead,

NY, Hingham, MA, and Herring Cove, NS, each one with a limited existence.

Recognizing that this area had its unique concerns, it was agreed that "A member of the Governing Board is to be assigned formation as a special area of concern, and Provincial coordinators of formation are to hold regular meetings for the purpose of coordinating formation at a congregational level" (F.1.b.). Sister Elizabeth Hayes took on the responsibility for this challenging area. The Chapter had also mandated the creation of a formation supplement to the *Covenant of Renewal.* Many people contributed to the project, especially formation personnel, provincial boards, and members of the Governing Board. In 1975, the Governing Board approved the contents in principle, mindful that chapter delegates at the July session would give final approval. They also suggested that the new material be printed separately from the *Constitutions* and referred to as a Directory. This would allow changes to be made without considering them constitutional changes.

The changes in the style of leadership – from local superior to contact person – also left a kind of vacuum for the formation of sisters in temporary profession. These members had arrived at the local communities either with their degrees or in pursuit of them, many as full-time students. Their initial formation experiences had been much broader and more open than the one that the older sisters had known. While some sisters welcomed the new perspectives and practices of the younger sisters, others found them unsettling. The roles of local coordinator and contact person did not include specific responsibility for these sisters. Instead, provinces developed formation teams whose members worked with the provincial coordinator of formation. These team members took on the role that superiors had formerly held, meeting with sisters in temporary commitment, encouraging them and helping them to continue their growth as new members. In some provinces, special nights were established where the young sisters could gather for liturgy and a presentation on theology or spirituality.

For the purpose of support and formation, the American formation team members established formation weekends that took place at

Mount Saint Vincent in Wellesley Hills. These events provided time for prayer, socializing, and input and strengthened the bonds among the young sisters. One of the developments that flowed from this new approach was the event known as "Formation '74," a gathering at the Motherhouse for sisters in temporary commitment. With the help of formation teams across the congregation, the committee planned an event that was spiritual, social, and informative. For some participants who had not entered the congregation in Halifax, this was their first visit to the Motherhouse. For others, it was a return to familiar territory and an opportunity for reunions with band members and friends they had not seen for several years. In the context of liturgies, lectures, social events, and a trip to Cape Breton, new friendships grew and old ones were renewed. The event bespoke the new mobility and freedom that sisters, especially younger members, celebrated.

As these developments were taking place in formation, the apostolic life of the congregation continued. The Gospel command to "Go forth and make disciples of all nations," is an integral part of the Christian message. From the missionary journey of Saint Paul to the zealous outreach of many women and men over the centuries, the Good News has been carried to all the corners of the world. In the twentieth century, the missionary call came again with new enthusiasm. Popes John XXIII and Paul VI called attention to the needs for evangelization in the developing countries of the world.

In 1968, in conjunction with an initiative of the Archdiocese of Halifax, the Sisters of Charity had begun their formal outreach to Latin America with the opening of a house in Victoria Nueva in the diocese of Chiclayo, Peru. The mission was staffed jointly with priests from the Halifax Archdiocese and became the first of several sites where the sisters served in that country. Sisters Zelma Le Blanc, Gabriela Villela, Catherine Conroy, and Agnes Burrows were the pioneers to the mission, facing the challenges and joys of life in a new culture. In addition to the Peru mission, the congregation also opened a site in Bani in the Dominican Republic, with Sisters Catherine McGowan and Sheila Anne

Nyhan. The sisters who served in these missions were considered part of the Halifax Province.

By the Chapter of 1972, the congregation had learned more about the needs of missionary life, and the delegates acted on the pertinent proposals. Enactments called for the Governing Board to "initiate a study and be empowered to implement recommendations regarding the status of missions in general, and regarding that of the Peru mission in particular in the event that the Halifax Archdiocese withdraw from the … project" (G.1.). In addition, the Governing Board was to assign one of the assistants to the area of foreign missions as an area for special interests and research, a role that Sister Rita MacDonald filled. This was a natural choice; during her term as provincial superior of Halifax, Sister Rita had served on the Halifax Archdiocesan Latin American Commission and had observed the developments of the mission. Recognizing that sisters from other provinces would be interested in serving in the missions, the chapter delegates agreed that the "needs for staffing of missions be channeled by the provinces through the Governing Board to the entire congregation" (G.4.). This last enactment was validated as, over the years, sisters from various parts of the congregation volunteered to serve in the missions.

While the Twelfth General Chapter had passed a number of significant enactments, the ongoing life of the congregation had its own positive energy as well as its own tensions and resistance. The amount of change and the speed at which the change occurred, the demands of renewal, and the daily needs of the congregation must have seemed rather overwhelming to the new General Superior and Governing Board, and it is not surprising that Sister Katherine, in her 1972 Advent message to the congregation, focused on hope. In her opening paragraphs, she wrote the following:

> When an organization or institution becomes conscious of being involved in rather widespread evolutionary change, a fear is often generated in the members … Caught up as we are in the post-conciliar era of change

> and its effects, we need the strong support of hope in God and in the Congregation to carry us forward. (November 27, 1972)

In notes that Sister Katherine made several years after she left office, she identified the three characteristics that marked her two terms as Superior General (1972–1976, 1976–1980): diminishment, diversification, and rebirthing. The diminishment was evident not only in the drop in membership, but also as the congregation sold or withdrew from major institutions. The Report to Twelfth General Chapter in 1972 stated that as of January 1, there had been 1,491 professed members (down from its highest number of 1,645 in the previous decade) and 23 women in formation; by the Report to Thirteenth General Chapter in June 1976, the number was down to 1,318, with 9 in formation. At the provincial level, the numbers are more specific. After the chapter of 1972, the Vice Province (two regions combined) had 255 members; by June of 1976, the number was 267, an indication of the number of members who were aging and withdrawing from ministry. The downward trend could be seen in the other provinces: Halifax Province went from 285 to 274; Antigonish from 139 to 115; Boston from 289 to 275; New York from 272 to 208; Western Province from 100 to 89; and Central Province from 96 to 85.

The numbers reflected the new reality: like many congregations, the Sisters of Charity were both losing members and attracting very few new vocations. The changes within religious life, the new ways of viewing human development, and the new freedom and new opportunities for women in society led some members to re-evaluate their lives and subsequently to leave the congregation. For many who left, this new sense of freedom was a gift of God. Simultaneously, potential members may have perceived the changes within religious life as being too tumultuous to inherit. In addition, the call to universal holiness and the new focus on ministry of the baptized may have deterred some from entering religious life.

The 1970s were a turbulent decade. Recreational drug use was rising.

News of liberation movements and calls for freedom filled the media. The changes in sexual mores had caused many in society to reconsider not only the value of vowed celibacy, but also of traditional perspectives on sexual intimacy and marriage. This era saw many men and women leave their congregations or the priesthood, and it was not rare for a former woman religious to marry a former priest. Many women who left the congregation took with them a deep love for the Sisters of Charity and for the Church and continued to use their gifts and their education in service to others.

While those who left the congregation in previous years might have done so without much recognition and may have severed ties, those who left during the 1970s had the opportunity to share their decisions with the sisters. Congregational announcements about departures changed from terse statements of fact to, as the Governing Board stated at its November 1975 meeting, a "message of appreciation of what the sister meant to the congregation and the people of God." Many continued their friendships, sometimes collaborating in ministries. On many occasions, provinces invited former members to gather in celebration of the friendships that continued to exist between members and former members. Each decision, both to stay and to leave, was a reminder of human freedom and of the uniqueness of an individual call and a personal response. While those who remained in the congregation often felt the loss of dear friends keenly, they inevitably were brought back to consider their own calls and responses.

The diminishment that the congregation experienced because of the sale of properties or withdrawal from institutions brought its own pain, even though those sales and withdrawals were meant to unburden the congregation and to provide a better financial footing, especially for retirement needs. In her book *Charity Alive*, Sister Mary Olga McKenna devotes an entire chapter, "Divestment of Institutions," to this issue, and much of the activity she chronicles took place in the 1970s. During Katherine's first term in office, major losses included the closing of Saint Anne's Hospital in Hardisty, Alberta, the transfers of the Halifax Infirmary and of Saint Elizabeth's Hospital in North Sydney to the

Province of Nova Scotia, and the closing and sale of Seton Hall in New York. Those years also saw the closing of Stella Maris Residence in North Sydney, the sale of Mount Saint Agnes Convent in Bermuda, and the transfer of ownership of Mount Saint Agnes Academy to the Diocese of Hamilton, Bermuda.

While financial concerns contributed to these decisions, the fact that fewer sisters were available to staff these institutions was also a consideration. Many wonderful women had given generously of themselves to establish and maintain these institutions, and it was not surprising that with the closings and withdrawals there would be an attendant grief accompanied sometimes by anger. Forty-one houses closed between 1972 and 1975. In writing about the sense of diminishment that these losses created, Katherine reflected on the impact on the congregation:

> Besides a possible lowering of corporate morale, I sense that this 'diminishment' brought us also to a new kind of corporate humility. Our worth was not to be in the institutions we own or operate … We ourselves, individually and corporately, would have to be the 'city on the hill,' the 'light on the candlestick' … Other closures – the Academies at Wellesley and in Halifax, several convents long associated with us: St. Sebastian's … Westmont, NJ … OLGC [Our Lady of Good Counsel], Staten Island … St. Patrick Convent, Arvida … Sacred Heart, Riverton … Our Lady of Charity, Montreal – the Bathurst Convents … all these further connoted a movement of diminishment, of endings. They had effects on ministry and other aspects of life.

So many closings and withdrawals would, of course, lead to changes in apostolic activities and living situations. An example of what one year brought to the New York Province serves as a reminder of the abundance of transitions: in 1975, this province of approximately 210 sisters reported to the Governing Board that "67 sisters will change either residence or ministry or both."

During these years, as the Sisters of Charity withdrew from institutions and convents, the number of local communities actually increased because of the establishment of small communities. Some of this was due to necessity, because private houses for large numbers of adults were costly or non-existent; but some sisters chose to live in small communities that seemed to offer more freedom, even as they paradoxically demanded greater responsibility and participation. Setting up and opening these smaller communities required a good deal of physical work, with sisters searching for and moving furnishings. Once the houses were ready, the members of the new communities often invited the sisters in the province to an "Open House" to celebrate the event. Such visiting kept alive the bonds of charity.

The transition from living in larger communities, sometimes within institutional contexts, to living in smaller communities in what had been private homes or apartments was not always easy. Sisters who had not had the responsibility of preparing meals on a regular basis found themselves preparing meals on a weekly basis, with varying degrees of success and anxiety. Such experiences often prompted awe and gratitude as they recalled the sisters who had prepared meals daily for large communities for so many years. In their new settings, members found themselves interacting in smaller settings, with few places to find sanctuary when tensions arose. Relationships within these communities sometimes caused unexpected pain. There was much to learn about human development, small group dynamics, power, and the elements that hold a religious community together. To assist with these new experiences of community living, the congregation and the provinces sponsored workshops for self-growth and group dynamics. Myers Briggs workshops and Rochais sessions aided many during that time, as did opportunities for psychological counselling. Those who persevered learned to celebrate together, to confront one another when necessary, and to work at becoming praying communities where gifts

and limitations were acknowledged, zeal for ministry was fostered, and the spirit of charity was renewed.

In addition to the small communities that began in houses or apartments, some were also created within established convents. These situations gave rise to unusual circumstances, and there were sometimes tensions between two groups living under the same roof, using the same chapel, and the same dining room. While this model would later work well in large institutions, it was not always an easy model for large convents where tensions could still arise over different ways of living the religious life.

The diversity which Sister Katherine described in her notes was evident in another new experience: in 1968, twenty-two sisters lived away from their local community, by 1972, this number was eighty-one, and in 1979, sixty-eight sisters lived away from local communities. There were many reasons for this shift, including ministry, study, care of a relative, and the need for psychological space, but this was a development that the Governing Board noted with some concern and would address in the future.

Diversity in ministry also flourished during these years, energizing some, but leading others who remained in traditional ministries to experience a feeling of abandonment. Sisters who had spent a number of years in a ministry to which they did not feel suited felt free to express their desires to enter a different ministry. As a result, a number of sisters once again returned to the classroom as students, earning advanced degrees in a variety of fields, notably theology and ministry, nursing, social work, and specific areas within education. Many sisters did remain in education, and decades later one of the highest compliments paid to them was that they were "great school women" who, sometimes in trying circumstances, formed students, learned to deal with school boards, teachers' unions, and pastors, and showed something of God's love in the world.

As sisters moved into diverse ministries, access to cars became a practical concern. Initially, several sisters shared one car. With varied schedules and destinations, it became clear that such an approach was too impractical and too taxing in terms of time and energy. Over time, often with the astute assistance of relatives, friends, and advisors, provinces began to purchase additional cars, some for the use of individual sister's ministries, others for general use. The congregation was becoming part of a very mobile society.

With the sense of empowerment, sisters began to consider their ministry locations, sometimes with what seemed like a narrow view. Governing Board discussions considered trends that included sisters choosing the province in which they would minister, decisions often shaped by the desire to move closer to home, thus limiting their openness to some missions. In contrast to the fairly limited ministries of the past, the array of ways in which sisters now served was extraordinary. Some worked individually in new fields, while others clustered together. For example, while some sisters had responded to the call to go to the Latin American missions in the 1960s, the 1970s saw a small number of sisters move to missions in the Yukon and the Northwest Territories. In several provinces, sisters created new communities for foster children in need and opened their homes to people awaiting medical care and their loved ones as they waited with them and supported them.

At the same time as such diversity was taking root, members of the congregation also began several new corporate ministries. During Sister Katherine's two terms, houses of prayer opened in most provinces: The Renewal Centre in Halifax (1972), the New York House of Prayer in Wantagh, New York (1973), Seton House in Quincy, Massachusetts, (1976), and Elizabeth Seton Prayer Centre in Quebec (1979). In the Western Province, sisters opened Seton House of Prayer in Summerland for the Diocese of Nelson, British Columbia in 1974.

In recognition of the needs of the church, especially of the poor, the congregation established a ministry fund that offered grants to sisters for ministerial projects. Over the course of Katherine's second term, grants were awarded to all the provinces: to Antigonish for the training of lay catechists; to Boston for the creation of WAITT House (We're All In This Together), a centre for adult education and advocacy; to the Central Province for a house of prayer for the English-speaking community of Metro Quebec; to Halifax for the development of lay ministers; to New York for a program to assist incarcerated women to develop skills that would lead to employment; and to the Western Province for the funding of a lay catechist who would train others. In Cape Breton, generous grants from the congregation led to the creation of Seton Centre Foundation, an organization providing interest-free loans to 250 families in need to procure housing.

Ministerial collaboration with lay colleagues (WAITT House), outside agencies (prison ministry), and priests (Seton Foundation) furthered the appreciation of the charism of charity. Within a few short years of the sisters being given the freedom to initiate new full-time ministries and to choose volunteer services, the Sisters of Charity could be found in diverse settings, serving a variety of people. Collaboration with colleagues from very different backgrounds widened horizons and created more opportunities for new friendships as sisters ministered with lay men and women and members of other religious congregations and dioceses in a host of new settings. Many local communities welcomed guests more easily than in the past, and in some cases welcomed the parish priests to share meals and prayer on a regular basis.

It was clear that although corporate ministries were decreasing, the desire to serve remained deeply rooted in the hearts of the sisters. What fuelled this generosity? No doubt it was fuelled by schooling in the Gospel and the spirit of the congregation, but in the years following the Vatican Council, there was also a new kind of spiritual renewal taking place. Faith sharing within the context of community prayer became more common, and sisters began to shape their own prayer services from a variety of resources. Sisters also joined prayer groups, such as the charismatic renewal movement and various renewal programs at the parish level. Books by Jean Vanier and Henri Nouwen and the periodicals *Review for Religious* and *Sisters Today* nourished new ideas.

In 1975, every sister received the *Christian Prayer Book* as a gift commemorating the canonization of Saint Elizabeth Seton. This book, a four-week cycle of psalms and readings, was a more complex version of the breviaries that had been in use. In the midst of so much liturgical change, this was another way to pray with the Church throughout the world and to deepen appreciation for Scripture. To facilitate their use of the books, the sisters in Halifax welcomed Archbishop James Hayes to address them on that topic. A well-respected friend of the congregation and brother of Sister Elizabeth Hayes, Archbishop Hayes was generous with his theological background and the insights that had been nourished by his participation in Vatican II.

Over this period, the liturgical changes at the Eucharist were becoming more familiar. Sisters joined parish liturgy committees and readily assumed roles as Eucharistic ministers and lectors, oftentimes providing the training for others. Due to the greater freedom and mobility, sisters also joined other worship communities where they found liturgies that enriched them.

Gradually new and better liturgical music than had been heard in the first years after the Council made its way into the repertoire of Church musicians. Inspired by the call to return to Scripture, composers penned melodies and joined them to Scriptural texts. Many Catholics painlessly learned Bible texts by singing many of the new Scripture-based lyrics. Composers such as the St. Louis Jesuits, Carey Landry, Suzanne Toolan, and the Monks of Weston Priory contributed to the repertoire of liturgical music, and the 1976 debut of Sister Susanne Abruzzo's album, *Sunburst Yellow and Orange* gave the congregation a sense of pride. "The Hebrew Blessing," joined Susanne's music to the words attributed to Aaron in the Book of Deuteronomy and provided the congregation with a hymn that members continue to sing on occasions of joy and sending forth, including at the time of final committal of deceased members. In addition to Scripture-based songs, Susanne also wrote "A Special Woman," a tribute to Elizabeth Seton, and "While I Live," based on the words of Elizabeth Seton.

The freedom that brought forth Susanne's gifts also allowed the congregation's visual artists to flourish. Talents expressed in a variety of media adorned the walls of residences and, in some instances, were displayed in public spaces. Liturgical renewal also opened the door to movement and dance for prayer services and, occasionally, for

liturgies. Sisters were nurturing and sharing their gifts and finding great satisfaction. That same kind of freedom enabled more sisters to find God in creation. In the Western Province, with access to the mountains, sisters found spiritual renewal in hiking and in savouring the beauty of the outdoors.

As the Sisters of Charity had returned to the spirit of Elizabeth Seton, so too had the Jesuits returned to the spirit of their founder. In their pursuit of that spirit, they began to offer directed retreats and the full 30-day experience of the Spiritual Exercises of Ignatius Loyola to the broader Church community. These offerings put the focus on the individual's relationship with God and invited the retreatant to speak with a director about her personal experiences in prayer. This was a dramatic shift from large group preached retreats, and for some it was an intimidating experience to reveal such an intimate part of their lives. Still, overcoming anxiety, many took the initiative to register for such retreats and to pursue spiritual direction. Retreat locations such as Guelph, Gloucester, and Monroe became familiar. Sister Paule Cantin recalled that when she was provincial superior of the Central Province she provided sisters with an opportunity to make a weekend directed retreat with the hope of allaying their anxiety and uncertainty about the experience.

In the ensuing years, a number of Sisters of Charity participated in programs to become spiritual directors in the Ignatian tradition of prayer, an approach that, although it was familiar to the congregation because of the strong influence of Jesuits over the years, now bore the influence of women directors. Other sisters found ease in spiritualties in the Franciscan and Dominican modes. Eventually a more structured approach to the Vincentian model of prayer took form.

The spirituality of Elizabeth Seton gained attention as the congregation prayed for her canonization over the years. That event was a milestone in the life of the congregation. As Elizabeth's status in the Church had moved from Venerable to Blessed, hope grew that the culminating event would eventually take place. When, on December 12, 1974, Pope Paul VI announced the decision to canonize her, the date selected for the ceremony was Sunday, September 14, 1975. The year marked the bicentennial of the founding of the United States, and it was fitting that the first American saint would be canonized that year. Within the Federation, plans that were in keeping with Elizabeth's spirit of simplicity took shape. The usual displays of pomp were omitted, and Federation members contributed $200,000, $50,000 of which came from the Sisters of Charity, Halifax, to care for the hungry of the world. This was in keeping with the Twelfth Chapter's statement on social justice.

The congregation established a lottery to determine who would make the trip to Rome, and any sister who could be available was invited to enter her name. In all, 105 Sisters of Charity, Halifax travelled to the event. As a means of spiritual preparation, Katherine asked those who would be traveling to Rome to make a triduum of prayer on September 11, 12, and 13. The journey to Rome proved to be not only spiritually uplifting but also culturally enriching, as sisters took advantage of the opportunity to savour the history, art, and beauty of Italy.

For those who did not travel to Rome, the day was marked by liturgies and joyful celebrations in their provinces. Many in the United States were able to view the liturgy in St. Peter's Square on television and watched with pride as Sister Katherine O'Toole read the petition for canonization. Among those assisting Pope Paul VI at the Eucharist was Archbishop James Hayes of Halifax. In addition to the celebration in Rome, each of the areas in which Sisters of Charity lived hosted a liturgy of thanksgiving, and a week later Rev. Edward McCarthy, CSC celebrated a liturgy of thanksgiving at the Motherhouse. The Canadian Broadcasting Corporation (CBC) televised the event and drew 30,000 viewers (McKenna 1998, 283). In addition, on October 4 in Halifax, Archbishop Hayes presided at a liturgy to which religious and civic leaders were invited. The canonization, which had long been the focus of prayer, was well celebrated.

As Pope Paul lauded the feminine spirituality of Elizabeth Seton, there was another dimension of feminine spirituality rising in the Church. The force of feminism in the Church had been growing, and

while this lead many to criticize the ways in which the Church had limited women's roles, others saw the insights of feminism as a reason to hope for change. The first Women's Ordination Conference took place in Detroit in November 1975, and many were optimistic that women's roles in the Roman Catholic Church were going to take on new and exciting forms. The Chapter of 1976 took place during that period of optimism. Within months of the Chapter's closing, however, the Congregation for the Doctrine of the Faith issued the "Declaration on the Question of the Admission of Women to the Ministerial Priesthood," in which the door was closed: "the Church does not consider herself authorized to admit women to priestly ordination … it would be difficult to see in the minister the image of Christ" (Quoted in Henhold 2008, 189). The topic did not disappear, however, and there were subsequent studies and conferences that kept the hope alive. In February 1977, the Governing Board took up the issue and asked Sister Donna Geernaert to chair a committee to study the Vatican's statement.

Although the ordination of women was the headline issue, the rise of women in pastoral roles created its own tensions. That "first generation" experienced many affirming moments in their ministry, but they also experienced numerous moments of frustration as they forged new paths. In a meeting with Bishop Francis J. Mugavero of Brooklyn, the sisters in the New York Province voiced their concerns, and the Archbishop acknowledged that some priests had difficulty accepting these changing roles. Despite the frustrations encountered, Sister Katherine Meagher was named Chancellor of the Diocese of Nelson in 1977, a clear indication that there were places for women within Church structures. This recognition of the gifts of nature and grace that women possessed prompted Sister Theresa Kane, a Sister of Mercy and President of the Leadership Conference of Women Religious[5] to raise the topic of full participation of women in the ministry at a televised event with Pope John Paul when he visited the United States in 1979.

Within weeks of the Women's Ordination Conference, one of the more controversial events of Sister Katherine's first term occurred: the

[5] For information on this conference, see https://lcwr.org/

issuing of a letter to the congregation on the topic of dress. It had been six years since the habit had become optional, and during those six years many sisters worked on balancing what was appropriate for a vowed religious with contemporary styles for women.

When Katherine, representing the Governing Board, issued a letter on December 1, 1975, she did so with the intention of dealing with the topic prior to the Chapter of 1976, lest delegates get distracted from more significant agenda items, as many sisters thought had happened at the Chapter of 1968 when the topic of religious habit had been discussed. In the letter, Katherine reminded the congregation that it was the Governing Board's role to interpret the *Constitutions* and that the *Covenant of Renewal*, the interim constitution, had stated that dress should be appropriate for religious women; that is, modest, simple, and suitable to the age of the sister and to the occasion on which it was worn. She wrote, "The wearing of formal dress such as evening gowns and the wearing of jewelry are considered inappropriate for religious women." But the letter also addressed those who continued to wear a veil. It was to be blue, black, or white, and "the rest of the dress should be in conformity with the wearing of a veil." More specifics of style and colour followed.

The question of dress raised issues of personal judgment and expression, and many sisters who were growing in these areas responded to the letter negatively. Sister Maureen Regan noted in her biography of Sister Katherine that "because Katherine had sent the letter, she received the blame; most of the resulting bitterness was directed to her" (1996, 318). Some wrote to Sister Katherine expressing their opinion and, in chapter the following July, she responded to questions on the topic. It was agreed that the topic of dress would be handled at the provincial level. Sister Mary Olga commented, "the Governing Board accepted the critique of its manner of handling the matter but not of its right and duty to speak to any matter" (McKenna 1998, 307). While the ways in which the letter was received by the sisters varied, it was a significant effort by Sister Katherine to mark the importance of simplicity.

It was out of this same concern for simplicity that Katherine sent out to the congregation an address on the topic that Pedro Arrupe, General Superior of the Jesuits, had delivered in Genoa, Italy at the end of 1973 to the Jesuits of that province as they prepared for their Thirty-Second General Congregation. During her second term, Sister Katherine would continue to raise the issue of simplicity of life in her presentations and in her written communications and discussions with the sisters.

These years also saw the first efforts of the congregation to gather large numbers of sisters from across the congregation for personal and spiritual development. In many instances, the sisters hadn't seen one another since first profession or tertianship, and the reunions, which often took place just inside the front doors of the Motherhouse, were joyful and oftentimes emotionally draining. Odyssey '75 was one such program. In August 1975, 178 sisters registered to participate. Topics for presentations included the vowed life, celibacy and sexuality, relationship with Jesus in prayer, and shared heritage and responsibility. Participants came away refreshed and energized by new insights and renewed friendships. Such events reflected greater mobility and the need and desire to provide ongoing formation for members, even at great cost.

As the changes of Vatican II took root, it was clear that religious education needed attention. Varied editions of the catechism came onto the market, new approaches to teaching arrived in classrooms, and sometimes those who taught religious education felt overwhelmed. In order to address this, the congregation offered a program for those who felt a need to update their knowledge and for those who had begun to consider full-time ministry in the field. The program, Good News, took place for the first time in the summer of 1977. One hundred and thirty sisters participated in that first offering. The program was also offered in 1978 and 1979 and brought together presenters, some of whom were Sisters of Charity or former members, to renew and inspire the participants.

The efforts to improve communication during this period are worth noting. The Governing Board had created an Office of Communications with Sister Cathleen Dunne as director. After her studies in the field of communication, Cathleen brought fresh ideas to the work, and congregational updates began to appear more regularly. The on-going changes and the growing desire for active participation in the life of the congregation meant that it was important for sisters to be connected and informed. To further these goals, the congregation, under Cathleen's guidance, published pocket-sized congregational directories for each sister. With hindsight, these directories reflect significant new realities: sisters were expected to be in easy communication with other Sisters of Charity, but they would often be traveling or working alone. There were also programs and workshops on communication as well as on caring for the elderly and on creativity in middle and later years. With a growing sense of collaboration, the congregation invited the public to participate in some of these programs.

Less than a year after the Chapter of 1972, plans were already underway to prepare for the 1976 Thirteenth General Chapter, with Sister Maria F. Sutherland serving as Chairperson for the Chapter Planning Committee. The previous chapter had mandated that there be a study of the General Chapter in all its aspects, and that the necessary changes be made. As members of the Governing Board did their homework, they became aware of the movements within other religious congregations to create chapters of total involvement. This approach reemphasized the importance of each member sharing her gifts and participating in the life of the congregation.

Preparations occurred throughout the congregation. In an attempt to use newer methods of communication to make the invitation to participate more personal, Sister Katherine made a video at the Motherhouse that was to be viewed in the provinces in January 1975. The new approach elicited positive responses. As the Chapter Coordinator of the Western Province, Sister Maureen O'Loane wrote, "There seemed to be unanimous agreement that this message had reached them in a way no written messages ever had." In the video, Katherine raised several questions: "Has the vision of a personal call and response to God in love and concern for the needs of the People of God become for us more than just words or concepts? … Are our communities prayerful enough and open enough to offer to people viable alternatives to the

values of a contemporary culture where the real meaning of life is so often obscured?" She referred to the Vatican Council's Decree, *Perfectae Caritatis,* and reminded the congregation, "The cooperation of all is required if the whole truth is to be discerned in our ongoing pilgrimage of faith into the future." Each sister was asked to sign an affirmation of commitment to participate as fully as she was able in the chapter process. Sisters would meet in provinces to identify areas of concern and these issues were synthesized to create the agenda for the chapter.

The official date for the beginning of the process was September 27, 1975, the feast of Saint Vincent de Paul. It was clear that participation would involve a great deal of sharing and small group discussions, something that Katherine referred to as "the asceticism of small groups." This format presented a challenge for some, and the various provincial committees laboured to balance warmth and expectation. The tone is detected in the invitation to the sisters of the Western Province: "[Y] ou are strongly urged and warmly invited to participate in the official opening of the General Chapter in the context of the Eucharistic liturgy."

The Chapter Planning Committee had determined that it would be helpful to separate the two segments of the chapter, with the Chapter of Elections taking place in March, and the Chapter of Affairs, that is the segment that dealt with other topics, taking place in July. After a conversation between Sister Katherine and Archbishop Hayes, the plan was solidified. In another step toward total participation, the Chapter Planning Committee agreed that sisters who were not delegates would be welcomed as observers at the general sessions.

Sister Bernadette McCarville served as Secretary for the Chapter. Part of her role was clarified by a statement from the Governing Board at their June meeting between the chapter segments: "It was agreed that there is no need for special communications to the congregation during the meeting because the session lasts only two weeks." Looking back at this decision from the age of computers, smart phone, and iPads, such limited communication seems hard to believe, although with elections taking place at the March session, much of the suspense would be dissipated before the summer session.

Fifty-one delegates who had been elected on a weighted ballot assembled at the Motherhouse on March 12-15, 1976 to conduct elections. As they proceeded to elect leadership for the next four years, they employed a new pre-election step: in an effort to provide delegates with an opportunity to get to know those whose names would appear on the ballots, the nominees agreed to speak candidly about their qualifications, their experiences, and how they envisioned themselves in congregational leadership roles – not an easy task for Sisters of Charity.

On March 14, the delegates re-elected Sister Katherine on the first ballot and, as local ordinary, Archbishop Hayes formally confirmed the election. Sister Rita MacDonald was re-elected Vicar General and continued as Treasurer General, a position she had assumed when Sister Mary Moore resigned midway through the previous term. Sister Elizabeth Hayes remained as Second Assistant and Sister Anne Harvey was elected Third Assistant. Sister Anne Hunter was appointed Secretary General.

When the delegates reassembled at the Motherhouse in July for the business segment of chapter, they accepted the four-year report from the Governing Board and considered the report's recommendations. They then turned to the proposals from the provinces and from individuals. These proposals covered a wide array of issues, some familiar and some the result of new consciousness and new experiences in community living. The recurring concerns about religious dress and a community symbol were evident among the proposals, as were concerns regarding congregational government and structure and life at the local level. But other issues were indicative of the new experiences within religious life, with some members still struggling to balance past experiences and new options, new developments in contemporary culture, and new demands of the Gospel's call to social justice.

One proposal addressed the issue of computerization within the congregation, raising a concern that as the use of computers spread, the congregation was losing some of its countercultural orientation. Others took on political issues: one proposal suggested that the congregation avoid any support for multinational corporations, another that we

support the role of women in the Church and encourage women religious to try to exert influence in decision-making within the institution. Some of the many proposals that went to the Chapter Planning Committee were amalgamated before they went to the floor of the Chapter. The final statements and implementation plans were organized into the following categories: Apostolate/Ministry, Community Living/Lifestyle, and Related Areas. The repeated phrases "each sister" and "an individual sister" served as a reminder that personal responsibility was of the utmost importance. Emphasis on the spiritual lives of members was obvious in the statements related to Apostolate/Ministry. This emphasis may well have reflected the concerns of older members for the prayer practices of sisters in formation, rather than simply representing the theological and spiritual renewal of the sisters.

The first statement reiterated the theme of the preceding Chapter by reaffirming the commitment to Jesus as Lord (I.A.1.). The delegates affirmed that "the corporate apostolate is to continue the saving mission of Jesus – the building of the Kingdom" (I.A.2.). In a variety of ways, the delegates reaffirmed the necessity of communities of faith and prayer focusing on Jesus (I.B.3. a, b, c, d, e, g). As diversity had taken hold and sisters' daily schedules had become more varied, it oftentimes took great efforts for the members of local communities to find a common time for prayer. Some met early each morning, others before or after dinner. Some designated specific days or nights each week. These efforts bespoke the value that local communities placed on common prayer, and the Chapter statements are a reflection of this.

For those sisters who did not live in community, there were other concerns. The Chapter described life in community as "an essential aspect of religious life" (I.B.2.). As the number of sisters living alone rose during these years, the Governing Board had spent a good amount of time dealing with this new reality and had formulated guidelines that became part of the congregation's Policy Manual in 1977. The chapter affirmed this work, encouraged local communities to keep communications open with these sisters, and called for the use of the guidelines, including "on-going mutual communication and evaluation" (I.B Implementation 2).

An examination of the topics in Apostolate/Ministry reveals keys to understanding how the congregation had changed since the previous chapter. The many statements that included the names of Saints Elizabeth Seton and Vincent de Paul are testimony to the ways in which the work on the spirit of the founders that had been implemented by the Twelfth General Chapter had taken root. Furthermore, the move away from top-down decision-making is evident in some of the statements. For example, Statement 3, "[D]iscern [the needs of the Church] and our ability to respond, in collaboration with authorities within the Church, as well as laity, and with social and civic agencies" (I.A.3.) invited a broad collaborative approach to establishing ministries. In addition, the phrase "dialogue and representation," during which an individual sister "discerns in matters affecting choice of ministry and local community," bespoke a more collegial approach to the apostolate and to obedience (I.A.5.).

Under the topic of Community Living/Lifestyle, the language was of rights and responsibilities, of goal setting and evaluation for the individual sister and the local community. One gets a hint of the possibilities and the challenges of community: "[O]ur communities should foster each member's growth in her total commitment and should challenge her to participate in the building of community characterized by love, simplicity, sharing and service" (I.B.3.f.). As groups of sisters were initiating the formation of new communities, the document reminded the congregation that "[l]ocal communities should be formed, increased, decreased, in response to personal and apostolic needs rather than from personal preference only" (I.B.4.). The element of simplicity is reinforced by reminding the congregation that "[e]ach sister, local community and province is called to give a counter-cultural witness by a simple lifestyle (I.B. Implementation 5.). And again, "We affirm that we should live simply – as followers of Christ" (I.B.5.).

In the section entitled "Decisions Arising from the Report of the Governing Board," the frequency with which the word "continue" appears is not surprising. The Governing Board had initiated a number of projects in the preceding four years, some mandated by the Twelfth General Chapter. Many of them, in that era of experimentation, seemed worthy of ongoing engagement: continued research regarding experimentation in various forms of extended community, continuation of the experimental vice provinces, and in the experiment of coordinated planning for retirement. All these practices seemed wise, as the congregation looked for ways to move into the future, including new approaches to finance: "The continuation of a system of centralized financial management which highlights stewardship, social concern, sharing within and outside the congregation" (II.K) linked financial stability to concerns for social issues. New initiatives approved by the Chapter included the creation of a congregational symbol and the establishment of a committee for the work of redrafting the *Constitutions*. Both initiatives would take time to come to fruition.

The congregation's Latin American missionary commitments were still young at the time of the Thirteenth General Chapter in 1976, and the needs of these missions in Peru and the Dominican Republic were becoming more defined. The hope for vocations gained new life when, in 1974, Martha Loo, a native of Peru, made her first profession in Lima. At the 1976 Chapter, the congregation affirmed "its intention of maintaining missionary involvement in Latin America as long as resources allow" (II.J.1.). The ministries focused on evangelization and development, and it was agreed that the missions "would remain under the jurisdiction of the Halifax Province" (II.J.3.). With hope for the growth of the missions, the delegates also determined that the staffing needs "would be communicated through the Governing Board to the entire congregation" (II.J.4.).

If the congregation's focus on evangelization and development addressed the needs of Latin America, its focus on social injustice addressed some of the needs of North America. Reinforcing the theme of social justice from the Twelfth General Chapter, the words of the Thirteenth General Chapter stated, "[W]e should develop social awareness which will help us to admit and strive to correct any racism and prejudice in our own lives and social injustice wherever it exists" (I.C.2.). At a time when the civil rights movement seemed to be facing new obstacles, the statement called on the sisters to consider if they had practiced discrimination in their own hearts and actions.

The broader term of social justice invited the congregation to consider systemic issues and led in 1978 to the action of boycotting Nestle products because of the deleterious impact of their infant formula in developing countries. In March of that year, after consultation with the congregation's attorney, Katherine addressed a letter to the president of the Nestle Company, in which she stated the congregation's perspective. This was an unusual example of activism. To nourish this movement, Katherine spoke about Biblical Justice and urged the sisters to be attentive to the call to Gospel living and the sources of the call to social justice.

Many of the enactments of the Thirteenth General Chapter related to congregational government structures. The previous four years had been a period of experimentation, and changes in government structures reflected new ways of recognizing human growth and new ways of dealing with the needs of the members of the congregation. Issues ranged from the Chapter role of the "superior general whose term of office has last expired" (IIIc), to possible additions to the vice provinces.

The *Covenant of Renewal* continued to serve as the congregation's interim constitution and the Chapter reaffirmed its importance, especially the five principles of the dignity of the human person, unity, diversity, co-responsibility/collegiality, and subsidiarity. But the Chapter also formulated several revisions relating to formation and government.

Among the enactments related to formation is one that serves as a reminder of the developments within that area. The process of forming new members had become much more personal and allowed for varied lengths of time for temporary profession. The enactment stated, "The first profession and the renewal of vows or promises are made for a definite period of time determined by mutual agreement of the candidate and the provincial superior" (V. Amendment 1.). This simple statement captures a great deal of the spirit of the times: fluidity, respect for the individual sister and her unique journey, and more personal relationships with the Provincial.

Once again the delegates returned to their provinces and to the generalate, and the work of integrating the Chapter decisions into the life of the congregation was underway. For Katherine's second term, and in some cases into the next administration, the provincial superiors who served as members of the Governing Board were as follows: Sisters Genevieve Morrissey (Antigonish, 1974–1980); Catherine Hanlon (Boston, 1974–1980); Paule Cantin (Central Province, 1974–1980); Maria F. Sutherland (Halifax, 1976–1980); Mary McGowan (New York, 1972–1978), succeeded by Barbara Buxton (1978–1984); Mary Therese Gavin (Western Province, 1974–1982); Romaine Bates (1979–1987); and Louise Kenney (Wellesley Vice Province, 1975–1977), succeeded by Mary Sheila Desmond (1977–1985). These women and their provincial boards worked to implement the pertinent chapter directives.

In many ways, Sister Katherine's three characteristics of diminishment, diversity, and rebirth seemed intermingled during her second term. The diminishment continued in some ways, with ministries ending, houses closing, and sisters departing the congregation; but these same movements led to new ministries and the rebirth of the charism in different settings. Ministerial openings throughout the congregation were published and provincial personnel directors assisted sisters as they made decisions about ministry and community life. Provincial celebrations of missioning became familiar as sisters came to a deeper understanding that even if they were the only Sister of Charity at a ministry site, they carried with them the responsibility of the congregational charism to show forth the love of God.

Among the recurring topics that the Governing Board addressed during the second term of Sister Katherine's administration was the creation of a congregational symbol. The minutes of March 1975 state that "the sisters at large seem to want a distinctive symbol." Since 1969, the habit had been optional and gradually the number of sisters wearing a veil or a habit was decreasing; a congregational symbol would identify and unite members, although the wearing of the symbol would be optional.

At the October 1976 meeting, the Governing Board appointed Sister Romaine Bates as chairperson of a task force that would establish criteria for the new symbol. The process for creating and selecting the symbol encouraged congregational participation, and in January 1977 Sister Katherine invited submissions. In October 1977, members voted, using a weighted ballot. Although many sisters favoured the simple Peru cross, more than eighty sisters abstained from voting. In February 1978, the Governing Board minutes noted "unreadiness on the part of sisters to accept a congregational symbol at this time." Later notes refer to "close results, lack of enthusiasm, bad timing." (Summary of Implementation by the Governing Board of Enactments of Chapter 1976). The topic was tabled until 1979, with the hope that the work on the writing of the new constitutions, then underway, would be helpful in assisting the sisters to choose a new symbol.

New designs and voting followed and in 1980, five years after the first mention of a congregational symbol in the Governing Board minutes, the sisters made a choice. The symbol, cast in pewter, consisted of a cross and a basin and towel. These reminders of Christ's service and sacrifice were set within an irregularly shaped heart, representing the willingness to adjust to changing times. Sister Florette Amyot, a talented artist, went to Sherbrooke, Quebec to oversee the production of the symbol. In the process of deciding on and creating the symbol, the congregation learned that broad-based participation in decision-making was a two-edged sword: it involved the membership, thus creating ownership of the outcome, but it also extended the period of decision-making.

During her first term, Sister Katherine had addressed the topic of simplicity and had urged the sisters to reflect on how they lived out that aspect of the charism. As sisters had more opportunities for individual decisions and an increased stipend for personal use, new questions arose around living in a manner that felt consistent with the spirit and vow of poverty. The Thirteenth General Chapter stated, "We affirm that we should live simply – as followers of Christ," and Katherine seemed to focus on the topic more frequently than others. At an Executive Council meeting the following April, members focused on the topic and agreed to ask for written reports from provincials and vice provincials on what had been done in response to the Chapter statement and to comment on positive and negative trends.

In an address to provincial treasurers in 1977, Sister Katherine urged them to help the sisters at the local level to see budgetary issues "in a broader appreciation of poverty rooted in faith, rather than in mere economics." Katherine also saw this issue in very practical terms, hoping that sisters would come to grasp the "R.Q." as she called it, the "reality quotient," asking, "Are we aware of the costs of rent, utilities, food, insurance, education, medical bills, and taxes?" And in the spirit of the vow, she suggested that sisters "adopt a policy of not complaining, of being grateful." In January 1978, Sister Katherine wrote about this issue again: "I believe that we are at a critical juncture in our personal experience of our commitment and of our credibility before others. I pray that we will have the vision to recognize this as a graced moment." She also included a copy of a talk on the subject given by Pedro Arrupe, the Superior General of the Jesuits, at the Third Inter-American Conference of Religious in Montreal in November 1977 in which he addressed consumerism and *homo consumens*. In a homily for the feast of Elizabeth Seton in 1978, Sister Katherine quoted the saint as she prepared to move from the Stone House to the White House in Emmitsburg: "Our moveables [sic] are not very weighty." Sister Katherine questioned, "Could we – you and I – say this with equal truth today of our possessions? If not, are we perhaps forgetting something of the detachment and simplicity [Elizabeth] taught and lived?"

The review of annual budgets in June 1979 also provided another opportunity to address the subject. Members of the Governing Board noted the sincere efforts of sisters to live simply, but they also felt concerns regarding poverty and lifestyle. There followed a listing of actions and attitudes that seemed contradictory to simplicity and the vow of poverty that "[caused] some sisters to accumulate money." There was a concern that sisters were "confusing needs and wants … moving away from the experience of common life … living more by middle-class values than by the Gospel call to simplicity." The topic is, of course, of perennial concern, but in those days of new personal freedom, Katherine saw the great importance of both the practice and the witness value of simplicity. Recognizing it as an essential part of religious life, she continued to urge members to consider their own commitment to a gospel life style.

During Katherine's second term there were questions about the development of the Latin American missions. Since they had opened in the 1960s, the number of sisters engaged in ministry there varied over the years. By the late 1970s, the Governing Board had asked sisters for a five-year commitment, but few sisters felt called. In 1978, the appeal for personnel listed the characteristics one should possess to respond to the call: personal health and maturity, genuine mission motivation, and an ability to learn languages. Such communications kept the Latin American missions in the sisters' minds, and several later responded to the appeal.

Both Canada and the United States felt political tremors in those years. In the Province of Quebec, during the 60s, the Quiet Revolution, had led to a new vision, a vision that was not dominated by tradition, the Church, and agriculture. The Church lost a great deal of institutional power and influence and the ramifications became obvious. One of the intellectual lights behind the Quiet Revolution was Pierre Elliott Trudeau. He was elected Prime Minister of Canada in 1968 and served in that position until 1979. He was re-elected in 1980 and served until 1984. Trudeau brought a liberal perspective to politics, and his energy and style brought excitement to the national scene. Although he was from the Province of Quebec, Trudeau was a federalist who supported a unified Canada.

In November 1976, the Province of Quebec elected separatist Rene Levesque as its Premier. The separatist movement gained support within the province, raising concerns among many communities. The Sisters of Charity, who ministered primarily to the Anglophones, began to feel tensions. In June 1977, Sister Paule Cantin informed the members of the Governing Board of the situation and the minutes note, "The political situation in Quebec has been a source of difficulty for the sisters in the Quebec and Montreal regions. At this point, the sisters are being encouraged to be a source of hope for the people of Quebec, particularly the English-speaking people."

Language became the flashpoint issue, especially with the passing of the Charter of French Language in August 1977. Anglophones began to feel isolated. Many moved to Ontario, with Toronto and its environs benefiting from the movement of commercial interests. This movement had implications for the Sisters of Charity in the Central Province, whose mission was primarily to the Anglophone community, both in schools and in St. Brigid's Home.

With tensions increasing, it became evident that the solution for some of the teaching sisters was to withdraw from schools. Fortunately, the Diocese of Toronto was eager to welcome them. The first of several communities in that area was established in Mississauga in 1977. For St. Brigid's Home, which, in 1973 had moved into a new building financed by the provincial government, the solution was a proportional one, with approximately one-third of the guests coming from English-speaking backgrounds. The house of prayer which had been established in 1979 primarily for the Anglophone community continued to serve that community in Quebec. As the political situation evolved, the separation of Quebec from Canada was averted, but the province had made its case forcefully, and French language and culture won an official place of prominence.

Within the congregation, the freedom that sisters were experiencing created new opportunities for understanding community life and the vows. The question of how to relate to authority in an era of personal freedom required focused consideration. In an effort to secure the authority vested in the position of the superior general, delegates at the Twelfth General Chapter emphasized that role, but the vow of obedience was acquiring new meanings in the years following Vatican II: the role of the local superior was decreasing, local coordinators or contact persons were more active, and local communities had certain expectations of members. Co-responsibility and accountability took on greater significance as women religious accepted the invitation to mature interaction.

In 1975, in response to this new reality, the Governing Board produced a three-page statement on the meaning, scope, and implementation of accountability. Clearly, this was a growing concern as sisters dealt with both freedom and privacy. Personal use of community cars and extensive time spent away from community with family or friends often triggered new concerns. The issue came to the fore in a letter from Katherine to provincial and vice provincial superiors dated May 10, 1977: "It is very important for each provincial/vice provincial superior to know the summer schedules of the sisters. This is very important for accountability but also for the very practical reason should contact be necessary at any time."

The topic of accountability and the related topics of obedience, authority, and government would surface in many ways and become a particular challenge with the writing of the *Constitutions*, one of the most significant projects of these years. Minutes for the Governing Board meeting in March 1975 state, "[I]t was agreed that work should be begun on the revision of the *Constitutions*. It was further agreed that new *Constitutions* should retain pertinent elements of the *Covenant of Renewal*." The Thirteenth General Chapter had formally mandated the work in 1976, and in September of that year a committee was in place. In keeping with the spirit of the *Covenant of Renewal*, the entire congregation was invited to participate in the work, completing what came to be called "Constitutions assignments" and attending related presentations in the provinces.

In August 1977, Sister Katherine wrote to the sisters to encourage their involvement:

> Your years of living and serving in and through the Congregation have given you the competence for participation in the task at hand ... You should then feel qualified to bring to the re-drafting of our particular law the fruits of your lived experience, your love and the

> results of your prayerful reflection ... I call each Sister of Charity now to enter into this work wholeheartedly in a spirit of faith and trust and love ... It is in fact only if each sister participates to the extent that she is able that the Father's will for the Sisters of Charity in this regard may be fully discerned.

To stimulate thinking on some of the issues involved in the work, the congregation invited noted theologians to speak in the provinces on key aspects of religious life. Ladislas Orsy, SJ, Jacques Pasquier, OMI, John Carroll Futrell, SJ, and his associates conducted workshops, and again Katherine wrote to encourage participation.

With Sister Anne Harvey as chairperson, the Constitutions Committee or its core committee met more than 100 times, preparing and reviewing provincial presentations and assignments for the sisters, working on drafts, and preparing reports to the General Chapter and the congregation. In 1977, provincial representatives were selected to form an extended committee; they assisted the core committee, serving as liaisons with the provinces. The core committee had studied preceding Constitutions, hoping to select the threads that would provide continuity. As the sisters completed their constitutions assignments, reflecting, praying, discussing, and responding to questions, Sister Anne found herself "listening for the language used by the sisters ... [for] recurring phrases, expressions, words," hoping that when the document was completed, the sisters would recognize it as their own, with its connection to their past and their present.

In 1978, the Governing Board approved a list of theological consultants, including three members of the congregation (Sisters Donna Geernaert, Katherine Meagher, and Elizabeth Bellefontaine) who would add additional expertise to the work of the Constitutions Committee. Lest details of the writing be overlooked, the Governing Board also approved the committee's recommendation for a subcommittee to review the draft for grammar and style.

In February 1980, each sister in the congregation received a copy of the draft of the *Constitutions and General Directives* and was asked to review the work and respond to the committee. Based on the sisters' responses, which were generally very positive, the delegates to the April session of the Fourteenth General Chapter determined that additional work on the government section was warranted. Committee members prepared an assignment on that topic and the results were published prior to the July session of the Chapter.

Many other religious congregations were also working on their constitutions during this period, and they willingly encouraged and supported one another in the work. As sisters from various congregations communicated with officials in Rome, they would often share with one another their insights and the issues that had been addressed. As the process went on, official reviewers in Rome seemed to find additional points to question, and so the insights that the congregations shared were helpful in resolving difficulties or preventing them from arising. The work on the *Constitutions* would continue into the next administration, reaching completion during Sister Paule Cantin's term. The effort to include the members in the process of rewriting the *Constitutions* was invaluable. It enabled the sisters to contribute to the very words that held the congregation together, words by which they lived.

If words helped to hold the congregation together, so too did works. While some ministry sites flourished, others were closing, including Saint Patrick's High School in Roxbury, Saint Mary's School in Randolph, and St. Peter's School in Lowell. Although the schools were the responsibility of the parishes, the Sisters had dedicated themselves to the education of the children and felt keenly the decisions to close the schools.

During the same period, the congregation considered its ability to sustain its support and involvement in Mount Saint Vincent University. Was it time to consider relinquishing its role in the University? When the delegates at the Thirteenth General Chapter addressed the question of the sale of Mount Saint Vincent University, Sister Mary Albertus Haggarty, who was then president of the University, pointed out its financial security. However, given the complexity of the topic, the Chapter delegates did not feel adequately prepared to discuss the issue,

and so they referred it to the members of the Governing Board for further research. Several months later, the board of Mount Saint Vincent University submitted a proposal. After consultation with the Treasurer General and the Advisory Board, the congregation's Governing Board rejected the proposal. Negotiations ceased for the duration of Katherine's second term.

Such discussions did not mean that the congregation took less interest in the University. To accommodate the University's growing need for student space, the sisters who taught on the faculty requested housing – some on campus, some off campus – and so the congregation constructed Walsh House and purchased a house on Marlwood Drive to accommodate their needs. Additional support for the University came from the congregation's Halifax Province, which created the Elizabeth Seton lecture series. With a gift of $50,000, the series, whose theme was "Christian Presence in the World – Past, Present, Future," was a concrete sign of the congregation's support and its intent to nourish the University's roots in the religious tradition.

Despite the University's roots, Mount Saint Vincent, like most universities in the 1960s and 1970s, faced new expectations about student life. Social values were changing, and the Executive Committee minutes of September 1976 hint at the tensions when old and new values clashed. When the University was negotiating the renewal of its lease for student housing within the Motherhouse, the congregation stated the concerns clearly: abuse of drugs and alcohol, the appearance of religious cults, and guests of the opposite sex. The University was asked to approve a policy that dealt with these issues as part of its new agreement. This did not resolve all of the conflicts on the campus, of course, and student opposition to the regulations that the administration sought to impose continued to surface in petitions and in an editorial in the student newspaper. Another sign of the times in 1977 was the University's choice of E. Margaret Fulton as president to succeed Sister Mary Albertus Haggarty. As the first president who was not a Sister of Charity, Dr. Fulton brought to her position a rich academic and professional background.

Other congregational institutions were at different stages of their development. In both Halifax and Wellesley, the retirement centres and infirmaries grew in many ways during the 1970s. With the establishment and reworking of the vice provinces, the congregation had shown sincere efforts to provide a government structure that would be helpful to the sisters who lived in these institutions. In addition, the creation of Boards of Management eased the administration of these large institutions so that they were directed in accordance with national standards in Canada and the United States, and the creation of small communities within the larger organization facilitated interaction among the sisters. Residents were the beneficiaries of numerous programs for their physical, spiritual, psychological, and social well-being. The sisters' ministry of prayer and their care for one another were sources of strength and inspiration, as were their many volunteer efforts. When Mount Saint Vincent, Wellesley opened in 1967, the nursing care section was relatively small. In March 1980, the adjoining Elizabeth Seton Residence opened, a nursing care facility to accommodate sisters in the American provinces, and, on a limited basis, family members.

The need to strengthen these centres was clear as the congregation faced the reality of an aging population and an increased number of sisters facing retirement. Accustomed to participating actively in ministry and contributing to the congregation, many sisters resisted the idea. As the minutes of the Governing Board meeting of October 1976 state, "[I] t was noted that the sisters are still averse to the term retirement."

There was also growing awareness that increasing longevity meant retirees could look forward to years of active living. How could the congregation assist sisters in that situation to age in a way that was helpful to them as apostolic women religious? Provincial meetings for sisters in pre-retirement presented opportunities to discuss and explore answers. One creative response came from the New York Province. With Sister Robert Marie as coordinator, Resurrection-Ascension convent became a residence for sisters who sought to continue in ministry on a limited basis. With a nursing home nearby, sisters were encouraged to visit the residents and to find other sites where they might bring

assistance. While the concept seemed on target, in hindsight it became apparent that more preparation would have been helpful to make the venture a long-term success.

In 1975, the Boston Province established a similar type of community under the leadership of Sister Miriam Constance at Immaculate Conception Convent in Winchester. Until 2004, these sisters continued their community life together in prayer and service to residents of nursing homes and to the parish in limited ministries. For many retirees, new opportunities for prayer and service enriched them in unexpected ways as they turned to visiting hospitals and nursing homes, tutoring, and a host of volunteer roles. Other provinces sought to address these issues and to assist those who were preparing for retirement to plan in a way that would be life-giving for them and for their concepts of ministry.

Since the Chapter of Renewal, the congregation had both absorbed and affected many changes. Deeper than the visible changes in name and dress were the altered ways of living together and the increasing variety of ministries. Growing collaboration with laity, priests, and religious of other congregations made these colleagues first-hand observers of the changes that influenced the life and mission of the Sisters of Charity.

With the Fourteenth General Chapter approaching, the congregation secured the services of Management Design, Inc. (MDI) to conduct a survey in order to gain some sense of how the congregation was viewed. Nearly 500 people who had some relationship with the congregation responded to the questionnaires, but it is interesting to note that few religious responded. Inevitably, the respondents' impressions were based on the individual sisters they had come to know; as a result, there were contradictory statements in the report, but several themes could be discerned. In the responses, the sisters' professional work, primarily in education, received generous praise, but respondents also desired to see the sisters extend their contributions into other areas within both church non-ecclesial settings. Conversely, others feared that too much diversity in apostolic commitments could lead to fragmentation, reducing the group's impact to the impact of one individual.

With the evolving diversity in community living, many respondents observed what they identified as a loss of a simple lifestyle, the growth of middle-class values, worldly attitudes, and materialism. As the summary states, "The strongest criticism … has to do with lifestyle … Such things as clothing, apartment living, expensive vacations and travel are mentioned specifically." Related to those criticisms, many respondents expressed "a desire for the sisters' involvement with the poor," and suggested a focus on the roots of the problem: an "emphatic group calls for analysis of the economic and political system, response to the Third World and confrontation of unjust structures." With regard to identifying members of the congregation, "most would like the sisters to show in some way that they are religious but none recommends returning to a traditional habit." Even as the questionnaire was collecting these critiques, the responses were already underway, as was shown by the consistent efforts of Sister Katherine to reinforce the significance of the Vincentian mark of simplicity and by the efforts of the congregation to arrive at a choice of a congregational symbol.

While the congregation's diversification in ministry enriched many apostolic efforts and brought satisfaction to sisters who sought to use their gifts in various settings, the comment regarding fragmentation was insightful; decades later the congregation still struggles with questions related to corporate identity, corporate mission, and corporate stance on issues. Furthermore, the call of one "emphatic group" for "analysis of the economic and political system," may well have been responsible for sowing seeds for later endeavours, as sisters turned their attention to the root causes of poverty and attempted to address them, by both congregational efforts and by collaboration with many other organizations.

From 1976 to 1980, the congregation continued to experience diminishment in the number of members, an experience not unique to the Sisters of Charity, Halifax. In 1976, congregational membership was 1,302, including 27 in temporary profession; by 1979, those numbers had decreased to 1,225 and 19. In an Executive Committee session in May 1977, the members looked at two questions: "Why was there no increase in the numbers of women entering the congregation?" and

"What could be done for sisters to develop a sense of purposefulness and pride in the congregation?"

Among the materials consulted was an article in the January-March 1977 edition of *Studies in the Spirituality of Jesuits*. The author, J. M. Becker, SJ, believed that there was a revolution "at the core of religious life. It involves a different view of reality, and it is likely to have profound long-term results" (3). He went on to cite intellectual development, new views of anthropology and history, and advancements in technology and communications as factors. As members of an apostolic congregation, the Sisters of Charity were part of the changing culture and the challenge was to find ways to address these changes in a manner that enabled the sisters to live their faith. This meant new approaches to attracting and forming prospective members and to providing education for those who were professed members.

Provincial formation team members continued their work, but their efforts seemed to attract only a small number of new vocations. Although team members made the rounds of parishes and schools on vocation days, only fifteen women formally affiliated themselves with the congregation during those four years. Among them was Sister Angela Stodolski, who in 1977 transferred into the congregation from a Franciscan congregation, an example of how vocations were being reinterpreted and reshaped during those years.

For those who were already in formation, the changes meant a much more personal approach. No longer lost in scores of postulants or novices, the candidates, now graduates of college or experienced members of the work force, brought new levels of self-awareness and maturity. When they joined as associates, they lived in small communities within the provinces, praying and recreating and sharing house responsibilities with professed sisters, but their theology courses, retreats, and personal development programs oftentimes took place outside the local formation community. Candidates shared many aspects of their formation with men and women from other religious congregations. During these years, it became common for individual sisters to make their profession of vows in parish churches. With the Superior General's approval, the sisters wrote their own vow formulas. These celebrations bespoke the values and tastes of the individual sister as she made her profession either by temporary commitment or perpetual vows. Many members hoped that with public celebrations of commitment other women would catch a glimpse of religious life and be inspired to consider this vocation for themselves.

During these years, several formation communities and novitiates existed in Canada (Herring Cove, Dorval, Glace Bay, Edmonton), the United States (Hingham and Hempstead), and Peru (Lima), indicating that the sisters were hopeful that new members would join them. In September 1977, Sister Elizabeth Hayes reported "that she was impressed by the priority being given to formation throughout the congregation; evidence of this is found in the fact that there will be four sisters doing full-time study related to formation as well as the importance being attached to the development of suitable formation communities." The collaboration of team members from across the congregation proved to be an invaluable resource to the sisters who assumed responsibility for formation. The congregational Formation Committee, with Sister Elizabeth Hayes as chair, usually met twice annually. Topics for discussion included an array of pertinent issues: vocation awareness, psychological testing, behaviour of young women in formation, expectations of professed members in formation communities, lines of communication among formation personnel, provincial superiors and provincial boards, and the questions of native vocations and formation of native candidates.

In the light of the many departures from religious life, ongoing formation took on new importance. Summer programs such as Good News, previously mentioned, were offered at the Motherhouse in 1977, 1978, and 1979. Passages, a program for those too old for Formation '74 and too young for Odyssey '75, took place at the Queen of Apostles Renewal Centre in Mississauga, Ontario. Individual provinces also sponsored courses, speakers, and programs, with sisters also initiating their own plans for updating and psychological counselling when that was considered helpful.

It was during these years that the early news stories were breaking

about the treatment of First Nations, Inuit, and Métis students at the residential schools across Canada. The schools had been established by the government and run under the auspices of various churches. Not surprisingly, many of them were staffed by religious congregations of the Catholic Church. While the intention had been to enculturate the students into the dominant Canadian culture, the effect had been to eliminate their ties to their native culture. There were also reports of abusive treatment. In 1978, Sister Katherine faced reports about the Shubenacadie Residential School in Nova Scotia, a school that had been closed for more than ten years. The reporter who spoke with Sister Katherine later interviewed some of the former teachers, but "the meeting was inconclusive" (McKenna 1998, 327). As Sister Mary Olga McKenna said in her book, "These events foreshadowed the efforts of First Nations people across Canada to express their experience of the residential schools" (McKenna 1998, 328). The national story would unfold and find some resolution, but it would take decades of memories painfully recalled, attentive listening, and restitution from the government and religious congregations.

As Katherine dealt with such challenging issues, once again the congregation prepared for chapter. In October 1978, the Governing Board appointed Sister Anne Fleming as Chairperson for the Fourteenth General Chapter Planning Committee, which consisted of representatives from the provinces and vice provinces. The effort at congregational participation that was begun with the Chapter of 1976 required careful attention. Much had changed in the intervening years, and the sisters had grown accustomed to consultation and involvement. The committee faced a significant task. Indicative of the developments in communication in the years since the previous chapter was the report made by Sister Cathleen Dunne to Sister Anne Fleming in April 1979 on possible modes of communication during chapter. Video and telephone were mentioned as possible choices.

On September 14, 1979, the Feast of the Triumph of the Holy Cross, Sister Katherine convoked the Fourteenth General Chapter and announced the theme: "Following Jesus in His Redemptive Mission:

Conversion and Service in Changing Times." This theme that would eventually find artistic expression in the congregational symbol. Mindful of the work on the *Constitutions*, Sister Katherine also informed the congregation that the delegates might have to reassemble in December of 1980 to approve the text before it was forwarded to Rome – a step that proved to be unnecessary.

To respond to the request for participation on the part of younger sisters, each province was invited to send one sister under 35. While these sisters were not considered official delegates and had no voting power, they could participate in the discussions and bring their insights to the issues. Again the Chapter was divided into two major sessions, with elections taking place during the first session in April at Mount Saint Vincent Motherhouse. On April 8, Sister Paule Cantin was elected General Superior. Once again, it was the role of Archbishop Hayes to confirm the name of the Superior General Elect of the congregation. Sister Paule brought many gifts to the position and her prior experiences served her well: having served as provincial of the Central Province for six years, she was familiar with the daily concerns of the sisters; her six years as a member of the Governing Board provided her with an overview of the congregation's workings. Following the election of the General Superior, the delegates elected Sister Anne Harvey as First Assistant/Vicar and Sister Mary Ellen Loar as Second Assistant. Sister Margaret Harvey was appointed General Secretary; Sister Margaret Molloy was reappointed General Treasurer, a position she had filled since the previous fall. The members of the new administration would assume their office on July 27, at the second session of chapter.

The General Chapter Planning Committee received numerous proposals. They provide a glimpse into the congregation and the issues of 1980. In some proposals, one senses efforts to reestablish a certain kind of order in the congregation: voices calling for the wearing of a habit, for fidelity to the pope, for specific spiritual practices and a return to the traditional vow formula; others calling for ministry solely within the works of the congregation, and for a novitiate located within the Motherhouse where vows would be professed; another advocated for particular practices as part of religious deportment. Other proposals, however, echoed the newer spirit of the Thirteenth General Chapter: concern that the congregation consider a response to the call for solidarity with the economically poor; that style of dress remain the choice of the individual sister; that language of congregational communication reflect sensitivity to gender issues; that the congregation deepen its consciousness regarding justice for women; that simple living be embraced; and that the idea of extended community become a reality. Proposals also addressed more structural concerns: that the independent standing of the Antigonish Province be reconsidered; that Bermuda be recognized as a mission territory.

There were also proposals that sought to establish a new approach to the election of delegates to general chapters. With a total membership in December 1979 of 1,244, the age bracket 60–69 was the most populous, and it was nearly inevitable that the sisters elected as delegates would be those who were better known by that age group. Younger sisters who were eager to participate in the life of the congregation were less likely to be able to share their experiences and their visions for the future of the congregation. Several proposals suggested ways to provide delegation from younger, more active members and helped to set the stage for significant changes for the way in which the meaning of the concept "chapter of total participation" would evolve.

As the delegates and observers gathered for the second segment of the Fourteenth General Chapter, it was clear that the seeds sown in the conversations in 1972 about chapter proceedings had taken root. As in other dimensions of congregational living, congregational input and participation had become the accepted mode for decision-making and governance. While this mode would continue to evolve, it was well established; congregational governance was forever changed.

The women charged with congregational leadership during these years, 1972 to 1980, had faced new challenges. Nourished by the spirit of the congregation they served, they helped to ease the Sisters of Charity into a new era. They themselves were also walking through that same unfamiliar terrain, charting their own renewal even as they worked out the congregation's needs and worked with other congregations. Sister Katherine took an active role in the International Union of Superiors General, in the Canadian Religious Conference, and the Federation; others worked with related committees. Sister Elizabeth Hayes conferred on issues related to formation. Sister Rita MacDonald extended her expertise to assist treasurers in other congregations. Sister Anne Harvey's work on the *Constitutions* kept her in touch with other congregations as they worked on their own.

These women also had to deal with personal loss. During her first term, Sister Katherine O'Toole experienced serious problems with her vision and, for a time, was forced to limit her work schedule. Members of the executive council stepped in to carry some of the work. Also during that first term, the resignation and subsequent departure from the congregation of treasurer-general Mary More touched the members of the Governing Board. Close to the end of Sister Katherine's second term in May 1980, secretary-general Anne Hunter, a very capable and humble woman, offered her resignation for reasons of health and died the following month. (Sister Margaret Harvey was appointed to complete the term of office.) Still the life and mission of the congregation continued.

In his book *Future Shock*, published in 1970, Alvin Toffler wrote about the phenomenal rate of change that was part of life in the twentieth century. Just as the wider society experienced rapid change and a resultant shock, so too had religious life experienced rapid change and shock. For those who lived through the changes incrementally, the realization dawned that the stability of the past was gone, and the ability to adapt to change was a significant key to living gracefully into the future.

The significant disequilibrium of the early years of renewal would be resolved, but because life is dynamic, there would be the new demands and trends of the 1980s. The challenge remained the same: to maintain the essentials of the congregation's tradition, rooted in the Gospel and in the spirit of Vincent and Elizabeth, while adapting to the needs of changing times.

General Administration (1972-1976).
Seated: Sisters Katherine O'Toole, Rita MacDonald.
Standing: Sisters Frances M. Fay, Elizabeth Hayes.
Absent: Sisters Mary Moore and Anne Casey.

Sister Anna Josepha Cox reading to students at St. Peter's, Lowell, MA (1975).

Sister Katherine O'Toole with Gabrielle Léger, wife of Jules Léger, Governor General of Canada (1974-1979).

General Administration (1976-1980). Sisters Katherine O'Toole, Elizabeth Hayes, Anne Hunter, Anne Harvey, and Rita MacDonald.

Sisters Margaret Murphy and Anne MacDonald, Renewal Centre, Mount Saint Vincent Motherhouse (1977).

Sister Margaret Flahiff in Mount Saint Vincent Motherhouse Archives (1980).

Selected Sources

Primary Documents

1-4-7 Enactments of the Twelfth General Chapter. August 24, 1972 and August 28, 1972 versions. Office of the Congregational Secretary fonds. Sisters of Charity, Halifax Congregational Archives.

1-4-7 "Statement on Social Awareness." Enactments of the Twelfth General Chapter. Office of the Congregational Secretary fonds. Sisters of Charity, Halifax Congregational Archives.

1-5-9 Executive Committee minutes, 1976-1980. Office of the Congregational Secretary fonds. Sisters of Charity, Halifax Congregational Archives.

1-5-13 13th General Chapter, Chapter Information Book, Office of the Congregational Secretary fonds. Sisters of Charity, Halifax Congregational Archives.

1-5-37 Governing Board Minutes, 1975. Office of the Congregational Secretary fonds. Sisters of Charity, Halifax Congregational Archives.

1-6-3 Planning Committee minutes, 14th General Chapter. Office of the Congregational Secretary fonds. Sisters of Charity, Halifax Congregational Archives.

1-6-20 1976 enactments - Implementation. Office of the Congregational Secretary fonds. Sisters of Charity, Halifax Congregational Archives.

August 22, 1972. Circular from Sister Katherine O'Toole to the Congregation. Sisters of Charity, Halifax Congregational Archives.

August 1977. Circular from Sister Katherine O'Toole to the Congregation. Sisters of Charity, Halifax Congregational Archives.

1.2 Homilies, conferences, talks given by Sister Katherine O'Toole, 1972-1980. Sister Katherine O'Toole fonds. Sisters of Charity, Halifax Congregational Archives.

1.10 Handwritten notes. Sister Katherine O'Toole fonds. Sisters of Charity, Halifax Congregational Archives.

1.13 Memos and Correspondence, 1972-1980. Sister Katherine O'Toole fonds. Sisters of Charity, Halifax Congregational Archives.

1.20 Talks, writings, and conference notes, 1971-1985. Sister Katherine O'Toole fonds. Sisters of Charity, Halifax Congregational Archives.

Published Sources

Abbott, Walter M., SJ (Ed.). 1966. *The Documents of Vatican II.* New York: Guild Press.

Becker, J.M. 1977. "Changes in U.S. Jesuit Membership, 1958-1975. A Symposium: Section I. The Statistics and a Tentative Analysis." *Studies in the Spirituality of Jesuits* IX (1, 2): 1–104.

Dirvin, Joseph, CM. 1962. *Mrs. Seton, Foundress of the American Sisters of Charity.* New York: Farrar, Straus and Cudahy.

Fay, Francis M., SC. 1972. *Hazard It Forward: Identifying the Charism with the Apostolic Presence of the Sister of Charity.*

Henhold, Mary. 2008. *Catholic and Feminist.* Chapel Hill: University of North Carolina Press.

Hollenbach, David. 1979. *Claims in Conflict.* New York: Paulist Press.

McKenna, Mary Olga. 1998. *Charity Alive: Sisters of Charity of Saint Vincent de Paul, Halifax 1950-1980.* Lanham, MD: University Press of America.

Melville, Annabelle M. 1951. *Elizabeth Bayley Seton 1774-1821.* New York: Scribner.

Regan, Maureen. 1996. *A Biography of Sister Katherine O'Toole, SC.* Halifax: Sisters of Charity of St. Vincent de Paul.

Sister of Charity of St. Vincent de Paul. 1969. *Covenant of Renewal: Interim Constitutions* Halifax, Nova Scotia: Mount St. Vincent.

Toffler, Alvin. 1970. *Future Shock.* New York: Random House.

2

Moving toward the People of God, Accepting the Call to Continuing Conversion: 1980–1988

Martha Westwater, SC

In a letter of September 14, 1979, Sister Katherine O'Toole convoked the Fourteenth General Chapter with the theme "Following Jesus in His Redemptive Mission: Conversion and Service in Changing Times." The times were indeed changing, and the rate of change was accelerating. In 1968, Stephen Hawking published his Big Bang theory, which is an attempt to give a scientific explanation of the beginning of the universe, and we Sisters of Charity held our Chapter of Renewal. By 1980, the full effect of Hawking's revolutionary theory had not yet been fully absorbed, and we Sisters of Charity had not fully absorbed the explosive changes that followed our Chapter of Renewal. Perhaps even more importantly, we did not yet fully understand the extraordinary changes in Catholic belief and identity that had followed the Second Vatican Council. It was not an easy task to dismantle pre-Vatican II religious life. It would take time – a long time.

The 1980s were a world away from the 1950s and 1960s, decades when vocations flourished in the Church. The aftermath of World War

II had seemingly brought peace, order, and prosperity to the world – how vastly different were the 1980s! This was the decade when poison gas escaped in Bhopal, India, killing thousands; when the nuclear plant at Chernobyl exploded, releasing more than a hundred times the radiation of the bombs dropped on Hiroshima and Nagasaki; when the space shuttle Challenger exploded only seconds after lift-off; and when Michael Jackson was King of Pop. A new awareness of the fragility of human life was engendered among the rich and privileged as well as among the poor and destitute. Even one of the most respected woman of the era, Queen Elizabeth II, could be threatened by an intruder (and her calls for help left unanswered), and the seemingly fairy-tale life of her daughter-in-law, Diana, Princess of Wales, was revealed to be one of depression and loneliness. This was the era when ordinary citizens became conscious of their global connections, and huge concerts were held to benefit victims of poverty and disaster. The world of the eighties was a world where both the dogmatism of the Church and the rationalism of the civic order were severely questioned. Sisters of Charity, like religious everywhere, found themselves adrift in a new world order.

Up until the latter part of the twentieth century, our identity as religious was grounded in obedience to the rule, which dictated every aspect of our lives from what time we rose in the morning, to what time we retired at night; from where we prayed in chapel, to where we sat in the refectory; even to where we lived and what work we did. It was not an unhappy life. After the Chapter of Renewal, we moved into a new world with an ever-expanding promise of freedom. No longer was the will of the superior accepted as the will of God; rather, the individual sister was expected to find God's will in prayer, in discernment, with the knowledge of the superior and in consultation with her. More significantly, far from fleeing from the world, we were called to find the Kingdom of God in the world. Just as Jesus acknowledged the socio-political circumstances of his day and challenged it, so too were we to transform our world and ourselves. We were to work for the Kingdom of God with the People of God. It was an astonishing change, a breath-taking leap – and there were casualties.

Many were leaving and few were entering religious life. Those who remained had to relearn that personal, communal, and ecclesial conversion is not a matter to be hurried and that the work of the Holy Spirit is always slow. Some of the hardest lessons to learn during this period were to respect one's own life experiences and to recognize the value of women's life experiences. Because most literature on the spiritual life was written by men, religious practices prior to 1968 emphasized reason and the mind. Emotions were the demands of "self," and the self was to be feared, denied. Although religious had come a long way from self-humiliation through the public admission of infractions of the rule and requests for penances, the body still had to be disciplined, natural desires modified, if not repressed. As Joan Chittister wrote in *The Fire in These Ashes*, "Men knew that what they could not control in themselves they needed to control in others. The solution became the eternal subservience of women" (1995, 169). In the years following Vatican II, religious women began to understand that the body was not the enemy. We were beginning to appreciate the interconnectedness between body and soul – between our natural and our spiritual lives – and it became abundantly clear that, though in heaven there might be no distinction between male and female, on earth there was certainly plenty of it. Leadership in the spiritual life was not the principal domain of men religious only; lay people were coming forth to take their rightful place in the Church and some lay people lived the gospel more faithfully, prayed more ardently, and worked more zealously than some religious. It took time, twelve years from the Chapter of Renewal, to realize that the old structures, put in place by men, protected us from much of the pain of the world and that the new call to "give joyful witness to love" would take a lifetime to learn. Sister Paule Cantin was to lead us through this climactic period, 1980–1988.

During this period, the charismatic Pierre Elliot Trudeau, Canada's Prime Minister, was shaking up the self-satisfied Canadian status quo. Ronald Reagan, as President of the United States, led the Reagan Revolution in economics and Margaret Thatcher, the "Iron Lady," dramatically challenged male political dominance. Saddam Hussein invaded Iran, sparking the Iran-Iraq War; Ted Turner established CNN, which attempted to satisfy people's insatiable appetite for news; and Mount St. Helens erupted. The volcano had given warnings, but scientists were still caught by surprise when the volcano caused avalanches, mud flows, death, and destruction. This last natural calamity might well have been a powerful signifier of the extraordinary shifts in political, social, and scientific stability that were taking place. The decade ushered in incipient chaos with the fragmentation of family life, the blitzkrieg of news, the increase in marketing and financial messages, and the onslaught of greed and corruption at all levels.

In the midst of this chaotic decade, science continued to prove that ours is an expanding universe. There was a deepening understanding of the scope and implications of the Big Bang Theory, which hypothesized that the universe began not with an explosion but with an expansion of matter that took millions of years. The Big Bang Theory led to the discovery of dark matter, an invisible force that exerts the gravitational pull that holds clusters of galaxies in place; twenty-five percent of the universe consists of dark matter. The astounding rapidity of change and the gravitational pull of dark matter became apt metaphors for the 1980–1988 period. We Sisters of Charity had our own black holes, areas of intense gravitational pull, and we had to use the energy they generated.

Unconsciously, but very forcefully, this vision of the slow expansion of matter and the pull of dark matter cast shadows on the congregational psyche of the Sisters of Charity of Halifax. If the Big Bang occurred 13.7 billion years ago, how insignificant was the twelve-year period between 1968, the time of our Chapter of Renewal, and 1980, the time of our Fourteenth General Chapter? Strong young voices were clamouring for speedier changes, while others (not necessarily old) cautioned that change does not always mean progress. Who could tell whether these changes in the habit, the horarium, the interpretation of the vows, community living, the concept of authority, and all of the other changes would ever stabilize; whether we would eventually return to more uniformity and regularity; whether vocations would again flourish. We did not yet fully realize the extent of the changes – the cataclysmic changes that had taken place after the Big Bang of Vatican II – in religious life, in the Church, and in the world. Only recently have we begun to appreciate something of the continuous but slow rate of change both in nature and in human nature. As the optimist Sister of Loretto, Elaine Prevallet, wrote,

> It was only in the latter part of the last century that persons of color "won" the right to vote … racism continues to disrupt human relationships across the world, and slavery keeps cropping up in new guises [trafficking]. We work to gain recognition for persons with disabilities. Women in every country must still struggle to be considered equal in humanity to men and to work out gender roles and differences. The effort to integrate differences in sexual orientation causes major disruptions. Yet, over centuries of struggle, our perspective on what it means to be a member of the human species has, little by little, become wider, more inclusive and more respectful of differences. (2007, 7)

Sister Paule Cantin and the council members who would emerge from the 1980 Chapter were energetic optimists who made two major contributions to the life of the Sisters of Charity: they moved us closer to the People of God and they broadened the concept of collegiality in leadership. They understood the intensifying nature of change and the need to break away from the restricting confines that hindered the development of religious life in a new age. But they also understood that the changes in religious life that we were attempting to integrate into our *Constitutions*, which were still being drafted, required time, and not just a decade, not even four decades. They would have only eight years as leaders of the congregation, and they would do their best to guide us in this difficult period of unrelenting change. Although all of the documents and letters proceeding from their tenure were signed by Sister Paule Cantin as Superior General, the content, in a sign of the developing collegiality, reflected the group's opinions.

The Most Reverend James M. Hayes, Archbishop of Halifax, was president of the Chapter, and on Sunday, April 6, 1980, after solemn vespers at 3:45 p.m., the Fourteenth General Chapter was formerly declared open. The following day was spent in prayer and reflection. On April 8, Sister Paule Cantin was elected Superior General of the Sisters of Charity on the sixth ballot, succeeding the charismatic Sister Katherine O'Toole. The election session of the Chapter ended on April 9, 1980, when Sister Anne Harvey was elected First Assistant and Sister Mary Ellen Loar, Second Assistant. Sister Margaret Harvey was appointed General Secretary, and Sister Margaret Molloy was appointed Treasurer. These five women formed the new General Council of the Sisters of Charity.

At this point in our history, leadership was still concentrated in the general superior. To reconstruct this period, we are relying chiefly on archival material – specifically, on the minutes of the Chapters and of General and Plenary Councils meetings. Minutes and letters signed by Sister Paule can never capture the differences that surface during meetings and the human pain and frustrations that leaders and members necessarily bear. It is to our credit that we are slowly breaking away from hagiography, and realizing that we elect human beings, very much like ourselves, to lead us. The miracle is that we still trust that the Holy Spirit is with us, helping us to build among the distinctly different groups of women who constitute the Sisters of Charity. The history of one woman, duly elected, reflects the history of the congregation during the 1980–1988 period. To exaggerate or to minimize her gifts is to destroy their significance.

Sister Paule (1938–2010) brought to her leadership intelligence, an open-hearted fearlessness in face of the truth, youthful energy, capability, stamina, and bilingualism (so important in a congregation serving primarily in Canada and the United States). She also brought her own, very human "dark matter," a trust in her own convictions that did not always meet the approval of others. But her cultured, Catholic, French Canadian family had nourished in her a deep love for God, the Great Mystery and the Great Lover. She was a woman of integrity. With all her human foibles, which she herself could laugh at, she believed implicitly in the sacredness of the call to religious life, which is essentially a call to discipleship. And it is a call that demands prayer and ongoing conversion. Furthermore, Sister Paule Cantin recognized the interconnectedness of all things and the interdependence of all humans, especially of all Sisters of Charity. She granted independence, the right for each sister to be an individual, but she also recognized that each was a part of the whole. The individual sister was part of the congregation; the congregation was part of the Church; and the Church was part of the world. The great difficulty for any leader during this period was that each and every sister was wrestling with her own personal conflict between individual liberty and responsible obedience to authority in the congregation. We are all "beloved sinners," as Paule would remind us. The individual sister's struggles were mirrored in what each congregation was wrestling with in the Church (and vice versa). The authority figure had to take the "slings and arrows" that "outrageous fortune" demanded of elected leaders during the climactic decade of the eighties.

It is revealing to look at a picture of Sister Paule taken just before she was elected superior general. She is holding the new logo, which consists of three components: an insignia with uneven pentagonal lines signifying the changing times; the cross, eternal symbol of Christ's redemptive love; and the bowl and towel, the emblems of service. Love and service are the constitutive, unchanging elements of religious life. But Sister Paule's teased, bouffant hair style and the eighties' penchant for large spectacles illustrate that change is endless. Above all, Sister Paule is smiling. She had boundless trust in Christ's injunction, "Fear not," even in the face of cataclysmic change. As Cardinal Newman expressed it, "To live is to change and to be perfect is to have changed often." And as Cardinal Pironio, in writing about the importance of chapters, counselled, "A chapter is measured not by the depth or beauty of its documents but by its capacity to transform (to change) the mind and heart of everyone." Sister Paule Cantin was unafraid of change or the demands of personal conversion. She was a woman of prayer. Her tenure as our congregation's leader gave her a good measure of pain, loneliness, and disappointment; we are not always kind to our leaders.

At the first session of the Fourteenth General Chapter, the elected council had not yet taken office. The Chapter of Affairs was to give them their mandate. The second session of the 1980 Chapter, the Chapter of Affairs, opened on July 14, 1980, with the celebration of Mass at which Monsignor Colin Campbell officiated, and it concluded on July 30. Because the format of this chapter was to be different from the format of other chapters, the planning committee inaugurated specific groups to study and formulate all of the issues that were to appear on the chapter agenda. Here, the congregation's new awareness of globalism began to reveal the groundwork spaded by Sisters Irene Farmer and Katherine O'Toole. The plan of the 1980 chapter followed the Berger Methodology of Prospective Planning, a method that was developed in France in the 1950s, but did not come into use on a significant scale until the early 1970s. At that time, the Movement for a Better World began to train teams in this kind of planning to facilitate chapters and other assemblies for renewal in the Church. The Berger Method emphasizes the prospective rather than the retrospective attitude of mind. It is future oriented, without denying the role that past and present experiences have in planning for the future. To support the Berger planning, delegates were supplied with a vast amount of information and reports on solidarity, the global poor, the local poor, the oppressor and the oppressed, economic systems, political systems, and lifestyles.

The 44 delegates to the Fourteenth General Chapter were elected from sisters in the congregation's six provinces and two vice provinces in Canada and the United States. They met at Mount Saint Vincent Motherhouse, Halifax, Nova Scotia. Among them were a canon lawyer, a medical doctor, a sociologist, and a theologian, and they exchanged ideas with educators, administrators, and sisters involved in pastoral ministry. However, as a reality check, we asked for outside help to clarify others' perceptions of the Sisters of Charity. Valuable insights were received from laity and clerics, in both the United States and Canada, who responded to questionnaires about their perceptions of the Sisters of Charity and the impact the sisters had on the professional and religious aspects of their lives. Engaging a public relations firm to study the impact of the

Sisters of Charity on their colleagues, students, parishioners, and others required courage. How one perceives oneself is far different from what others perceive, so the congregation's decision to discover how outsiders perceived them was an unprecedented risk. The opinions that emerged from the questionnaire were compiled and studied by Management Design, Inc. (MDI) of Cincinnati. Their final report was reassuring: "You have many friends." MDI's input was accepted with gratitude and the findings highlighted many of the issues that needed to be studied by the chapter delegates. This was just part of the monumental effort that went into the preparation for the 1980 Chapter of Affairs.

The principal work of the Chapter was preparing a draft of the revised *Constitutions* for submission to Rome. The constitutions of any religious order try to embody the spirit and mission of the group. For example, the very first entry of the *Constitutions* over which the Chapter laboured explains, "We, Sisters of Charity of Saint Vincent de Paul, are a congregation of consecrated women sharing the gift of a call to give joyful witness to love: the love of God, of one another and of all persons" (C.1). How can mere words apprehend the life of deep faith that defines what it means to be a "consecrated woman" and what it means to "love" all people? Yet, that is what constitutions (or what in older days we called "the rule") try to do. Constitutions try to capture the spirit behind the law. Delegates wrestled with the problem of the meaning of the vows of poverty, chastity, and obedience, which are the signifiers of our consecration, and how these vows are to be lived in an ever-expanding world within a conservative church that is totally male-dominated.

The importance of the delegates' work at the 1980 Chapter should never be underestimated. All of the sisters in the congregation had an opportunity to be personally involved in the writing of our new *Constitutions*, which incorporate the ideal of how Sisters of Charity live their commitment to continue Christ's work on earth. Before the Chapter, the reflective and efficient Sister Anne Harvey, chair of the Constitutions Committee, led the sisters through the entire process of revision. It was a major undertaking. How were we to move our personal, consecrated life with Christ into the life of the world as it was

lived at that time? Each sister was asked to reflect on the many aspects of religious life: service, community, and lifestyle. Written assignments focused our thinking on the spirit and mission as found in the gospel, in the congregation, and in the vows and prayer. Sister Anne and the committees studied and summarized these responses and prepared a draft to be reviewed and amended by the chapter delegates.

The discussion most central to the mission of the Sisters of Charity was that on service, because love of God is characterized by service to others. Under the topic of service came proposals on the missions, on solidarity with the economically poor, on the equality of women, and on social justice. The previous Governing Board had recommended that a task force be set up to consider expanding our missionary activity in the Latin American church, with particular attention to the formation of native vocations. What became one of the major tasks of the newly-elected general council, however, was the proposal on solidarity with the economically poor. This would become the congregation's major focus for the next four years.

Pope Paul VI in his *Evangelica Testificatio* [Apostolic Exhortation on the Renewal of Religious Life] called on Christians to hear the cry of the poor, to reach out to those oppressed, and to use all means possible to heal the wounds of injustice and to leaven the world with love. The call was not new. The Twelfth General Chapter of 1972 had called us to be "visible means of healing in the time in which God has placed us." It was easy to assent to the call, but how would we transform that call into a reality? For over 125 years we, as Saint Elizabeth Ann Seton's daughters, had been educators, homemakers, and nurses. In these three ministries, we served God in the poor. But how different was the poverty of the late twentieth century from that of the early nineteenth! In an age of ecological awareness, growing racial diversity, economic disparity, and moral ambiguity – a world of a vastly increasing population – the varieties of poverty increased dramatically. Were we too deeply ensconced in our comfortable ivy-clad towers? Was it time for us to take our part in controlling the melting of the ice cap? Could we help to eliminate the racial, social, and moral conflicts between white and black?

Between rich and poor? Between advocates of birth control and those sick of male domination? Between the desperate poor in Africa and India and the poor in Halifax and Boston? Were we teaching the economically and socially marginalized classes who really needed our help? These were the questions that had to be answered by each sister individually; these were questions that could not be handed over to a superior general or to a governing board. Perhaps no other proposal has met with such veiled uneasiness as the one that called us to be in solidarity with the economically poor; perhaps no other proposal has had such a long-term effect on the work of the Sisters of Charity.

Most sisters were challenged by the new thrust to engage actively in working with the economically poor. But for some sisters, there was the strong conviction that we had always worked with the poor in schools and hospitals. They saw nothing new in our mission; we would continue to go on as we always had. For still others, there was the lurking feeling that eventually we would return to a more stable form of community living, and that new women would join and carry on the work of an aging and decreasing population of Sisters of Charity. Given the loss of cherished institutions and the continued diminishment in our ranks, the significance of this proposal to commit ourselves to the economically poor proved enormously meaningful.

Since Vatican II and the renewal chapters in religious congregations, it was better understood that each congregation's general chapter must consider not only the members of the congregation, but also the members of the Church and of the world. In 1980, one such focus of team discussions and shared insights between delegates was a heightened awareness of injustice to women. Tension between the Church and religious women was not new. Our own Saint Elizabeth Ann Seton, for example, had her nemesis in the Sulpician priest Father William Dubourg. Religious women had always been in the forefront of presenting new ways of serving the People of God. In Saint Vincent de Paul's time, the Daughters of Charity feeding the poor of Paris met with fierce opposition. The Church by its very nature must be conservative, the guardian of tradition, while orders of religious women are more forward thinking, searching new ways of carrying out gospel living. Canon law rules, but religious women have always been adept in interpreting canon law in liberal ways. In 1980, the Sisters of Charity were conscious of the emerging changes in the position of women in the Church. Religious women were seeking more equality; the Church was under attack and religious women themselves were in the forefront of that attack. Once very docile nuns, who had demurely served "Father" breakfast after the seven o'clock Mass, gobbled their own breakfasts, and then ran over to school "yard duty" at eight-thirty, were now embracing women's rights, liberalism, and emancipation. The sudden change of habit, the freedom of action, and the presence of religious women in many fields of professional endeavour had made this identification more visible.

Conscious of the gospel imperative that we be people of justice, the 1980 Chapter affirmed the need for ongoing education within the congregation with regard to the status of women. Sister Joan Holmberg commented that we must be open to the face of God in women. She asked delegates to be mindful of women in agricultural societies who still serve as "beasts of burden" and of the marginal women in industrial societies who are exploited in factories even as they attempt to respond to their call to care, love, and nurture. In our own day, Sister Sandra Schneiders, IHM, has gone so far as to claim that even the Church has looked on religious women as "an ecclesiastical workforce" (2009).

Most powerful, however, were Sister Katherine Meagher's words on the role of women within the Church. As recently as Vatican II, the Church has taken steps to express equality between men and women. While men and women were believed to be spiritually equal, women, because of their sex, have often been considered inferior in other ways, particularly intellectually inferior. In the past, and in many subtle ways today, women are excluded from leadership within the Church structure. Sister Katherine, a sensitive and intelligent woman, reminded the delegates that there were no women in the public structure of the Roman Catholic Church at that time; no women in any official ministry; no women in the decision-making segments; no women officially recognized as able to give the grace of Christ. Twenty-four years later, in her book

In the Heart of the Temple, Joan Chittister, OSB, would reiterate Sister Katherine's indictment: "There are no women at the altar, no women in the Cardinalate, no women prefects of curial offices, no women expected in liturgical processions or as spiritual directors in seminaries or as the anointers of the dying whom they catechized" (2004, 100).

Sister Katherine, one out of several spiritual "feminists," opened the doors to feminism for the rest of the Sisters of Charity. As Diarmuid O'Murchu so cogently explained,

> In terms of spirituality, feminism, more than any other contemporary movement, throws open doors that have been not merely closed, but tightly bolted—and not just for centuries, but for millennia. Its re-naming (and in some cases, naming for the first time) is highly creative, provocative, subversive, primordial and archetypal. A whole new world, for long subverted within the enclaves of staid and stultifying religiosity, and aborted by the 'sins of the Fathers' … is now claiming our attention and allegiance. (2000, 103)

By the end of the 1980 Chapter, most sisters had been made conscious of sexist language. It was decided that all communications from the Chapter would be in non-sexist or inclusive language. This might seem a slight change, but it was of major importance to the Sisters of Charity.

Later in her time as leader, Paule shared a very interesting, seemingly trifling incident, revealing how she used her subtle charm to break the chasm between women and men in the Church. While she was president of the Canadian Religious Conference (CRC) (1982–1984), she was invited to attend the annual meeting of the Canadian Catholic Conference of Bishops (CCCB) held at the Chateau Laurier, Ottawa. She was to be both an observer and a participant in the workshops. On one occasion, she joined a bilingual group and found herself the only woman. Around mid-morning, a trolley was sent up with coffee, tea, and muffins. Naturally, the waiter placed the trolley by Paule's chair, which was close to the door, and then he left. Paule, wisely, made up her mind that she would not be the one to serve the coffee, since she considered herself the guest of the bishops. All eyes were directed on her for what seemed an eternity. After less than a minute, a bishop on the opposite side of the table got up and began to serve, offering her the first cup of coffee. Of course, he had earned Paule's gratitude so, in a very low voice, she offered to help. He responded for all the men in the room to hear that the sisters had served the priests long enough – it was time for them to return the favour. The position of women in the church was changing – slowly. The notion that we women were called to service – particularly service in a male-dominated church – carried an underlying tension as we emerged from the Fourteenth General Chapter. The major concerns of this historic chapter and the leadership that arose from it were the revision of the *Constitutions*, a switch of focus from education and nursing to working with the economically poor, and an honest study of the injustices dealt to women.

The enactments of the Fourteenth General Chapter, expressing the hope and the vision of the delegates, would form a blueprint for the leadership of Sister Paule, her council, and the Governing Board (consisting of General Council and provincials), as they led the congregation through the next four years. First and foremost, the Chapter approved the revised draft of the *Constitutions and General Directives*. The draft, under Sister Anne Harvey's astute supervision, was to be submitted to Rome for approval. Second, in order to reflect the chapter theme of conversion and service in changing times, the chapter logo was to be used as the congregational symbol. Third, the sisters' lifestyle was to continue being modified, so that it would more evidently reflect our awareness of the Gospel, of limited natural resources, and of the poor and needy of the world. Since then, we have learned how difficult it is to become what we were meant to be.

Furthermore, the enactment on community mandated that provinces, in consultation with the Governing Board, develop structures to receive persons interested in being part of an extended community. We had only a vague idea at the time of what an "extended community" might entail, but the seeds of the associate movement were sown. Perhaps the most demanding thrust of the chapter enactments emerged under the topic of service. Under this heading, the Chapter decreed that we take the call for solidarity with the economically poor as a major focus of concern over the next four years; that there be ongoing education within the congregation to deepen our consciousness of justice for women; that a task force be set up to consider the expansion of our missionary activity in the Third World, with particular attention to the formation of native vocations; that Bermuda be considered a mission territory and that the congregation encourage sisters to consider the need for a congregational presence there; that we keep under advisement the question of ownership of Mount Saint Vincent University; and that inclusive language be used in all congregational communications and in liturgical and para-liturgical services where options were available.

If nothing else, the enactments of the Fourteenth General Chapter showed how far we had moved from particularity to universality, from debating whether to keep open an individual, private school like Mount Saint Agnes Academy in Bermuda, to the expansion of our ministry in third-world countries. The enactments also indicate how long it takes for chapter enactments to bear fruit. We were ever so slowly learning that change is a process and that conversion is a process that requires time – unimaginable time. Furthermore, chapters were taking on a new form that involved every member of the congregation who was able and interested in being involved.

Two further enactments under the topic of formation indicated that we were beginning to realize that formation itself is a life-long process, as necessary in old age as in youth. These enactments mandated that the ongoing formation efforts of the congregation at all levels be directed to strengthening the following: our commitment to Christ, our personal and corporate identity, a theologically sound and updated sense of the Church, and an awareness of the world in which we live and serve. The second enactment recommended that ongoing formation efforts include programs intended to help us grow in our ability to analyse and reflect on our social-ecclesial situations and to further help us to move from mere words to conversion and responsible action. (In other words, we were urged to "walk the talk.") These programs were to include ministry experiences among the poor in emerging countries. As a result, many sisters were to experience the benefit of living among the people of third-world countries in Latin America and Africa.

The new Governing Board was asked to consider the possibility of an assembly to consider the future of the congregation in terms of ministry, lifestyle, and support systems. They were also asked to study the number of delegates for the next chapter and to assist the Antigonish Province in looking to the future, in collaboration with the neighbouring province of Halifax and the Halifax Vice Province. (Already we were thinking of down-sizing.) Finally, and perhaps more pivotal for future leadership teams, under the topic of administration of temporal goods, it was decreed that a certain percentage of our income be used annually for apostolic projects and for the poor of the world. There was one final injunction: that the congregation continue a system of centralized financial management that highlighted stewardship, social concern, and sharing within and outside of the congregation according to policy guidelines approved from time to time by the Governing Board. In hindsight, we can see that the vow of poverty was to have a more personal yet more universal impact on the poor of the world. These wide-ranging tasks were to be borne by the young, willing, enthusiastic teachers and social workers of the in-coming General Council.

After this blueprint was articulated (but certainly not fully digested) by the new leaders, it was with a spirit of deep joy and a little relief that the momentous Chapter of 1980 ended on July 30, 1980, with Evensong presided over by Archbishop James Hayes. The passage from Jeremiah, proclaimed by Sister Paule, seemed to express her attitude as she was called to leadership: "I know not how to speak" (Jer:1:6). She looked on her new position with awe and misgivings, and on herself as one called not only to leadership but also to discipleship, to ongoing conversion. The cross took on a personal meaning. But the passage goes on to assure her, and us, that God's presence is ever abiding: "You shall go … you shall speak … do not be afraid." (Jer. 1:7-8).

In his homily, Archbishop Hayes reminded all that that the message of Jeremiah is not just for the sisters but for the whole Church. Sister Paule took her oath of office and the new General Council moved to the sanctuary to reaffirm their will to serve in the congregation and to be blessed by Archbishop Hayes in the name of the Church. In an article she had written for *Chapter News* (1980), Sister Paule wrote, "As women religious, we have accepted Jesus' invitation to be agents of change. If our message is to be heard; if it is to find a home in the hearts of men and women of good will, we must be characterized by certain qualities."

In an unstable world, we should witness to the constancy of a life of love centred on Jesus by joyful and selfless service. More than ever before we need to bring to the ministry personal concern, reverence, and respect for the giftedness of all persons.

Her deeply personal concern for all her sisters and her reverence and respect (and humble recognition) of the giftedness of others, were to be the hallmarks of Paule's first tenure of office. She was not interested in finding flaws (because she recognized her own), but rather in celebrating differences.

Certainly, when Paule entered the Sisters of Charity in 1956, at our high point of membership, she had no idea that a bright, fun-loving, energetic, young French-speaking girl from a French-Irish background, would one day emerge to lead the sisters whom she first met when she entered the English-speaking Leonard School in Quebec. Along with her precise French, Paule mastered English and came to admire the sisters who laughed at her mistakes in usage and enabled Paule to laugh with them too. With her clear intelligence, Paule mastered English and spoke it with just a trace of a charming French accent. But by the time she was missioned at St. Paul's in Wellesley, Massachusetts, even the trace of her French accent was beginning to disappear. Her ability to laugh at herself, even when she set the kitchen afire while cooking supper, endeared her to everyone – including the Pastor at St. Paul's who had to pay for repairs in the kitchen.

A characteristic of Paule's style of leadership was her ability to trust and love her sisters even when they disappointed her. She realized that the "Pyramid Church" must change, so she never relied on herself alone to accomplish God's work. The image of Moses praying for his people while Aaron and Hur held up his arms was always with Paule. Her "Aaron and Hur" were the members of the General and Plenary Councils. She claimed that she could love and trust her sisters because she knew they loved, trusted, and would uphold her. Paule trusted the insights of her councils and admitted that she was given a valuable gift from her own superiors – the challenge to accept her talents and to stretch beyond what she was able to do. She believed that when people recognize our gifts, help us to own them, and allow us to use them, even at the risk of making mistakes, we grow. In her first years as superior general, she pledged to herself that she would help her sisters recognize their gifts and help them develop them, just as she had been helped.

Sister Paule was not a novice in leadership. Since 1974, she had been Provincial of the Central Province comprising both New Brunswick and Quebec, and later Ontario. Her sisters there testified to her compassion and to her discernment of gifts. She was non-judgmental. She moved in trust through the risks that change creates, and she maintained a sensitive respect for each of her sisters' calls and responses within the far-reaching charism of charity. Perhaps she had an intuitive response to the Pentecostal gift of tongues. People speak not only by their words but by their actions. One needs to study and pray not only over what one says, but also over what one does. She combined a bouncy sense of humour with a no-nonsense approach to gospel living. That no-nonsense attitude was affirmed by Sister Irene Amirault, Paule's secretary, who averred that "externally Paule appeared impatient but underneath she was a very caring woman." Paule did not suffer fools gladly. No leader is ever without difficulties, complaints, dissatisfaction of one sort of another. It's difficult to bear these problems when you are alone; it is easier to share them with a governing council of four competent, God-centred women like Sisters Anne Harvey, Mary Ellen Loar, Margaret Harvey, and Margaret Molloy – all very intelligent, very different women. Sister Paule avowed that whatever good came from her term in office was the result of the sharing of gifts among these women. She depended on them and gave them responsibilities.

A fellow resident of Quebec, Sister Anne Harvey was born in the Gaspé at Chandler, but she entered the congregation from Edmonton in 1957. Living in Montreal, Quebec City, Sherbrooke, and Edmonton gave her a rich, bilingual education. Perhaps her greatest gifts were an incisive, comprehensive intelligence and profound prayerfulness. In her work on the *Constitutions* over the course of several years, Sister Anne had refined a thoughtful respect for the insights, grace, and contributions of each sister. As First Assistant, her gifts were much appreciated. She chaired the Constitutions Committee and the Committee for Ongoing Formation.

When Sister Mary Ellen Loar was elected Third Assistant, she brought with her a passion for the poor that was to intensify during her tenure. She spearheaded the works for justice and chaired the Committee on Solidarity with the Economically Poor. She was deeply concerned that, as a congregation, we continue to develop a corporate response to the needs of the poor. Her message sometimes met with deep reluctance. A graduate of Seton Hall High School, Mary Ellen entered in 1957 and began her teaching at St. Patrick's, our oldest school, in Roxbury, Massachusetts. Her kindness and keen sense of humor were gifts to all, but especially the Wellesley Novices when she served as formation assistant to Sister Francis Lillian Riley. No matter what the problem, no matter what the calamity, Mary Ellen could find some humour and share it with others.

Sister Margaret Harvey, appointed Secretary, hailed from Grand Falls, Newfoundland. A graduate of Mount Saint Vincent College with a degree in secretarial science, Sister Margaret received her master's degree in philosophy and later returned to teach philosophy at the Mount. Her degree in secretarial science made her a logical choice for the position of general secretary. She was a good listener who had an authentic respect for confidentiality.

Another Newfoundlander and lover of the Mount was Sister Margaret Molloy, appointed Congregational Treasurer to the Governing Board by the Fourteenth General Chapter. A graduate of Mount Saint Vincent College, Margaret earned her liberal arts degree and a degree in library science from the Mount. She also held master's degrees from Windsor and

Boston College. Having taught as a member of the history department and served as Academic Dean at Mount Saint Vincent University, Margaret brought deep insights into human nature. As general treasurer, she had a special relationship with the Mount workers, and was gifted with the ability to call out the best in them and to create a collaborative spirit.

It should be noted here that the Church in Canada, particularly under Archbishop James Hayes, was at the forefront of change during this decade; it was exciting, innovative, and inspiring. Archbishop Hayes, a firm believer in the work of Vatican II and always a friend of the sisters, assisted the congregation in understanding the changes that needed to be made in the Church, and supported the sisters in the changes that were to be made in their congregation.

The Governing Board members became very conscious of the extraordinary evolution in chapter styles since they had joined the congregation. Before Vatican II, chapters were bureaucratic, even autocratic. They were closed to most members, there was limited communication of the chapter's results, and a very strong centralization of the agenda. Given the importance of each chapter – it is the ruling body of the congregation while it is in session and is a moment to pause and reflect on the past, consider the present, and plan for the future – one wonders if any changes in chapter procedures would have been introduced without Vatican II, which, it must be remembered, was a conservative institution's trust in the reality of the present. But Sister Paule and her councillors were Christ-centred women who valued the contributions religious women had made to the Church. The Fourteenth General Chapter had given them clear, direct mandates to follow. Their four-year term was characterized by a new, more open, more participative model of chapter procedures.

As a superior general and as an individual, Paule had natural qualities that enabled her to bridge differences. She had successfully bridged the French and English-speaking world and she would prove herself capable of bridging the Canadian-American divide. Perhaps it was simply a matter of style, of youth, of humour, but Paule's outgoing manner embraced everyone. Even a perusal of her letters (and it must be remembered that these letters were written with input from her councillors), reveals an ability to form bridges: between Halifax and Rome, for example; or between the rich countries of Canada and the United States and the poor countries of Central America; even between the educated and the uneducated. In a letter to Rome, specifically to Sister of Notre Dame Mary Linscott who was shepherding the draft of our *Constitutions* through the Sacred Congregation, Paule revealed her ability to break down barriers. Her letter focuses on the recipient as she cites Sister Linscott's "remarkable attentiveness," her "willingness to be of service," and her "sisterly availability," qualities which Paule would "carry in her heart." Paule could make the official, personal. It was no small tribute to her graciousness that when the Prince and Princess of Wales, Charles and Diana, visited Halifax in 1984, the Prime Minister, Pierre Elliot Trudeau, requested that Paule say grace at the state dinner held at the Nova Scotian Hotel, even though there were three bishops present at the event.

Solidarity with the economically poor was touchingly revealed in the many social justice conferences attended by members of both the Plenary and General Councils, and in the letters (again with council input) written by Paule during her tenure. However, Sister Mary Ellen Loar, as Paule admitted, was the power behind the social justice issues. For example, Mary Ellen's voice is in Paule's letters about the rupture between the "Princes of the Church" and the Sandinistas in Honduras. These letters were particularly effective in making the congregation more aware of the sufferings of the people in that country and our need to be aware of them. Poignantly, in a letter of February 21, 1981, in the name of the congregation, Paule wrote of the brutal murders of four missionaries in El Salvador: lay missionary Jean Donovan, Maryknoll Sisters Ita Ford and Maura Clark, and Ursuline Sister Dorothy Kazel. With her compassion for the deaths of these four women came her down-to-earth practical conclusion that we in our comfortable niches must continually work for justice in great ways or small. She wrote,

> Our experience in the face of this crisis and our desire to act responsibly brought to the attention of our General

> Council the need to consider a congregational policy making possible the involvement of every Sister of Charity in a decision to take a corporate stance on an issue of justice.

This was a call to arms for the Sisters of Charity; they were urged to work directly with those living in poverty in the improvement of their lives, to become socially aware of human rights issues, and to study and to live out the Church's social doctrines by writing letters and voicing solidarity on issues that affect their lives. In general, they were discovering ways to better the lot of the poor. Any action in the pursuit of justice makes us participative in the transformation of the world and in a constitutive dimension of gospel living. In other words, it was the Church's mission and the mission of every Sister of Charity to work for the development of the human race and its liberation from every oppressive situation: "to right in great ways or small the injustices we see around us" (C. 43).

If letter writing on the part of the Superior General and other members of the Governing Board was time-consuming, it paled in comparison to the time demanded for meetings. And the time spent at the meetings was minimal compared to the time spent preparing for them. In addition to meetings with her council, Sister Paule also had meetings with the Plenary Council, which consisted of members of the General Council and the provincials. The provincials were Sister Anne Fleming, Halifax; Sister Louise Bray, Antigonish; Sister Frances McLaughlin, Central Province; Sister Mary Therese Gavin, the West; Sister Barbara Buxton, New York; Sister Mary Sheila Desmond, Wellesley Vice Province; Sister Catherine Hanlon, Boston; and Sister Romaine Bates, Halifax Vice Province. Provincials were required to report on these meetings to their provincial boards. In addition to these "in-house" meetings, there were many local and political ones. As Chair of the Mount Saint Vincent University Corporation, Sister Paule had countless meetings with Dr. Margaret Fulton and Dr. Naomi Hersom,

Presidents of the University during her term of office, as well as with various political leaders.

There were also meetings associated with the Leadership Conference of Women Religious Conference (LCWR) in the United States, its Canadian counterpart, the Canadian Religious Conference (CRC) of which Paule was president (1982–1984), as well as various meetings in the city and diocese. From 1982 until 1986, Paule was our representative on the International Union of Superior Generals (UISG). One of Sister Paule's significant contributions to this group was a paper entitled "Two Challenges" in which she highlighted essential aspects of prayer. This paper is important both for an understanding of Sister Paule's own spirituality and for comprehending the subtle yet profound changes occurring in the prayer life of every Sister of Charity.

Before Vatican II, the communal aspect of our spirituality was ritualized, in the sense that we all prayed the same prayers at the same time – morning, noon, and night. We meditated at the same time, took spiritual reading together, and we had a half hour of "adoration" before the Blessed Sacrament. As novices in formation, we had "adoration" together, but "on the mission," we prayed privately at our own convenience. Most Sisters of Charity received extraordinary nourishment from this regimen, and some sisters were loath to relinquish the type of spirituality emphasized in the beloved small prayer book. Devotion was sustained in the private period of prayer in which we encountered the personal Jesus in the Eucharist, and in the "examination of conscience," which emphasized a compilation of weaknesses (and strengths). Both exercises took place before the Blessed Sacrament – always reserved in our chapels. With the new theology, some sisters became less formal in their approach to the sacrament. They insisted, rightly, that Jesus the Lord was present not only in the tabernacle but in each other, and in those we encounter among the poor and in our daily experiences. It was a mind-bending change. Some wanted to retain the old method of prayer, which had enriched the prayer life of each Sister of Charity for over a hundred years, while others wanted to enter into the changing way of thinking about the transcendent in the life of a Sister of Charity living in the eighties.

As in so many other endeavours, Paule sought for a balance between the old and the new.

In her paper on prayer, Paule emphasized communal prayer, but more specifically faith sharing, as an essential means of achieving unity in the midst of diverse lifestyles and ministries. Faith sharing is a more demanding form of prayer because it instructs us to give up preconceived notions and to be open-hearted in accepting the different needs of different people. Some sisters would never be able to practice this form of prayer because they felt that privacy was the key element of one's spirituality, that "it was good to hide the secrets of the King." Nevertheless, faith sharing opened up the lives of others and gave many sisters a new appreciation of how one's life's experiences informed one's spirituality.

Communal prayer or faith sharing, Paule wrote, embraces the needs of the global community and call us to personal and communal conversion. The diversified apostolic energies necessitated prayer to ensure fidelity to the spirit of one's institute and to verify with one another the authenticity of our ministerial efforts. Prayer as a survival technique in a fast-changing world was a constant theme in Sister Paule's writings, whether she was addressing (*en francais*) the CRC *Reunion de l'Assemblée Générale* (1984), or in a homily at a missioning liturgy for Sister Doris Schoner as the latter was about to embark for Bani in the Dominican Republic (1982).

In 1982, to ease the burden of typing conference papers, letters, and reports, the first computer or word processor was purchased. The computer was especially helpful in view of the upcoming Emmaus and Futures programs, which were intended to cultivate a deeper spirituality among younger members of the congregation. The adoption of new technology continued to advance both at the Motherhouse and at Mount Saint Vincent University. On May 6, 1983, Sister Paule was invited to attend the first satellite video-teleconference for educational purposes. Yes, times were changing, and fast.

One particular project that demanded a great deal of Paule's energy and time, and that of her council, was the implementing of Enactment

VB from the Fourteenth General Chapter: "That the Governing Board in its planning for ongoing formation reflect on the possibility of an assembly to consider the future of the congregation in terms of ministry, lifestyle and support systems." Some questions that had to be considered were as follows: What place would the Sisters of Charity have in a world characterized by the wasteful consumption of limited global resources, increased international competition, unequal distribution of wealth, and increased marginalization of large groups of people?; What place did a Sister of Charity have in a male-dominated Church where there is a decline in the male clergy?; Will the increased participation of the laity in Church matters crowd out the Sisters of Charity?; and What will our unique charism as Sisters of Charity be for the global community in 2000? A planning committee held a series of weekend-long meetings from April 23–25, 1982 until April 9–10, 1983. The pamphlets, essays, documents, statistics – the sheer amount of reading material contained in the minutes of these meeting – attest to the work done in preparation for the Futures Assembly, which was held at the Motherhouse on July 10–15, 1983.

In her opening address to the Futures Assembly, Paule metaphorically cited Jesus as the Navigator who will lead us into the future. She counselled a loving trust in this Divine Navigator: "Let us be confident that this week is meant to be for us a very special experience of community … [I] n the total group the spirit resides." Paule had a unique gift of applying scripture to every day relationships: "Whatever you bind on earth will be bound also in heaven; whatever you loose on earth will be loosed in heaven" (Matt 18:18). This passage, Paule applied to interpersonal relationships – forgiveness and freeing one another from the guilt of grudges. Furthermore, she insisted that a genuine response to gospel living demands "in some instances, a radical break with what I have grown accustomed to, with what brings me security, with what I believe I can no longer do without." Quoting Henry Miller, Paule affirmed that "we are not kept alive by legislators and militarists … We are kept alive by men and women of faith … They are like vital germs in the endless process of becoming."

The principal presenters at the Futures Assembly were Ruben Nelson, a futurist, Patricia Mische, co-author of *Toward a Human World Order*, and Sister Mary Ellen Sheehan, IHM, Professor of Moral Theology at St. Michael's College, Toronto. The assembly was primarily composed of workshops and working sessions that used the interactions of individuals to shape the group process. Input focused on the future, the global reality, and women in ministry. The assembly began and ended with a celebration of the Eucharist, after which the participants broke out into song, dance, and loud applause. The program was energizing and life giving for the younger members of the congregation.

At the end of their term in office, the members of the Governing Board could report to the upcoming Fifteenth General Chapter that, in addition to having worked to bring our *Constitutions* towards final approval and adopting a congregational symbol, they had begun to implement expanding ideas on community. Coming to grips with individual differences meant that the old practices of the common life had to be modified, and these modifications needed to make evident our awareness of gospel living and of limited natural resources.

The number of sisters living alone at that time was minimal, but began to steadily increase. Sisters were beginning to realize that community was to be found not only with those with whom one lived in a convent or house, but with lay workers and with colleagues. At the same time, by 1984, some provinces had developed structures to invite people who shared the charism of charity to form extended communities – the beginning of the associate movement.

The associate movement illustrates how long it takes for the seed of an idea to germinate. Associates were envisaged to be lay people, mostly women, who would share in the life and mission of the Sisters of Charity, but who would not take vows. The idea of "extended community" did not generate much support in 1980. It was not until 1989 that the Friends and Associates of the Sister of Charity of New York Province began as a pilot program at Our Lady Help of Christians, and the first associate, Susan McMahon, made a commitment in New York on January 4, 1991. Later, another group started in Halifax, but the program did not gain full momentum until the 1996 Chapter. However, the germinating idea of an extended community indicates how fast we were moving to embrace the laity. The structures between women's religious congregations and the clergy were weakening, while the ties between lay women and women religious were strengthening.

The report submitted by the General Council in 1984 made it very clear that we needed a new and updated sense of the Church that had an awareness of the world in which we live and serve. The catastrophic effect that the worldwide abuse of children by Catholic priests and brothers would have on the credibility of the Church and on vocations to the religious life cannot be exaggerated. The horror of so many innocent victims first attracted notoriety in the 1980s (although cases of abuse occurred at least from the 1960s onwards – and perhaps for generations before), when the abuse at Mount Cashel in St. John's, Newfoundland, became public. It was a humiliation for the Irish Christian Brothers and devastating to the hierarchy of the Church. Because of the hierarchy's cover-up of the scandal, trust in the Church as an institution was notably eroded. The participants at the 1984 Chapter had no idea of the worldwide scandals that were to be revealed in the years to come, and there was no mention (in the minutes) of the abuses carried out by the religious congregations (of whom we were a part) who ministered at the Indian Residential Schools. However, the Sisters of Charity, together with all Catholics, tasted shame and anger when newspapers fed us reports of physical and sexual abuse. Saint Elizabeth Ann Seton counselled us to "Be children of the Church," but in light of the sexual abuse scandals, a new idea of Church was considered necessary. Power should no longer be vested in a few – let alone in one. The "Pyramid Church" had to be reformed.

At the close of their 1980–1984 tenure, the council members recommended changing the composition of general chapters to make them more representative of the sisters. They proposed that at the Fifteenth General Chapter, there be an equal number of delegates from each of the provinces with a smaller number from each of the vice provinces. In the first intimation of the restructuring that would

eliminate the provinces, they suggested that individual provinces further collaborate with each other. The decreasing numbers and the increasing age of the sisters made this collaboration necessary. In December 1980, there were 1,246 sisters in the congregation; on December 31, 1983, the number was 1,173.

In response to the needs of the world, the General Council had contributed to the needs of countless poor missions that had asked for aid, and the number requesting financial help increased in this time of social upheaval. While African leaders were wresting control from colonial powers, the poor of those countries were requesting help. There is a touching letter, dated May 12, 1982, from a sister in Kisuma, Kenya, East Africa, thanking Sister Paule (and the Sisters of Charity) for money they had donated – money which enabled the Kenyan sisters to build three water towers for the convent (a mud hut), the school, and the hostel. There were many such letters from missionaries in developing countries thanking the Sisters of Charity for their assistance. To the poor and vulnerable, Paule responded, but she also wrote to the rich and powerful.

There is another letter, dated January 5, 1984, addressed to the Right Honorable Pierre E. Trudeau, in which Sister Paule, representing the congregation, congratulated the Prime Minister on his appointment of Mme. Jeanne Sauvé as Governor General. It pleased Paule (and the congregation) that a woman was appointed, and she proceeded to praise Trudeau for his peace initiatives throughout the world. There are the sad letters announcing departures from the congregation and happy letters announcing appointments of new provincials. There are letters illustrating the burgeoning development of land once owned by the congregation, and there were even a few anonymous crank notes with which Paule and her council had to deal. Certainly, these letters make it obvious that the world was changing fast. But there was an exultant moment when Pope John Paul II came to Halifax, the first time that a Sovereign Pontiff had visited Canada since the Church began on Pentecost Sunday some 2,000 years ago. Sister Paule Cantin was invited to serve on the national planning committee for the Pope's visit – the only woman on the committee. Because she believed that the Sisters of

Charity were in closer harmony with the laity than with the clergy, Paule wanted the sisters to meet the Pope as members of the People of God, as members of the laity, and she wrote a letter to the CRC expressing this wish. This visit of the Pope was especially meaningful because there had been an attempted assassination of the Pope in 1981. Rain (torrents of it), mud, soggy clothes – nothing could dampen spirits on that memorable day on September 14, 1984, when John Paul II celebrated Mass with us on the Halifax Commons.

But alongside the comfort and joy of a Pope's presence, or the appointment of Sandra Day O'Connor as the first woman justice on the Supreme Court of the United States, there would be many instances of "dark matter" – of murders, diseases, plagues, and assassinations – in Sister Paule's term of office. An attempt was made on President Reagan's life in 1981, and in 1984, Indira Ghandi was assassinated by two of her guards. AIDS was identified as the new plague and the Falkland Islands were invaded by Argentina. The world seemed to have gone mad. The ugly seemed to be replacing the beautiful; disorder replacing order. No doubt the changes in society reflected the move from a mode of conformity to one of individuality. Streakers could disrupt a college convocation and the shock would evoke laughter. Changes were also being made in religious life. The guitar replaced the organ in liturgical services – especially among the young. A skilled organist like our own Sister Teresa Campbell could masterly perform a prelude before Mass, going from Handel's classical "Largo" to Schutte's "Table of Plenty," and both would blend harmoniously.

For the most part, religious life among the Sisters of Charity moved peacefully enough. However, by 1984, although the majority of sisters were still engaged in education, their mindset had shifted from local problems to global issues like disarmament, refugees, the position of women in the Church, abortion, decolonization, and political problems in Ireland and the Middle-East. Part of this shift was due to the rapidly advancing position of women in the modern world. In Terrence Fay's, *A History of Canadian Catholics*, Ellen Leonard is quoted as saying "The history of western civilization until recently has been the preserve of white male scholars who have written little about women, aboriginals, or the marginalized people of the world" (2002, 310–311). But now women, and especially sisters, were champing at the bit to advance the position of women in the modern world. And while some were thus absorbed, others were just as avidly content to discuss these issues and seek answers to world problems in prayer. The House of Prayer Ministry continued to grow in the provinces because the sisters realized that working with those in need could be overwhelming, and that it was necessary to free themselves from the workaholic syndrome. These houses of prayer became increasingly popular with the laity. Most sisters wanted to "walk the talk," and their works prove it. Provincial annals abound with stories of sisters exercising their Vincentian charism with renewed vigour. WAITT (We're All in This Together) House in Boston, "Women Helping Women" in New York, and Adsum House in Halifax were begun by Sisters of Charity to help women in abusive relationships, women struggling with addiction, homeless women, and women without formal education, women without work or means of support. Retired sisters from local convents boarded the ferry to visit Camp Hill Hospital in Halifax; others boarded buses to take them to nursing homes and hospitals in New York and Boston; still others left traditional ministries such as giving music lessons to take positions in homes for the elderly. In every province and state there were instances of sisters serving those living on the margins—especially women. In Boston, there was "Rosie's Place," and in Dorval, Quebec, Sister Carmelita Currie used her teacher's salary to found a home for boys. Another such home for girls was founded in Halifax by the Sisters Deal. Both Canada and the United States saw an influx of immigrants at this time. New York, Halifax, and Boston are major entry ports and container ships were homes for thousands of immigrants seeking a better life. The Asian Center in Lawrence, Massachusetts is a case in point. Sisters began working with immigrants by teaching them English and ended up by providing food, shelter, and furnishings.

Part of Sister Paule's ministry was addressing church groups, educational groups, and women's groups. Whether it was addressing the 370 members of the CRC (June 17, 1984), "Women for What World and What Church," or the Royal Commission on Post-Secondary Education (February 8, 1984), Paule brought her enthusiasm, passion, and commitment to religious, educational, and social issues. Her ideas had a vitality that inspired. Paule had "class." She gave her sisters a healthy pride and immeasurable hope.

The general superiors and their councils refused to get locked into an unreal world of insubstantial meetings; they studied, counselled, and approved of countless new ministries. At the same time, they had to look out for the continuation of these good works by finding new membership. Formation was a major concern. There were eight novices in October of 1980, and seven others beginning formation, but 358 of the total 1,221 sisters in the congregation were in the 60–69 age bracket. Obviously, membership had decreased since Vatican II, works had expanded, and fewer women were entering the congregation. Although most sisters were in education, ministries were becoming more diverse and would continue to diversify to alleviate the effects of oppressive economic and social structures and to work to eliminate them. From the minutes of the meetings of both the General Council and the Plenary Council, it is evident that much enthusiasm had been generated by the new projects. Council members expressed pleasure at the openness displayed in the sharings at meetings, and all acknowledged the amount of reading on global and local issues that formed the background for these meetings. The notes of the General Council meetings indicate that the Sisters of Charity had no identity crises. They did not see themselves on some vague threshold between the clergy and the laity. They were solidly entrenched in the midst of the People of God. The sisters were challenged to be with others – especially those living in poverty – in their human struggles. The "otherworldly" demeanour of pre-Vatican II religious had transformed itself to suit a world where injustice had to be confronted. Thus, in December 1980, Sister Paule wrote to the Prime Minister Pierre Elliott Trudeau on behalf of the congregation:

> We are asking that the Canadian government clearly state its condemnation of the massive human rights violations of the military and Christian Democrat junta in El Salvador which have led to over 8,500 deaths this year, to the assassination of six leaders of the opposition Democratic Front, to the creation of more than 80,000 internal refugees, mostly poor peasants, and in the last two weeks to the deaths of two more Salvadoran priests and four American missionaries.

There were many such letters written in the name of the Sisters of Charity and addressed to government leaders both in Canada and in the United States on behalf of oppressed peoples, particularly the children of El Salvador and Nicaragua.

It is evident that during this decade there was a growing awareness of the connection between corporate and political power; consequently, a congregational corporate policy began to slowly emerge. We were beginning to find our corporate voice. Every province had standing committees that spearheaded new ministries. These committees might include groups working for social justice, government, heritage, ongoing formation, or finance. Of these committees, the social justice committees were perhaps the most empowering. They required social analysis to root out the causes – the dominant structures and historical patterns – of the ills of society. Through these social analyses, sisters began to recognize the economic, political, and social structures that are key elements of the problem, but also that it is culture that carries meaning and shapes values. Added to the fears of the 1980s – the proliferation of weapons, the danger of the nuclear arms race, and the rising power of big business – was the plight of children in third-world countries. World problems challenged our thinking and the relationship between politics and wealth frightened us more than a little. Take, for example, the workings of the World Bank, which, in pre-Vatican Council days, few of us even knew existed.

At the time of our Chapter of Renewal (1968), the World Bank, which emerged after the Bretton Woods Conference in 1944, provided loans for reconstruction and development after the disastrous ruins of World War II. The United States and Great Britain were the most powerful members of the World Bank and they shaped the negotiations. With the creation and success of the Marshall Plan, first implemented in 1947, which had provided aid to Europe after the war, the bank's focus shifted to non-European countries, which were given loans for projects such as the building of ports, highway systems, and power plants – but now the recipient countries had to repay these loans. From 1968 to 1980, the bank focused on alleviating poverty in third-world countries; thus, bank funds went towards the building of schools and hospitals, raising literacy rates, and instigating agricultural reform. One consequence of this period of lending for poverty-alleviation purposes was the rapid rise of third-world debt. By the 1980s, structural policies within the World Bank were refocused on streamlining the economies of developing countries, and usually this was done at the expense of health and social services. In the late 1980s, it became increasingly evident that the restructuring policies of the World Bank resulted in reduced health, nutrition, and educational levels for millions of children in Asia, Latin America, and Africa. The Sisters of Charity were beginning to understand more fully the pain of the world.

The 1980–1984 period of government was nearing its end. Sisters Paule Cantin, Anne Harvey, Mary Ellen Loar, Margaret Harvey, and Margaret Molloy could look forward to a new era when others would assume the responsibility of leadership. Although Sister Paule and the General Council could take solid comfort in their study and confrontation of the world's problems, there were matters much closer to home that had to be addressed, namely, planning for another general chapter.

Scheduled for July 1–16, the theme of the Fifteenth General Chapter was "Called to Continuing Conversion." The Fourteenth General Chapter had also emphasized conversion: "Conversion and Service in Changing Times." Why was the conversion theme so dominant in both sessions? Part of the reason is to be found in a new understanding of Christology,

a dramatic conversion to a new idea of who Jesus was. Previous chapters, under the guidance of Sisters Irene Farmer and Katherine O'Toole, had recognized the importance of theological reading, study, and reflection. As a result, sisters were becoming aware of a new understanding of Jesus's relationship to the Father, and consequently experienced a change in their own relationship. Under this framework, Jesus and his teachings were humanized and modernized. A very provocative book at the time was *Jesus before Christianity*, by the Dominican Albert Nolan, which threw new light on the gospel message. For example, in explaining the multiplication of the loaves and fishes (Matt. 6:35–44), Nolan remarked, "The miracle was that so many men should suddenly cease to be possessive about their food and begin to share, only to discover that there was more than enough to go round" (1978, 52). Before Vatican II, the divinity of Christ and his message were stressed; his humanity was down-played. Fresh theological investigations such as Nolan's studied Jesus as a free human being, who had to make choices and had human limitations. Jesus had to learn he was the Son of God. This understanding developed gradually. Raymond T. Bosler suggested that Jesus's union with God was unique; it might have begun with his baptism in the Jordan, but "he only fully knew who he was at the resurrection" (1992, 103). This new thinking engendered a profound change in the way we related to the Godhead. It gave us a greater understanding of our own limitations and a greater tolerance for those of others. At the same time, our human weaknesses seemed to become more visible, less protected by convent rules, especially the rule of silence.

Consider for a moment the life of a Sister of Charity before Vatican II. Obedience, to which we freely surrendered, ruled. Individual choice was almost non-existent. Sisters (in their twenties, thirties, forties, or fifties) were assigned their work chiefly in schools and hospitals. (No choice there.) They were awakened from their sleep at five in the morning (no choice there, definitely), and by five-thirty, all dressed alike, they assembled in the chapel, before the Blessed Sacrament, ready to begin their day. There was a silent, intangible reminder that "We were all in this together," and this created a powerful bond of unity. Sisters were followers of Christ and Christ surrendered his will to the Father. As young girls, sisters had been "called," and that call was real to them because, usually by adolescence, they had established their own faltering relationship with Christ in prayer. Then came the shattering Chapter of Renewal in 1968. Sisters could now make choices; they were free to follow their consciences. Superiors could no longer assign their ministry without consultation, dictate the hours of rising and retiring, or interpret God's will for them. But it is unsurprising that when eleven hundred people suddenly had to face their own personal, different choices – and the consequences of those choices – difficulties arose, not only in the individual sister, but also in the "authority" that had to regulate choices, in this case, the General and Plenary Councils of a religious congregation. No wonder "conversion" was stressed in both the Fourteenth and Fifteenth General Chapters.

At this time in our history, the General Council consisted of Sisters Paule Cantin, Anne Harvey, Mary Ellen Loar, Margaret Harvey, and Margaret Molloy. In 1983, the Governing Board included the General Council members and the provincials, Sisters Romaine Bates, Louise Bray, Barbara Buxton, Sheila Desmond, Anne Fleming, Elizabeth Hayes, Francis McLaughlin, and Sally McLaughlin, who represented sisters in Canada, the United States, and Latin America. These were caring, conscientious women who voiced their concerns about the quality of life lived, the choices made, both individually and communally, and the impact of these choices on the People of God. Plenary Council members recognized that the emphasis of the Chapter was to be on conversion, but they stressed that *personal* conversion in community life was crucial. In her letter to the sisters accompanying the "new look" of the Governing Board report, Sister Paule wrote,

> Community is not an end in itself ... Let us honestly and courageously look at the quality of our life at the local level; let us assess our ability and our willingness to share our life at the local level ... to learn better how

to be signs of God's love to each other and consequently
to the people we serve.

The freedoms in religious life in which we revelled after Vatican II had brought their own share of problems to sisters living in various houses of the congregation. Gone were the days when we all dressed the same and followed the same routine. There were different ideas on the vows, on community living, on charity. What Christ's life meant to some was not what Christ's life meant to others. Community living was becoming more and more problematic. There were some extravagances in dress and in deportment. More seriously, there were a few occasions when unfair and odious comparisons were made between the living standards of one group of sisters and those of another. There was suffering. It was becoming obvious that while the old rule had made us more or less equal, all sisters in the same way, we were now free to be our own person and sometimes that "person" was not accepted. Now, when a sister tried to change from one small community to another, she might be rejected. We needed conversion to the mind and heart of Christ.

The input of members of the Plenary Council of the Sisters of Charity was of major importance in planning for the Fifteenth General Chapter, which would be different in form from previous chapters. After the Twelfth General Chapter, the election and the business sessions were separated, but in the 1984 Chapter the business session preceded the elections, so that delegates could discern the direction of the congregation for the next four years and then, in view of that, call forth people to serve in leadership. In preparation for the chapter, the Plenary Council looked to the enactments of the 1980 Chapter and to the work done by the standing committees. Of primary importance was the Constitutions Committee, but there were other committees with significant contributions, such as committees on solidarity with the economically poor, on the enactments concerning the status of the Antigonish Province and of Bermuda, a task force for the expansion of mission activity, the committee on justice for women, the committee to study ownership of Mount Saint Vincent University, and the projections committee on retirement and housing.

Despite the personal and congregational problems related to "conversion," and the serious business to be discussed, in his homily at the beginning of Chapter, Archbishop Hayes sounded a theme of hope and encouragement that would pervade both sessions of the 1984 Chapter:

> I am grateful for the chance you give me to stand by your door today as you begin your Chapter. I am grateful for the sake of all the Children of the Church, because you have so much to offer them. You have the ability to call them back to new life again and again. I wish that more and more of them could see the great variety and effectiveness of your apostolate. The education, religious ed., the pastoral ministry, the spiritual renewal and direction, the service of family life, the serious promotion of women's rights, the insistent demands for justice, the leadership in calls for peace and disarmament, the advocacy on behalf of the poor, the friendly and tender care you give to the infirm and the aged, the missionary thrust in Latin America, the clear choice of an option for the poor—and so much more ... Yes, you are doing a wonderful thing in the Church.

Despite the "wonderful" scope of the work done during the previous four years, the 1984 Chapter was not satisfied with the status quo. We were called to *continuing* conversion. One aspect of gospel-centred, congregational living that was challenging (and changing) was the concept of leadership in government. This section is only one example of the meticulous work done by Sister Anne Harvey and the Constitutions Committee, which presented the refinements, revisions, and clarifications of the draft *Constitutions and General Directives* to the Chapter. When examining the issues on government, particularly the role of the general

superior, it is interesting to look briefly at the history of leadership and the concept of collegiality.

The Sisters of Charity arrived in Halifax in 1849. Confirmation and approval of the establishment of the House of the Sisters of Charity of Halifax was decreed by the Sacred Congregation on February 17, 1856, in the Pontificate of Pius IX. Approval of the Constitutions for five years was given on May 7, 1908. Definitive approval came on July 24, 1913, under Pius X. Fifty-one years later, after the congregation had established provinces, the constitutions were revised and approved on July 18, 1964. In the period after Vatican II, we were governed by the *Covenant of Renewal*, adopted at the 1968 chapter. When one considers the role of the general superior in the 1964 document, one sees a considerable expansion in the concept of leadership. The 1964 *Constitutions* reads, "The mother general governs and administers the entire congregation according to the sacred canons and these constitutions" (*C.* 374). At that time, there was no disputing the power of "Mother General." The *Covenant of Renewal*, with its emphasis on the dignity of the human person, subsidiarity, collegiality, uniformity, and pluriformity, especially collegiality, shifted government to a Governing Board as "the highest legislative body of the congregation." Chapters thereafter continued to explore the relationship between the superior general and her council, but did not lose the spirit of government (*CR.* 44). In both the 1980 and 1984 Chapters, authority had shifted again. The *Constitutions* approved in 1985 reveal that authority had moved from a Mother General to a general superior who "is the spiritual and apostolic leader of the congregation and has a prime responsibility for its life and mission ... She has authority over all the provinces, local communities and sisters of the congregation, and is accountable to the general chapter for the exercise of her office" (*C.* 91). The concept of government had expanded to embrace the spirit of collegiality, so that reaching a decision by consensus rather than by voting seemed to embody our spirit of government. However, the superior general has the *prime responsibility* for the life and mission of the congregation. There were lingering doubts about putting too much confidence in collegiality. In a letter, dated June 1988, Father Francis Morrissey wrote to Sister Irene Farmer,

> I would say that if a decision is reached by consensus it has less weight than one taken by vote, particularly if the result is not recorded in the minutes. If the minutes record that the decision was finally made unanimously, then fine. However, I have a worry about certain forms of 'consensus' which can be quite close to manipulation.

At the 1984 Chapter, leaders of the congregation shared their experiences of team leadership; this was to deepen and broaden, as would be evident in the 2003 edition of the *Constitutions* which states, "Our efforts to be a community of faith should be based on respect for the dignity of each person and the practice of co-responsibility, subsidiarity and accountability" (*C.*74). Recent chapters have laboured over similar regulations, always seeking the spirit behind the rule. Who could count the hours of prayer and thought that went into our *Constitutions* before its final approval by the Sacred Council for Religious and Secular Institutes (SCRIS) was received on December 8, 1984?

Following the approval of the *Constitutions*, each sister was presented with her personal copy. Sister Paule asked Sisters Irene Farmer, Margaret Flahiff, Frances Fay, and Betty Hayes each to prepare a reflection booklet so that the sisters might interiorize the spirit of the *Constitutions* during their annual retreat. The approval of these *Constitutions* brought immeasurable peace to Sister Paule and to her council at the conclusion of their first term in office in 1984. The new *Constitutions* also brought with them a deepening understanding of conversion and an awareness of the choices involved in becoming a Sister of Charity of Halifax.

One of the greatest tasks of the Fifteenth General Chapter was to address the issue of Mount Saint Vincent University. On July 31, 1969, the delegates of the Eleventh General Chapter and special Chapter of Renewal unanimously adopted the recommendation of the finance committee: the Sisters of Charity should withdraw from ownership of hospitals and educational institutions. When and how the principle of withdrawal was to be implemented would be dependent on the need for funds to reduce debts and to provide an adequate pension program for all sisters. The congregation had already begun to divest itself of the ownership of property, including the following: Halifax Infirmary; the Academy of the Assumption, Wellesley; Mount Saint Vincent Academy, Halifax; Seton Hall High School, Patchogue; Saint Elizabeth's Hospital, North Sydney; Stella Maris Residence, North Sydney; and Mount Saint Agnes Academy, Bermuda. But relinquishing ownership of these institutions, from which so many vocations had come, difficult as it was, was easier than relinquishing "The Mount," which had been educating teachers since its earliest days.

The Sisters of Charity had been associated with Mount Saint Vincent University in a major way since its inception in 1873 as an institution dedicated primarily to the education of women. In that year, the sisters' concern for the education of women had begun with the opening of a small academy in Rockingham. In 1895, Mount Saint Vincent Normal School was recognized by law as equivalent to the new Teachers College in Truro, and in 1925, a bill of the Nova Scotia legislature established Mount Saint Vincent as the first and only degree-granting college for women in Canada. With the granting of a new charter in 1966, the name of the institution was changed to Mount Saint Vincent University. We had basked in this accolade during the time of the gifted University President, Sister Alice Michael (Catherine Wallace), who might well be representative of the development from the "Jesus and I" philosophy of the 1950s and 1960s, through the "Jesus in Everyman" of the 1970s, to the new "Building the City of God" philosophy of the 1980s.

However, a major transformation had taken place at Mount Saint Vincent University. Provision was made for both a University Corporation, comprising the Sisters of Charity, and a Board of Governors, which included a variety of people with a wide range of expertise. It was the congregation that supported the Mount up until 1956, when funding from the government began. Up to 1966, the college was directed solely by the general superior and her assistants, and until 1951, the college was staffed entirely by sisters. The sisters held all of the major administrative positions until the 1967–1968 academic year. Beginning with Sister Alice Michael Wallace, there was a period of unparalleled growth; however, by 1983, of the 186 total faculty, only 15 were full and part-time sisters.

In addition to financial considerations, it was the catholicity of the college that had to be examined. No courses in philosophy or in religious studies were required for graduation, and the 1966 Charter of the university explicitly stated that "No religious test shall be required of any professor, lecturer, teacher, officer, student, or employee of the university, nor shall any religious observance according to the regulations of any denomination or sect be imposed upon them." Mount Saint Vincent University had become completely secularized, and the last Sister who served as President was Sister Mary Albertus Haggarty. The "University Question" was a flashpoint of the Fifteenth General Chapter. In the enactment that followed from the Chapter deliberations, it was moved "[t]hat the General Chapter authorize the Plenary Council to move toward the relinquishing of the ownership of Mount Saint Vincent University at an appropriate time" (IIB). The appropriate time did not come until 1988, when, once again, the sisters were convened in Chapter. While engaged in prayer together in front of the Motherhouse, another significant building which they anticipated leaving, the Sisters of Charity looked down from the Motherhouse at the expanding university and sadly, very sadly, relinquished it.

At the suggestion of some members of the university's Board of Governors, Sister Paule invited the Premier of Nova Scotia, the Honourable John Buchanan, and his ministers to hold their regular meeting at the Motherhouse. The General Council's board room was placed at their disposal and an invitation to lunch in the penthouse was accepted. After lunch, the Premier and his ministers toured the Motherhouse, particularly the sisters' infirmary. It was at this time that the official announcement of the transfer of ownership of the university was made public. Joel Matherson, ministerial representative of the Rockingham riding, had worked diligently with Sister Paule to bring this transfer to completion, a completion due in part to Sister Paule's skill and diplomatic grace.

Sister Paule also revealed those characteristics that same year when the CRC held its annual national assembly at Mount Saint Vincent University. The assembly was attended by Cardinal Jean Jérôme Hamer, OP, the Prefect of the Congregation for Institutes of Consecrated Life and Societies of Apostolic Life, and his presence was a cause of tension to many CRC members. There had been friction about a statement on abortion and freedom of conscience, published in the *New York Times* on October 7, 1984 that some sisters had signed and the Church's response.[6] Sister Paule, who hosted the Cardinal at the Motherhouse, calmed the troubled waters by what Cardinal Hamer later called her "gracious hospitality."

The preceding events were consequents of the Fifteenth General Chapter, but consideration of the Halifax mission to Peru was another item of business for delegates to the 1984 Chapter. The mission was a joint venture between the Sisters of Charity and the Archdiocese of Halifax. In 1968, the first mission was established in Chiclayo, 800 kilometres north of Lima. Here Sisters Catherine Conroy, Gabriella Villela, and Zelma LeBlanc laboured. In subsequent years, Cecelia Hudec, Mary Beth Moore, Mary Kay Brady, and Mary Anne Foster joined the mission. A second house was established in Cajamarca (1983), located high up in the Andes Mountains, where Sisters Catherine Conroy and Zelma LeBlanc relocated and were later joined by Carmen Foley. In 1984, a third mission was opened in Lima. Here Sisters Jeanne Cottreau, Pamela Oatway, Barbara Tracey, and Martha Loo worked. Missions were opened in the Dominican Republic at Bani and Descubierta among whose people Sisters Margaret MacDonald, Catherine McGowan, Doris Schoner, Maureen Lynch, and Cecelia Sacca attempted to alleviate suffering. These were our missionaries at the time of the 1984 Chapter at which the delegates determined that the congregation should continue its work of service with continued attention to the development of lay leaders and the formation of native vocations. It was also deemed necessary to study the possibility of establishing a separate "missionary region." Because of

[6] For a discussion of this ad and the response to it, see https://www.ncbi.nlm.nih.gov/pubmed/12178920

the significance of the missionary region, it was suggested that they put forth a delegate for the Sixteenth General Chapter.

The business session of the Fifteenth General Chapter proceeded peacefully, and Sister Paule thanked the delegates for the overall spirit that prevailed over the chapter, a spirit "of gratitude for our history, trust in who we are as a congregation and great hope for the future." July 12, 1984 was a day of prayer and fasting in preparation for the elections. On Friday July 13, 1984, Sister Paule Cantin was re-elected general superior on the first ballot, and she freely accepted the election. Sister Mary Ellen Loar was elected First Assistant, and Sister Carol Evans was elected Second Assistant. Carol's areas of concern were the health and formation of the sisters. Her compassionate nature would be shown when the UISG asked us to adopt an Ethiopian family, and Carol became the overseer of this project. Sister Theresa Corcoran was elected General Secretary and her organizational skills quickly became evident. Her respect for confidentiality and her deep, unobtrusive compassion, especially for the unrecognized, made her a confidante and a comfort for many. Sister Margaret Molloy was now an elected member of the council, the General Treasurer. The theme of the chapter had been "Called to Continuing Conversion," and the eleven enactments proceeding from the meetings echoed that theme. We had begun to realize the extensive time required for any change, personal or congregational, and the eons needed to transcribe concepts into reality.

Sister Paule believed that conversion began at the personal and the local level, but the new concepts of freedom of choice and independence were taking their toll on the common life. Simple things, like differences in styles of dress, were causing some division. Some sisters took the high road of style and shopped at high class stores; others travelled the low road of economy at "good will" outlets. We had yet to learn to ameliorate and to accept differences – and not to be judgmental. Sister Paule understood that gospel living challenges all the People of God: "The principles of unity in diversity, adopted at our 1968 chapter, has yet to be appreciated and accepted by all." Furthermore, she reminded

us that, "to follow Jesus is to embrace the cross." We were (and are) slow learners.

The new General Council was to lead us to reflect on the nature of Christian community and its role in realizing both the mission of Jesus to establish the reign of God and our unique identity as Sisters of Charity within the Christian community. The Fifteenth General Chapter counselled us to continue sharing a life of faith, to practice communal discernment, and to deepen our understanding of diversity in unity. Again delegates returned home leaving the members of the General Council the tasks of leading us to make charity come alive, dealing with problems in formation, assisting us in deepening our study and reflection on the *Constitutions*, and encouraging us in more theological reflection. Added to these duties, the new council had to wrestle with matters of finance: relinquishing ownership of properties and making sure provisions were made for the young in formation as well as for the aged and aging sisters. But the major emphasis was on service. They worked to ensure that both communally and individually we continued to integrate faith and action on behalf of justice, respecting and promoting the dignity of the human person with a particular focus on peace, the marginalized, and women. It was a tall order that the delegates left for the leaders of the congregation to execute.

A new council signifies a new beginning. The call to continued conversion to authentic gospel living had to be lived individually and in the community. By forming itself into a small community living at the Motherhouse, the new council tried to concretize the ideal as expressed in the *Constitutions:*

> Community living requires a spirit of faith.
> To nurture this spirit
> we accept each person
> with her gifts and limitations,
> recognize the reality of diversity, respect one another's need for privacy and quiet
> as well as for presence,

support one another
in trying to maintain a proper balance
of work, leisure, prayer and rest.
We also share in the common tasks of the house. (*C.* 23)

This establishment of the General Council as a local community might seem a small step forward, but it was a giant leap in bridging the gap that had existed between "authority" and the individual Sister of Charity. The gap was ingrained by the pre-Vatican II rule wherein those in authority were enthroned as a special species. "Superiors" were given great deference by their "inferiors." The new council mixed more readily with the larger community at the Mount. As Sister Laura Buckley and other members of the Motherhouse community would testify, "They took their trays to table and shared the noon meal with us," a small act but with an enormous impact for unity in community. In their own small community, council members themselves became simple sisters who had to do the shopping, prepare a meal, wrestle with the demands of finding God in the day-to-day living of a group. Besides the joy and the fun, like all of us, the new leadership had to face loneliness, disappointments, anxieties, misunderstandings, and ingratitude. Accepting individual differences is not easy, but it might well be what teaches us how to love.

One quiet but gnawing anxiety for the General and Plenary Councils, indeed for all members of the congregation, was the decline in numbers. The fact had to be faced that religious life as we had known it was dying. Not to examine this situation would contribute to the dying process. It was a frightening thought. However, for new life to be born, the old must be forsaken. New ways of training those interested in joining religious life had to be fostered, ways which were very different from those of the 1950s and 1960s. Innovations in the training of novice mistresses had to be envisaged. Sister Mildred Crowley, novice mistress for the Boston-New York novitiate, and Sisters Maureen Regan and Nancy Brown, novice mistresses for the Canadian provinces, were key figures in the formation meetings in Canada and the United States, and in implementing new models of initiating novices into the religious life.

All these new formation directors were unanimous in praising Paule and her council for their support in this difficult period of formation – or more exactly reformation. Women entering at this time were certainly not the same breed as the young women, usually recent high school graduates, who entered in the 1950s and 1960s. The women who entered in the 1980s were accustomed to independence and their own lifestyles. They were not easy to mould. (Indeed there was no mould.) The changes wrought in formation over a twenty-year span were striking. Compare the homey details accompanying a novice entering the congregation in the 1980s with one who entered in the 1960s. Before the mid-1960s, novices left their relatives at the train, boat, or air terminal where they waved a sad, lonely, reluctant goodbye. One incident illustrates the extraordinary shift from congregational to familial influence. A young women who entered the American novitiate around this time was accompanied by her father to the house, where he personally installed at least three electrical outlets so that his daughter would not be deprived of her electronic heritage. A similar shift could be seen in the Canadian novitiate, located in Herring Cove, a small village on the outskirts of Halifax.

The turbulence in formation training at this time cannot be exaggerated. There was a tremendous turnover in young people entering the congregation; some were leaving as soon as they entered. At this time, we began to realize the importance of inter-congregational communication. Sisters Maureen Regan and Nancy Brown attended formation meetings in Saint-Jérôme, Quebec, and Halifax, Nova Scotia. Sisters Mildred Crowley attended the Intercommunity Religious Formation Program (IRDP) in St. Louis, Missouri. The IRFP was a nine-month program designed to prepare sisters, brothers, and priests to meet the needs of initial and ongoing formation personnel, but it also increased congregations' appreciation of each other. A new program begun by the Daughters of Charity in 1985, entitled "From These Roots," invited formation directors from congregations belonging to the Federation of Sisters of Charity to become acquainted, discuss formation programs, and explore further collaboration. It was an invigorating experience. One participant averred how strange it was that in the days when we had many people entering religious life, we did not appreciate each other; now, in our poverty, we have come to recognize and respect the beauty, history, and works of other congregations. The Roots program proved a very successful approach to sharing the Setonian and Vincentian charisms among all the branches of Saint Elizabeth Ann Seton's daughters.

Another idea percolating at this time was the plan to establish a centralized North American novitiate to replace the existing houses of formation in the provinces and states. Despite these efforts, in 1980 there was only one associate (formerly called a postulant), seven novices, and ten sisters in temporary profession. In 1980, there were 1,255 Sisters of Charity, but by 1984, there were only 1,164. In a four-year period (1984–88), one hundred and seven sisters had died. However, it is worth remembering that the apostolate of charity began with only four Sisters of Charity who came to Halifax from New York in 1849. We could take comfort in the fruits of these four sisters' endeavours in education, health care, social services, religious education, pastoral ministry, campus and hospital ministry, and internal ministries such as administration, secretarial work, and dietary and health care. Despite the falling numbers, a prevailing mood of optimism characterized the years from 1984 to 1988.

The decreasing numbers in the provinces led the Plenary Council under Sister Theresa Corcoran to conduct a collaborative study with the provinces to explore the possibilities for future restructuring within the congregation. Sister Theresa drafted a questionnaire seeking information and statistics from all the provinces on pertinent information such as numbers, ministries, and living situations. She compiled the information for presentation to the Sixteenth General Chapter, and the ensuing recommendations would initiate a gradual restructuring of the provinces, which were encouraged to explore and experiment with the possibilities for sharing services, personnel, and resources at local and provincial levels. The Plenary Council was to ensure that steps be taken towards eventual restructuring, the aim being to "strengthen the living of our spirit and mission; foster bonding and communication; facilitate sharing of services, and provide for the eventual change of structures."

From the minutes of the Plenary Council meeting, held at Sillery in November of 1985, we get a glimpse of the apostolic works going on in the provinces. The Plenary Council that year was composed of Sister Paule Cantin, Chair, and Sisters Mary Ellen Loar, Carol Evans, Margaret Molloy, Theresa Corcoran, Sally McLaughlin, Romaine Bates, Elizabeth Hayes, Barbara Buxton, Carol Swan, Anne Fleming, Louise Bray, and Gloria Garbarini. At this meeting, after Sister Carol Evans reported on the visit of herself and Sister Mary Ellen Loar to the Dominican Republic, the idea of printing memorial and special occasion cards to support the missionary fund was launched, and "holistic aging" and "pre-retirement" topics surfaced.

The minutes of subsequent meetings reveal plans for the future use of the Motherhouse, for restructuring the provinces, and for the retirement and care of our aging sisters. Paradoxically, many older sisters, after forty or fifty years performing the spiritual and corporal works of mercy, increasingly turned to global problems. Their focus was on working for justice, remedying in great ways or small the injustices they saw in their own shrinking world and in the world around them. A wide range of concerns can be seen in the topics discussed at the meetings, such as plans for the Federation novitiate and naming a future archivist. Financial matters like the sale of land, the approval of budgets, the purchase of houses, requests for money to assist the various ministries in the provinces were also discussed, and the idea of establishing congregational ministry funds was proposed.

Sister Paule accepted her second term as Superior General as a much more confident leader, because she placed more freedom and responsibility on her General and Plenary Council members. In October, 1985–1986, had been declared an International Year of Peace, and the sisters were encouraged to pray and fast for the success of the Geneva Summit Meeting (November 16–21, 1985). The election of Mikhail Gorbachev as leader of the Soviet Union created an opportunity for President Reagan to offer an olive branch to end the Cold War and to stop the build-up of nuclear weapons. Prior to Reagan, U.S. presidents had supported a policy of deterrence based on the principle that if the United States and the Soviet Union maintained a nuclear arsenal, both countries would be restrained from using them. The threat of mutual annihilation deterred both countries. It was for the success of this Summit Meeting that the sisters were asked to fast and pray. "More things are wrought by prayer than this world dreams of" wrote the poet Tennyson, but, added to prayer and fasting, Sister Paule, with support and input from her council, sent a letter to President Reagan of the United States and to General Secretary Gorbachev of the Soviet Union to inform them of our corporate voice in seeking world peace. On November 7, 1985, Paule urged the two superpower leaders "to enact new arms control limits which would ensure a peaceful, secure planet for future generations." Along with thousands of others, these two letters might have had just a little bit of weight in encouraging Reagan and Gorbachev in their crusade for peace and for the non-proliferation of atomic weapons. There is no doubt that Pope John Paul II, skilled diplomat that he was, played a pivotal part in the fall of communism and the break-up of the Soviet Union, but how often, believing in Mary's promise at Fatima that Russia would be converted, had the sisters prayed the rosary for the conversion of Russia. Prayer and action worked. The Berlin wall crumbled at the end of 1989, one year after Sister Paule left office. By the end of 1991, the Union of Soviet Socialist Republics (U.S.S.R.) was dissolved.

More and more Plenary and General Council meetings shifted from the congregation's "household" matters to global problems. There was an increasing understanding of global concerns and our need to connect with them. We were more aware of the workings of the World Bank and now the International Monetary Fund. Both these institutions aimed to alleviate the plight of poor nations by assisting national governments in financing environmental, agricultural, and industrial projects. However, the debts held by both the World Bank and the IMF actually prevented national governments from financing such projects. Furthermore, these and other large banking institutions that loaned money to poor countries did not provide adequate supervision for its distribution. As a result, money was diverted from needy countries into the pockets of dictators like Ferdinand Marcos and Jean-Claude Duvalier; what was worse, money landed in the private accounts of narcotics dealers who relied on poorly supervised banking facilities to launder their intake. The leaders of the congregation became more conscious of the threat of greed and corruption on all levels in public and private institutions. We had an obligation, a social responsibility, to insure that our financial investments were not aiding and abetting the proliferation of greed in the marketplace. Consequently, we joined the Taskforce on Churches and Corporate Responsibility (TCCR), based in Toronto, and the Interfaith Center on Corporate Responsibility (ICCR) based in New York. Sisters Therese Moore and Mary Elizabeth Finn were our Sister Representatives who attended meetings, raised questions, and made presentations at the annual shareholder meetings of the companies in which we held investments: the Bank of Nova Scotia, American Home Products, Citicorp, J.P. Morgan, and Bankers Trust.

How different were the 1980s meetings of the Superior General with her General and Plenary Councils from the meetings in the 1940s or 50s of a Mother General with her Council. The General and Plenary Council meetings of the 1980s demanded long hours of reading reports and studying documents. Time-consuming, fact-filled meetings followed one after another. In addition, there were personal meetings with sisters in the different provinces and states, meetings with the university's governing board, and meetings with the government. What long, long hours went into the preparation of reports to be presented to the Council, the follow-up letters to be written. The hours Sister Paule spent at her desk far exceeded the 9-to-5 work day of the ordinary labourer.

The hours of work, however, would bear fruit. The growth of the missionary region in Latin America is a case in point. January 20–26, 1986, witnessed the first missionary conference attended by all the sisters from the Dominican Republic and Peru, who were joined by Sisters Paule Cantin, Mary Ellen Loar, Carol Evans, and Anne Fleming – a total of nineteen sisters. In 1982, there was only one house in the Dominican Republic and one house in Peru, with a total of eight sisters, a number that had remained relatively stable since 1970. By Christmas, 1984, there were fifteen sisters in five local communities: Bani and La Descubierta in the Dominican Republic; Lima, Chiclayo, and Cajarmca in Peru. The idea of a missionary region was born. Indeed the birthing metaphor was symbolic of the process of formation. As Sister Martha Loo expressed it, "We are pregnant … and we've already felt some of the dislocation and discomfort of the first months. The region is our 'child' born of a North American father and a Latin American mother."

By 1987, Sister Paule realized that her time in office was nearing completion. She could reflect on so many works done by the sisters that were coming to fruition. In 1987, under the leadership of Sister Mary Jean Burns, the Home of the Guardian Angel celebrated its one-hundredth anniversary. The work of providing a home for unmarried mothers had expanded to include, besides the nursery, counselling for unmarried mothers, advancement in adoption procedures, rigorous screening for the placement of children, and the Single Parents' Centre in Spryfield, N.S. (renamed the Chebucto Family Centre in 2010). That the people and the government, particularly of Nova Scotia, recognized the work of the sisters is attested to by celebrations in Government House, by the Mayor's Tea, a commemorative flower bed in the public gardens, a commemorative painting, and an anniversary Mass and reception at the Motherhouse.

Respecting the rights of the unborn was of passionate concern not only in Halifax but in all the provinces. Like Sister Miriam Patrice who worked with "Friends of the Unborn" in Boston, some sisters helped found and volunteered in privately endowed homes where young women, mostly immigrants, were provided with a home, counselling, and safety during their pregnancy and even after the birth of their child. Some Sisters of Charity were among the quiet protestors outside abortion clinics or among the silent writers of letters addressed to local representatives pleading to curtail the overwhelming number of abortions perpetrated in Canada and the United States. In a letter dated May 11, 1988, and addressed to Sister Paule, Howard Crosby, M.P. from Halifax West reported, "I have received many representations from Sisters of Charity concerning the abortion legislation which has been declared invalid by the Supreme court of Canada ... I have prepared a 'Report on the Status of Abortion Laws in Canada' which may be of interest to you." Paule herself wrote on behalf of the sisters to the Chairman and Chief Executive of the Royal Bank of Canada, distressed to read in the press "that the Royal Bank has provided financial support, in the form of a mortgage loan to a free-standing abortion clinic in Toronto" (March 11, 1987).

Sister Paule's letters indicate the countless hours dedicated to the apostolate of letter-writing. Her voluminous correspondence echoes all the interests dear to every Sister of Charity. She wrote countless letters like the one to the government protesting the deportation of illegal aliens (April 2, 1987) and to major corporations protesting their involvement in the policy of apartheid in South Africa (December 17, 1985). Sister Paule could see that sisters who once had been constricted by the four walls of a classroom were now sailing up the North River in Gambia, distributing fishing nets made by the fishermen of Nova Scotia to the fishermen of a tiny village of Mandina, Africa. Pictures that once appeared on television about poverty and famine had now became real experiences.

Many sisters from several different provinces and states had become involved in the charismatic movement, ongoing in all Christian churches at this time. It was one of the ways whereby prayer, once thought to be the domain only of priests and religious, was enriched by lay people who saw in it a way of transforming reality. Ordinary housewives and ordinary workers began to experience all stages of the spiritual life: the honeymoon time of consolation; the desert time of solitude; the testing time when people walk the way of the cross. People from all walks of life were involved in this ministry, often founded and directed by Sisters of Charity. Another gap between religious and the laity was bridged, and the sisters found themselves among the People of God.

Moreover, the development in ordinary women's prayer life led, very quietly and very slowly, to two different movements: the associate movement and the revival of the consecrated life. The Associates of the Sisters of Charity are women and men who seek to live the charism of charity while continuing to live their own vocations. As in any call, it is the existence of a personal relationship with God in prayer that leads to a call to the life of an Associate or of a Consecrated Virgin. Only time will reveal how both these movements, perhaps outcomes of the charismatic movement of the 1960s, will play out. But, as of this writing, there are approximately 300 Associates of the Sisters of Charity, Halifax.

The situation with regard to consecrated celibacy is much different. The revival of consecrated life is another outcome of increasing spirituality among the laity in the latter part of the twentieth century. It should be remembered that the Church had consecrated virgins long before there were nuns and religious. And perhaps religious life will return to this simpler form of religious life in the Roman Catholic Church. The tradition died out around the ninth century. But after Vatican II and during the time of the charismatic prayer movement, the idea was reseeded. Vatican II emphasized that everyone is called to holiness. A few women began to consecrate themselves to Christ, under the guidance of a Bishop, and felt themselves called by God just as much as any priest or nun did. In a *Boston Sunday Globe* article (2009), Liz O'Donnell reported that these women take a vow of celibacy but do not take vows of obedience or of poverty; they live in their own homes and support themselves by working in jobs outside the Church. Moreover, interest in the consecrated life "is on the rise." These two developments in modern-day religious life were seeded, tentatively, during the 1980s.

At the close of her tenure, Sister Paule could not foresee the future, but she could look to the past and see how the Sisters of Charity were still living out the Vincentian ideal. Sisters were intent on looking after those in need, whether that be in schools in the poorest sections of our cities, or looking after the homeless – runaway children, homeless men, abused women. These services were not new, because the Sisters of Charity were founded by Saint Vincent de Paul, the Apostle of the Poor; however, they were new in the sense that they were no longer an after-school endeavour, but a full-time occupation.

In another area of need, extraordinary advances had been made in the treatment of the mentally challenged, and perhaps an overly optimistic reliance on medicine caused many mental health hospitals to

be closed. Families were often unable to cope with adults who refused medication and left home for freedom on the streets. Added to this, there was widespread disillusionment following the cataclysmic ending of the Vietnam War. Main Streets in the major cities of both Canada and the United States were now the domain of the homeless. Thus, the United Nations declared 1987 to be the Year of the Homeless. Sisters of Charity were working, sometimes founding or co-founding homes, and volunteering among the homeless who could be found in nursing homes, prisons, and overnight shelters.

Since June 5, 1981, when the Center for Disease Control and Prevention reported that five gay men in Los Angeles had come down with a rare kind of pneumonia, the first cases of what later became known as AIDS (Acquired Immune Deficiency Syndrome), our sisters have been counselling AIDS victims. Who can calculate the degree of goodness wrought by our own Sister Cathleen Dunne among the victims of the disease in Halifax, Nova Scotia? Charity had a new name and its name, in one case, was simply "Cathleen."

In 1987, many dioceses and parishes were celebrating centenaries of Sisters of Charity in their midst. Stella Maris parish in Meteghan, Nova Scotia, celebrated the 150th anniversary of its founding, and St. Patrick's in Roxbury, Massachusetts, the first house of the Halifax Sisters of Charity in the United States, celebrated its centenary. This was an especially joyful occasion, because it marked the anniversary of the return of Saint Elizabeth Ann Seton's daughters to the land of her birth. On October 11, 1987, Sister Paule greeted a burgeoning crowd of sisters, relatives, former students, and friends at the historic Cathedral of the Holy Cross in Boston. Her warm, gracious, thought-provoking welcome made her sisters proud of their leader.

The history of St. Patrick's illustrates convincingly the changes that had taken place in society and in the congregation by the end of Paule's term. At the beginning of the Sisters of Charity's time at St. Patrick's, they lived on Mount Pleasant Avenue, an idyllic name for an upper-level community in Roxbury composed mostly of Irish Catholic immigrants who were beginning their rise to success. As those residents moved to new neighbourhoods, families of colour moved into the area. After the Civil Rights movement of the 1960s, Boston faced a crisis in racial tensions, particularly ugly when a federal judge mandated busing students to better neighbourhood schools to insure equal opportunity for a good education. Buses carrying black students were pelted with rocks, particularly when they were bused into South Boston, the enclave of white Irish Catholics. Boston had always prided itself on being a city of neighbourhoods. But some of these neighbourhoods were breeding grounds for negative exclusivity and the growing drug culture. The antagonism on both sides of the racial divide was certainly evident at St. Patrick's in Roxbury and in other schools, both public and parochial, for although the Catholic school students were not bused, they, like everyone else in the city, were observers, sometimes participants, in the tension, the anger, and the fear.

The atmosphere in the schools had changed. Some sisters found it difficult to continue to teach, given the tension and the problems of the students and their families, and so they chose to work outside the traditional parochial school system, contributing to congregational support with their salary rather than their labour. Whereas before Vatican II, a sister would not dare test the "obedience" that placed her in a classroom, in 1987, sisters themselves played a major role in their choice of ministry. Saint Patrick's Convent, for instance, once dedicated exclusively to the ministry of education, now became the domain of sisters serving in several ministries, some secular. However, our dedication to Saint Patrick's is still strong. At the present writing, two Sisters of Charity are still on staff at St. Patrick School, Roxbury; one Sister of Charity as well as several from other congregations – including congregations from Africa – are still living in a convent that was once the domain of more than thirty Sisters of Charity.

Another aspect of the 1980–1988 period was the availability of programs in human development intended to make the adjustment between old and new aspects of religious life more comprehensible. Sisters participated in workshops on the Myers-Briggs personality inventory, and there was serious hilarity as we discovered our dominant characteristic: intuitive, extrovert, intellectually controlled, or sensitivity programmed. There was also the Enneagram. These workshops helped us respect our differences and recognize how changing just one member of a group could change the whole group. Each member brings her presence, which forms an essential part of the whole group. But the local community to which each person belongs is part of a larger whole (the congregation), which itself is part of the Church. We were beginning to understand our dependence and independence, our interconnectedness. It would take much more time for the understanding to take firm root in our collective consciousness.

But even as most of us came to find our place as consecrated religious, bound by the ever-expanding merits of the vows of poverty, chastity, and obedience and of working side by side with the laity, our numbers continued to dwindle. The National Conference of Religious Vocation Directors published a report in 1987 entitled "Who's Entering Religious Life." They found for every three persons of Anglo origin entering the religious life, there was only one person of Black, Hispanic, Asian, or Native American origin and that female communities were accepting fewer candidates per community per year (1.1) than male communities (2.9). Twenty percent of the women's orders and eleven percent of the men's had not accepted one person into postulancy/residency during the 1980–1985 period. But in 1988, the Halifax Province newsletter "The Net" recorded that Marcia McQuaid of the Boston novitiate was doing ministry work at the Izaak Walton Killam Hospital in Halifax. Marcia and Edna Walsh of the Canadian novitiate were learning the history of the congregation from Sister Margaret Flahiff. Muriel Kranabeter was volunteering at Hope Cottage, a home where the homeless were fed. Gertie Jocksch was doing volunteer work at Adsum House, and Giselle Baxter was working with Sister Evelyn Williams in the city courts ministry while she and Gertie were taking courses at the Atlantic School of Theology. Indeed, we had surpassed the norms reported by the National Conference of Vocation Directors.

However, whether voiced out-right or asked silently within, religious congregations especially in the English-speaking world, were coping with a striking irony. When religious were given more independence and freedom, numbers became fewer. Why? Is religious life dying? Were we going to sit back and calmly accept demise, or should we realize that only the religious life of the cloister had died? Perhaps, a new life witnessing to gospel values, a life lived in humility, simplicity, and charity with the People of God, was being born.

Meetings of the General and Plenary Councils of the Halifax Sisters of Charity continued to be upbeat. There was a greater sense of "togetherness." Sisters were trying to accept differences, to own their gifts, to disavow labels of conservative or liberal, to embrace action and contemplation, to work quietly to enhance the quality of life one for the other. So, as the Sixteenth General Chapter was approaching, the Chapter at which Paule and the General Council might finally lay down the burden of office, there was a spirit of optimism and hope.

"Celebrating Our Spirit – Proclaiming Our Mission" became the theme of the Sixteenth General Chapter, which had three parts. The chapter of elections took place from April 1–4, 1988. The chapter of business was held in two phases. In the first phase, July 3 to July 15, as many sisters as possible were invited to attend so that we could indeed celebrate our spirit and proclaim our mission. In inviting the sisters to attend, Paule wrote in the name of the Plenary Council, "It is our hope that as we grow in awareness of God's goodness to us throughout our history in the midst of the many dyings and risings, we shall be challenged to proclaim our mission as Sisters of Charity with a renewed commitment born of a common experience of God in our lives." More than 400 sisters accepted the invitation.

On Friday, April 1, 1988 at a formal prayer service, Sister Paule Cantin formally declared the Sixteenth General Chapter open. Good Friday fell on April 1 that year, and the prayer service reflected the poignant struggles of the Sisters of Charity in trying to live out their mission.

> We sit at the feet of Jesus, on Calvary,
> At the foot of the cross … in darkness … pain … absurdity
> failure … lack of power …

And we ask to know the broken Jesus in the moments of this day:
in our struggle during the election process,
in our stumblings toward unity in sisterhood,
in our at times half-hearted witness to justice and peace,
In the visions we only half-dare to dream,
And fear putting into reality.

A spirit of quiet, humble prayerfulness pervaded the election process. The capitulars then moved to the chapter hall to begin the process for the election of the general superior. On Holy Saturday, April 2, 2008, Sister Louise Bray was elected on the fourth ballot, and she freely accepted the election and was to take office on July 7, 2008. Subsequently, Sister Mary Louise Brink was elected General Assistant/Vicar; Sister Helen Danahy, General Assistant; Sister Theresa Corcoran, General Assistant/ Secretary; and Sister Patricia Mullins, General Assistant/Treasurer. Archbishop James Hayes celebrated Mass on Easter Monday at the close of the election session. He retold the story of Jesus meeting with the women after the resurrection and he challenged the delegated, "Go back to Galilee – form the community again, and then be prepared to walk the way of the cross. That, after all, is the only road that leads to resurrection."

The new administration was not to take office until the end of the first phase of the business session to which all sisters were invited. This full participation aspect of the first phase was deeply appreciated by the sisters who found it a "great improvement" in chapter proceedings, a "learning experience" and one which "enhanced my self-image to go out and be a better Sister of Charity." It would be the prototype of future chapter meetings.

Sister Paule's tenure of office was not without its losses. Surely the transfer of ownership of Mount Saint Vincent University from the Sisters of Charity to a Board of Governors was painful to Paule and to all the sisters, but it signalled a willingness to let go and let others lead. There was also the pain of conflict in the process of unionizing the lay staff at the Motherhouse and the faculty at MSVU (with Sisters of Charity among the advocates). There was also the sense of betrayal in the leak of confidential information to gossip-mongering newspapers like *Frank* or the *Daily News*. But Paule could leave office knowing that she coped valiantly with the accelerated aspects of change. God had always been her Great Mystery, her Great Lover. He was enough.

In 1989, after relinquishing leadership, Paule made a thirty-day retreat at Guelph, Ontario. Surely during those thirty days of solitude, Paule could communicate and celebrate with her God. Her life was her own once more. She had put her whole being into her role as community leader and during those fast-changing years from 1980 to 1988, she had found energy in those black holes that can only lead to light and a new creation. During her long retreat, Paule might not have considered the impact her term in office would have had on the congregation; and, although she might not have realized it, when she decided that the Sisters of Charity would not be isolated but would stand firmly, unequivocally with the laity during the Pope's visit to Halifax in September 1984, she had moved us from our status as "other-worldly" nuns to our rightful place with the People of God.

For over one hundred and fifty years we Sisters of Charity had tried to be "in the world but not of it." Vatican II reversed that axiom and we were caught in a difficult, almost painful, identity crisis. Before Vatican II, specifically before our Chapter of Renewal in 1968, we were content to retire from the world and to be known but to God – to be the daughters of God, the spouses of Christ. But after the historical Chapter of Renewal in 1968, the spirituality of the Sisters of Charity shifted dramatically. Now we were called to be known to the world by our loving service, especially among those in need. During Sister Paule Cantin's term, we finally recognized that we had to carve a new niche for charity in this world and that would take time. Sister Paule Cantin was an optimist, an enthusiast. She was content to wait because she was totally in love with God. We were fortunate in having this woman as our congregational leader during this time of responding to the call to continuing conversion.

General Administration (1980-1984).
Sisters Anne Harvey, Margaret Harvey, Paule Cantin,
Margaret Malloy and Mary Ellen Loar.

Sister Mary Corona MacDonald directing the Sisters' choir during a liturgy at the 14th General Chapter in Mount Saint Vincent Motherhouse (1980). Sister Frances Teresa Martin is the organist.

Sisters in procession with banner of Congregational symbol during the 14th General Chapter, Mount Saint Vincent Motherhouse (1980).

Sister nurses at Elizabeth Seton Residence, Wellesley Hills, MA (1980). Seated: Sisters Agnes Catherine Coyle, Evelyn Clare Quinlan. Standing: Sisters Mary Christina Scanlon, Margaret Leo Nonnano, Marjorie Higgins and Paul Christine Houlihan.

Sisters assembled at protest march against United States military aid to El Salvador, Point Pleasant Park, Halifax, NS (July 1981).

Sisters Margaret Molloy and Paule Cantin on a walk around Mount Saint Vincent Motherhouse (1982).

Sisters and General Council in Whitehorse, YT (1983).
Back Row: Sisters Margaret Harvey, Joan Butler, Paule Cantin, Anne Harvey, Frances Elizabeth, Susan Smolinsky, and Margaret Malloy.
Front Row: Mary Palardy, Mary Ellen Loar, Claire Murphy, and Helen Danahy.

General Administration (1984 - 1988).
Standing: Sisters Carol Evans and Margaret Molloy.
Seated: Sisters Paule Cantin, Mary Ellen Loar, and Theresa Corcoran.

Missionary Conference II in Lima with Sisters from Peru and Dominican Republic (January 1988).

Sisters Romaine Bates and Mary Aquin Doyle during a reunion dinner for Sisters missioned at St. Brigid's Home in Quebec City, QC (1988).

Selected Sources

Primary Documents

Paul VI, 21 November 1964. *Evangelica Testificatio* [Dogmatic Constitution of the Church]. Vatican.va Available at http://w2.vatican.va/content/paul-vi/en/apost_exhortations/documents/hf_p-vi_exh_19710629_evangelica-testificatio.html

1-6-1 Letter of Convocation, 14th General Chapter, 1979. Office of the Congregational Secretary fonds. Sisters of Charity, Halifax Congregational Archives.

1-6-2 Planning Committee records, 14th General Chapter, 1978-1980. Office of the Congregational Secretary fonds. Sisters of Charity, Halifax Congregational Archives.

1-6-3 Planning Committee records, 14th General Chapter, 1978-1980. Office of the Congregational Secretary fonds. Sisters of Charity, Halifax Congregational Archives.

1-6-23. Enactments, 14th General Chapter, 1980. Office of the Congregational Secretary fonds. Sisters of Charity, Halifax Congregational Archives.

1-6-30 Governing Board, supporting documents/reports, 1981. Office of the Congregational Secretary fonds. Sisters of Charity, Halifax Congregational Archives.

1-6-31(2) Governing Board, supporting documents/reports, 1982: July, 1982; Constitutions, SCRIS; Oct. - Nov., 1982. Office of the Congregational Secretary fonds. Sisters of Charity, Halifax Congregational Archives.

1-6-32 Governing Board, supporting documents/reports, 1983: Jan. - March, 1983. Office of the Congregational Secretary fonds. Sisters of Charity, Halifax Congregational Archives.

1-6-33 Governing Board, supporting documents/reports, 1984. Office of the Congregational Secretary fonds. Sisters of Charity, Halifax Congregational Archives.

1-7-1(1) Chapter Minutes, July 1-15, 1984. Office of the Congregational Secretary fonds. Sisters of Charity, Halifax Congregational Archives.

1-7-2 Chapter Planning Committee records. Office of the Congregational Secretary fonds. Sisters of Charity, Halifax Congregational Archives.

1-7-3 General Chapter expenses, 1979-1984. Office of the Congregational Secretary fonds. Sisters of Charity, Halifax Congregational Archives.

1-7-4 Chapter Planning Committee Proposals. Office of the Congregational Secretary fonds. Sisters of Charity, Halifax Congregational Archives.

1-7-5 Chapter delegates evaluations. Office of the Congregational Secretary fonds. Sisters of Charity, Halifax Congregational Archives.

1-7-6 Chapter Planning Committee meeting minutes, supporting documents/reports, 1983. Office of the Congregational Secretary fonds. Sisters of Charity, Halifax Congregational Archives.

1-7-7 Chapter Planning Committee meeting minutes, supporting documents/reports, 1984. Office of the Congregational Secretary fonds. Sisters of Charity, Halifax Congregational Archives.

1-7-8 Videotapes: Segment on Aging Part I and Part II. Office of the Congregational Secretary fonds. Sisters of Charity, Halifax Congregational Archives.

1-7-9 Letter of Convocation, 1984. Office of the Congregational Secretary fonds. Sisters of Charity, Halifax Congregational Archives.

1-7-10 List of deceased Sisters, 1980-1984. Office of the Congregational Secretary fonds. Sisters of Charity, Halifax Congregational Archives.

1-7-11 Planning Committee: correspondence. Office of the Congregational Secretary fonds. Sisters of Charity, Halifax Congregational Archives.

1-7-12 General Chapter preparation material. Office of the Congregational Secretary fonds. Sisters of Charity, Halifax Congregational Archives.

1-7-13 Governing Board report to General Chapter, 1984. Office of the Congregational Secretary fonds. Sisters of Charity, Halifax Congregational Archives.

1-8-41 Official minutes, Chapter of Elections, April 1-4, 1988. Office of the Congregational Secretary fonds. Sisters of Charity, Halifax Congregational Archives.

1-8-32 Enactment IVA, and "Collective Study by Provinces on Possibilities for Future Restructuring." Office of the Congregational Secretary fonds. Sisters of Charity, Halifax Congregational Archives.

Correspondence, 1980-1988. Sister Paule Cantin fonds. Sisters of Charity, Halifax Congregational Archives.

Sisters of Charity, Halifax. *Constitutions.* 1964 edition. 1985 edition. 2003 edition.

Published Sources

Bosler, Raymond T. 1992. *New Wine Bursting Old Skins: Memories of an Old Priest Longing for a New Church.* Indianapolis: Criterion.

Chittister, Joan, OSB. 1995. *The Fire in These Ashes: A Spirituality of Contemporary Religious Life.* Kansas City: Sheed &Ward.

----- *In the Heart of the Temple.* New York: Blue Ridge, 2004.

Fay, Terrence J. 2002. *A History of Canadian Catholics.* Montreal & Kingston: McGill-Queens University Press.

Mische, Gerald and Mische, Patricia. 1977. *Toward a Human World Order: Beyond the National Security Straitjacket.* Mahwah, NJ: Paulist Press.

Nolan, Albert, OP. 1978. *Jesus before Christianity.* New York: Orbis.

O'Donnell, Liz. 2009. "The Forever Virgins," *The Boston Globe Magazine,* 24 May, 20-23.

O'Murchu, Diarmuid. 2000. *Reclaiming Spirituality.* New York: Crossroads Publishing Co.

Prevallet, SL, Sister Elaine. 2007. *Making the Shift.* Nerinx, Kentucky: Prevallet.

Schneiders, Sandra. 2009. Quoted in Laurie Goldstein, "Vatican conducting Sweeping Investigation of American Nuns." *The Boston Globe.* 2 July, A2.

In-person Interviews by Author

Sister Laura Buckley, June 13, 2008.

Sister Irene Amirault, June 12, 2008.

Sister Gertrude Callahan, June 16, 2008.
Sister Paule Cantin, September 5-7, 2008.
Sister Mary Ellen Loar, March 7, 2009.

Telephone/e-mail Interviews by Author

Sister Mildred Crowley, June 5, 2009.
Sister Maureen Regan, June 5, 2009.
Sister Mary Anne Foster, June 9, 2009.
Sister Nancy Brown, June 10, 2009.
Sister JoAnn Bonauro, July 7, 2009.

3

Refounding the Congregation, Creating New Structures: 1988–1996

Elaine Nolan, SC

> Called to a radical refounding of our life as Sisters of Charity, we will continue to explore, creatively and responsibly, ways of bonding and restructuring that will strengthen community and the living of our spirit and mission.

In 1988, this was the mandate of the newly elected Superior General, Sister Louise Bray and her council, Sisters Mary Louise Brink, Patricia Mullins, Theresa Corcoran, and Helen Danahy. As Sister Louise wrote, "The Sixteenth General Chapter (1988) was a salvific act … it is the beginning of our transformation, our refounding."[7] This refounding took place between 1988 and 1992, eventful years in the history of the congregation and elsewhere.

Ronald Reagan was the President of the United States and Brian Mulroney was the Prime Minister of Canada. Flight 103 exploded over

---

7 Unpublished materials discussed in this chapter are from the Sisters of Charity, Halifax Congregational Archives or from interviews conducted by the author. For more detailed information see the Selected Sources.

Lockerbie, Scotland; Osama bin Laden's Al Qaeda movement emerged in Pakistan; pro-democracy demonstrators in China fought for their cause in Tiananmen Square; Iraq invaded Kuwait; an earthquake in northern California caused widespread damage and loss of life; and the Exxon Valdez oil spill was an environmental disaster in Alaska. The Berlin Wall fell; the Cold War ended; Nelson Mandela was freed from prison in South Africa; and the Solidarity movement defeated the Communist Party in Poland's elections. After ten years of fighting, the Soviets withdrew from Afghanistan; the Canadian Space Agency was born; Burma became Myanmar; the leaders of Canada, Mexico, and the United States signed the North American Free Trade Agreement (NAFTA); and a Grammy winning popular song was "Don't Worry, Be Happy."

Women made strides in the area of leadership during this period. Benazir Bhutto was elected the first female president of a Muslim nation; in Nicaragua, Violetta Chamorro became the first woman president; Mary Robinson served as the first female president of Ireland; Canada had its first female provincial premier, Rita Johnson of British Columbia; Janet Reno was the first female Attorney General of the United States; Carol Mosely Braun became the first black female United States Senator; and Jeanne Sauvé, who visited the sisters and attended Mass at Mount Saint Vincent Motherhouse in 1989, became the first female Governor General of Canada.

Another woman with leadership qualities became General Superior of the Sisters of Charity. Sister Louise Bray (1932–2016) was born in Boston, one of five children. She entered the Sisters of Charity in 1950, and in 1953 began her active religious life at Saint Agnes Convent in New Waterford, Nova Scotia. This first experience of Cape Breton would leave a lasting impression upon Sister Louise. She would spend most of her time of ministry there, growing to love the land and the people. She looked upon her ten years at Seton Centre in Glace Bay as the period of her most profound spiritual growth. She and the sisters of her local community, the parish priests, and a core group of lay people, joined in a corporate venture that assisted families struggling for better living conditions. The group helped provide new housing and improved the quality of life of people affected by the then-troubled economy.

Sister Louise later became Provincial in Cape Breton and then General Superior of the congregation. She considered those periods of service a gift. She cherished the deep connections she established with many sisters and her affection for them enriched her life and was reciprocated by them. As General Superior, Sister Louise faced many serious challenges, but she had help. Her willingness to delegate tasks to capable team members indicated her support for them, which enabled them to undertake their responsibilities and use their extensive gifts with confidence. The General Council's approach to its 1988–1992 term of office reflected this spirit of teamwork.

A letter Sister Louise Bray wrote to the congregation on September 13, 1988 gave some indication of what the search for refounding might embrace:

> Jesus calls us to be compassionate prophets, transformers of society. Our *Constitutions* call us to respond to the same challenge ... In our search for the meaning of refounding, let us focus our energy and being on what we say we are for: Love, The Poor, Community, Women, Peace, Justice. May the God who unites us, move us to renewed vision.

This mandate was a bold call for transformation, a word that would be echoed in the years to come. It seemed to be a particularly profound task, because the call was not merely to change this or to adapt that, but to refound, to reclaim, to start anew. The leadership members' commitment can be seen in the frequent references in subsequent Plenary Council minutes to the idea that "the call given to this Plenary Council differs from those of the past. Consequently, the mode of acting, the emphasis on reflection, the sharing of experience, the crystallization of ideas, and the grappling with obstacles to our vision are part of the evolving style of responsible leadership" (Plenary Council Minutes [hereafter PCM] October 1989).

Not surprisingly, at their first meeting, the Plenary Council (made up of the General Council and the Provincials of the provinces and vice–provinces) devoted much time to strategizing the implementation of the chapter mandate. They planned an in-service workshop facilitated by Gertrude Foley, SC, a Greensburg Sister of Charity. Keeping in mind a quotation from Gail Atchinson used by Sister Gertrude, "Visions without action are fantasies," they set about their work.

Strategies for Growth in Religious Life by Gerald Arbuckle proved to be a good reading resource during these times. Another book Sister Gertrude used was *The Image,* by Kenneth Boulding, which proposed that culture is rooted in images, and that shared images create a reality and help people see meaning. Building on this idea, Sister Gertrude suggested that the challenge of renewal is to change our shared images.[8] Before discussing ways of implementing the chapter mandate, members of the Council explored the necessary and basic topic of leadership. At the Plenary Council meeting in September 1988, Sister Gertrude posed some challenging questions: What is a leader? and Does leadership make a difference in a group? After much discussion, the group concluded that "a leader is one who listens, who hears the group and can articulate its ideas; a leader is one who enables others to be and to do; a leader helps others to grow; a leader has the courage to challenge and compassion to reassure." The next question each member asked herself was "What do I want for the congregation in the next four years by way of moving the congregation toward radical refounding?" By the end of their first week of meetings, a four-pronged vision had surfaced. The two main items were valuing one another and embodying love for the poor. These were

---

[8] The Plenary Council minutes from November 1989 mention several books and articles that served as valuable resources for the congregation during this process: a chapter from *Ecclesiogenesis*, "The Reinvention of Church," by Leonardo Boff; "Kung: Church not so much Roman as Global," an article from *National Catholic Reporter*; "Towards a Fundamental Interpretation of Vatican II" by Karl Rahner, from *Theological Studies;* "New Skins: A Legacy for the Third Millennium," by Sandra Schneiders from *Delta Epsilon Sigma Journal*; and "Empowerment: Personal and Social," a chapter from *The Emerging Laity* by Evelyn Eaton Whitehead and James D. Whitehead.

to be supported by the third and fourth prongs, energizing participative structures and communal discernment of mission. Further exploration identified the possible challenges to achieving the vision: unexamined obstacles to growth, unclear corporate identity, and an underdeveloped habit of personal and communal reflection. The council members realized that they could not implement the enactment on their own, and that it would require not merely consultation but the active involvement of all the sisters.

At that same meeting, the Plenary Council members said that they "felt strongly drawn to call on each sister, each individual member, to grow toward wholeness of life and to create for herself and for her sisters an atmosphere where this growth will be possible." This led them, on October 5, 1988, to send a letter to each sister in the congregation in which they described their vision along with their pledge "to foster interprovincial communication and participation, to engage in in-service training for the kind of leadership that refounding requires, and to use a reflective process in dealing with Plenary Council agenda." Written in a box within the letter was this challenge: "We call you to the personal healing and growth that refounding demands and to the creating of an atmosphere in which this can take place." The letter ended with these words: "We see this as the essential first step in facing the challenge of the enactment. Let us respond together to this challenge with hope, confidence and enthusiasm." The letter was signed by each member of the Plenary Council: Sisters Anne Harvey, Catherine Conroy, Rose McNeil, Mary Louise Brink, Carol Swan, Louise Bray, Patricia Mullins, Helen Danahy, Theresa Corcoran, Catherine O'Leary, Sally McLaughlin, Maria Sutherland, and Elizabeth Hayes.

One of the council's conclusions was that "to be in a refounding mode, our leadership style must be collaborative, focused, empowering, future oriented" (General Council Report [hereafter GCR] 1992). Some suggestions for collaboration were to participate in the Federation (the association of various congregations of Sisters of Charity), to promote inter-province gatherings, to support social justice networking, and to explore the possibilities of communication among provinces and with

the generalate. They felt that a focus could be generated by setting goals and evaluating them in light of the vision statement and by developing skills in communal discernment. Continuing to foster healing and growth among the sisters and being attuned to formation, health care, and provincial councils would be means of empowerment. To achieve the goal of being future-oriented, a study would be needed to determine who would be most in need of the services of the Sisters of Charity in the immediate future. Planning was needed to ensure there was money to embody love for the poor and for the personal empowerment of sisters.

Council members realized that membership as a relationship with others who share the same call was a topic that needed further study. Closely connected to the idea of membership was that of corporate goals, that is, the articulation of their mission. The idea of a corporate mission or focus demanded serious attention, particularly since numbers were declining and very few women were entering the congregation. Furthermore, sisters had more freedom in choosing ways of serving. The Plenary Council, at its October 1989 meeting, maintained that "Even in acknowledging our diversity, we must name who we are, what we are about, and why." The General Council, at a January 1990 meeting, decided to again engage Gertrude Foley, SC. With her facilitation, they set a goal for themselves for the next four years: "Using the vehicles of the Plenary Council and other congregational groups, we want to motivate and facilitate our sisters, individually and collectively, to take responsibility for the present and future life of the congregation." From this flowed a two-step plan that embraced the ideals of this goal. As a first step, they proposed that a small group explore fresher and deeper answers to the question of what belonging to the congregation actually means. A second group would explore alternative retirement lifestyles.

Thus, in March of 1990, the members of the General Council asked Sisters Donna Geernaert, Joan Holmberg, and Mary Manning to initiate a study on models of authentic belonging. They felt the work of this small group would "open up the links between where we are and where we choose to go." It would also motivate, open up questions, facilitate thinking, and lead to action. This trio worked for over a year on the project and produced a summary of their findings in a 44-page book entitled *Seeding a Future Rooted in Charity.* In the introduction, the writers explained the genesis of the work:

> At our initial meeting (with the General Council) we designed a threefold process. It included researching current and emerging models of authentic belonging, examining the relationship between belonging and corporate identity, and listening to dreams of what inclusive community might look like in the 21st century. Hopefully, our report provides you with an opportunity and a challenge to examine reflectively current understandings of what it means to belong to the Sisters of Charity and to envision the shape that authentic belonging might take in the future. (5)

The team researched not only other communities of vowed religious women, but also groups that began as lay communities oriented to mission, groups who had less formal communities with a specific local mission, and also two self-help women's groups in the Peruvian barrios. There were questionnaires for the sisters, thanks to Sister Joan's sociological background, which prompted much pondering as well as discussions on a myriad of topics that had a direct bearing on their future. Some of the questions were as follows: Who do we say we are? Who are we together? How do we say who we are? The simplicity of the wording belies the depth of the thinking these questions evoked. Because they approached the project from the theoretical perspectives of psychology, sociology, ecology, and theology, the study was expansive and rich. Sisters Joan, Donna, and Mary each wrote papers that were later included in abbreviated form in the final printed product, *Seeding a Future Rooted in Charity.* Sister Joan Holmberg's title was "Sociological Perspectives on Community," Sister Donna's was "Theological Perspectives on Community," and Sister Mary's was "Belonging, Ecology, and the Implications of the New Story." The entire project was a gift that Sisters Joan, Mary, and Donna gave to the Sisters of Charity, a gift whose benefits are still being reaped. The authors made it clear that it was not meant to be a finished product. In the introduction, they wrote, "Deliberately this report is not conclusive. Rather, it remains open-ended as each of us is called to continue to speak our word as the congregation prepares for its 1992 General Chapter. We believe that together we will discern how best to respond to our call to 'radical refounding' – how best we can engage in the task of *Seeding a Future Rooted in Charity*." The Plenary Council thanked Donna, Mary, and Joan not only for the high quality of their research and the perceptiveness of their conclusions, but also for their dedication and persistence in accomplishing this task in addition to their ordinary full-time ministries (PCR, October 1991). Sadly, Sister Mary Manning, who made countless contributions to the congregation and to many of the people of God, died before her time in 2005.

When asked about how she felt when she was asked to be part of this undertaking, Sister Joan Holmberg said, "I had mixed reactions about being asked to participate in this project – it meant a major time commitment but it offered an opportunity to offer the congregation a bit of my expertise as a sociologist; I was also delighted to hear that I would be collaborating with Donna and Mary." Joan also reflected a common reaction by saying, "It really made me rethink how I desired to be in relationship to the congregation and its members – in some ways it made me ponder what had drawn me to the Sisters of Charity in the first place – the project clarified for me my own sense of 'belonging'." Sister Donna recalled, "Working with Joan and Mary was a great experience. We became good friends; we formed and modelled community as we worked together." Donna also remarked that the broad-reaching attempt to clarify the meaning of "belonging" might well have paved the way for the formation of clusters in the life-giving structures adopted at the 1996 General Chapter. With the completion of this project, packaged in an attractive green booklet replete with clear and informative graphs, council members met their first goal.

While the General Council considered launching the project to model authentic belonging as the first step towards their leadership goal, the second step focused on assuring the quality of life for senior sisters by seeking alternative retirement lifestyles. In the letter of September 1988, Sister Louise wrote, "We have come once again to that moment of our history, to pause in whatever it is we are doing, to ask ourselves how we are doing it, to think about where we are, and to plan where we need to go. This moment is an awesome one, for it calls each of us to take seriously the challenge to active participation in examining our present reality and in creatively shaping our future." Shaping the future for the aging senior sisters was a major concern. There was a growing realization that large numbers of sisters were in their senior years. In 1988, there were 1,066 sisters in the congregation and 405 were under the age of 65. In 1992, there were 975 total members, with 339 under 65. According to projections prepared by congregational personnel for an in-house study, by 2005 there would be 587 sisters, 106 under and 481 over 65. This knowledge led the General Council in October 1990 to ask the following questions: How can we create and sustain an atmosphere that gives our senior sisters the opportunity to continue a life of healthy interdependence and freedom? What life style models will promote this? What models are viable options for us now? The provinces held discussions around these topics, giving everyone the opportunity to contribute ideas.

One of the enactments of the 1984 Chapter on the topic of aging recommended that the general administration assign someone to lead in this area. The congregational leadership following that Chapter did much of the groundwork for the discussion, assessing both the needs of the sisters and the tools the congregation might use to fulfil those needs. At the 1988 Chapter, they presented a plan, approved by the Plenary Council in June of 1987, that listed the responsibilities of the newly created position: to be aware of the trends in aging in the congregation, in gerontology, and in ethical issues related to long-term care; to be familiar with the spirituality of aging; and to collaborate with provinces in issues of pre-retirement and retirement planning. In addition, the person assuming the role would keep the Plenary Council aware of issues of aging in the congregation and work as liaison between the general administration and the administrators of the healthcare centres in regard to the following issues: the quality of life for sisters in long-term care; long-range planning; evaluation of major policies; membership on appropriate boards; and updating of general council during interim between annual meetings with administrators (Enactments of Sixteenth General Chapter 1988). The person to whom Sister Louise Bray and the council entrusted this imperative was Sister Helen Danahy.

In the minutes of the Plenary Council meeting of February 1990, Sister Helen reported on the formation of a resource team called Aging into the 21st Century. Sister Helen felt that it would be helpful if the members of this team were persons who were willing to work collaboratively and creatively to develop plans that would address the needs of the congregation as it "aged into the 21st century." She recommended that the team be a good mix of older, middle-aged, and newer members interested in the mission and future of the congregation and willing to serve and actively participate in strategic planning in the area of aging. Sister Helen also suggested that representatives from various provinces would enrich and enable the group to communicate with the total congregation. This team drew up a list of belief statements among which were the following: that all life is a gift; that the first moment of life is also the first moment along the path to aging; that the gift of life brings with it dignity and uniqueness, and a responsibility to care for and respect that life – in oneself and in others; that we use research, analysis, and planning to meet our needs in the years ahead and that we "undertake this apostolic commitment in a spirit of faith and obedience … in accordance with the spirit of the congregation" (*C.* 46); and that collaboration with government and other agents (such as religious communities) is essential to providing these services.

The Sisters of Charity were responsible for three healthcare facilities: Immaculata Hospital, Westlock, Alberta; Elizabeth Seton Residence, Wellesley, Massachusetts; and Mother Berchmans Centre, Halifax. At one time, the Sisters of Charity staffed three Alberta hospitals. One of them, Immaculata Hospital in Westlock, an active treatment hospital, was incorporated in 1964. The congregation had relinquished ownership of the hospitals in Hardisty and Jasper in 1972 but, for a variety of reasons, Immaculata Hospital stayed in the hands of the Sisters of Charity. One reason was that the bishops wanted to maintain some vestiges of a Catholic presence in the Alberta medical scene. The hospital had sufficient personnel, including Sisters Florence James Klein, Clare Fitzgerald, and Eileen Therese Boyle, and it was not a financial drain on the congregation.

Elizabeth Seton Residence, a nursing home providing quality health care for sisters from Massachusetts and New York and a small number of sisters' parents, was incorporated in 1978. Sister Catherine Hanlon was its administrator in 1988 and throughout the first four years of Sister Louise Bray's administration. Many sisters in the adjoining Mount Saint Vincent were volunteers at ESR. They fed patients, helped with transporting them in wheelchairs, made beds, and offered companionship. Because salary costs and other related expenses were a drain on finances, the congregation formed a task force to study the situation. The sisters researched the government programs that could offer assistance and saw that enrolling eligible sisters in Medicaid would be a good route to follow. This alleviated some of the financial strain the facility was experiencing due to the rising cost of health care.

On November 22, 1989, Sisters Helen Danahy and Moira Gillis, the administrator of Mother Berchmans Centre (MBC), met with the Chief Supervisor of Homes for Special Care, as a first step toward licensing MBC. Because a fire marshal's report needed to accompany the application form, the sisters began taking steps to comply with the requirements, such as the installation of sprinkler systems, checking building codes, numerous inspections, and various upgrades to the building. When in the February of 1990 Sister Helen inquired about the status of the application, she was told that it was going to be presented to the Cabinet as soon as possible. Mother Berchmans Centre was incorporated in Nova Scotia in 1990 under the Companies Act. The official document identifies the Sisters of Charity, Halifax, Nova Scotia as the owners who have legal responsibility and authority for the overall operation of the Centre. It also identifies the Board of Directors as responsible for managing and directing the operation of the Centre in accordance with recognized standards and federal and provincial requirements, in the spirit of the Sisters of Charity. The ex officio members of the board were Sisters Louise Bray, Helen Danahy, Teresa Torley, and Moira Gillis. But this was only the beginning of the licensing saga that would continue into the next administration and beyond.

At the beginning of her tenure in office in 1988, Sister Louise wrote that the Sixteenth General Chapter had been a "salvific act," the "beginning of our transformation." That "transformation" would be made tangible in the disposition of the Motherhouse. No other endeavour would tax her ingenuity and that of her council more than this monumental task. The 1988 Chapter urged "that the Plenary Council continue to take action on options regarding Mount Saint Vincent Motherhouse." Such a clear and direct mandate required much attention and that is what it received. In February of 1989, the Plenary Council asked Sister Mary Louise Brink to shepherd this task. She was part of the Motherhouse Task Force with Sister Rita MacDonald, Sister Margaret Molloy, and Finance Director Greg Walsh, along with some local businessmen.

Sister Mary Louise reported on the task force's suggestions for the better utilization of the Motherhouse. She circulated a study projecting the number of sisters in Canadian provinces and the vice province by 2005. This information would help evaluate future congregational health care and individual retirement needs related to the use of the property at Mount Saint Vincent Motherhouse. A similar survey of the American sisters would take place shortly after this time. The task force was looking for imaginative and comprehensive uses for a significant portion of the Motherhouse building and its surrounding acres. Sister Mary Louise felt that communication with sisters was vitally important, so she met with the sisters of the Halifax Province to explain the goals of the task force, and planned to send letters of information to the congregation. She said that in such important decisions, which touch the lives of every member of the congregation, prayers for wisdom, prudence, and opportunities were vital.

As a first step, the task force reviewed the study prepared for the 1988 Chapter with the intention of implementing its recommendations. The task force then began to consider systematically the following options: 1) sell the building and land, 2) develop the Motherhouse land, 3) raze the building and construct a separate new healthcare centre and residence, 4) continue to occupy the building and consolidate the space occupied, 5) rent or sell the surplus space to other tenants, or 6) "mothball" the surplus space.

From October 1989 to July 1990, the task force invited fifteen major local development companies to submit proposals indicating their ability and interest in taking on a large-scale project like the Motherhouse. Four companies responded; two dropped out early on, and the plans of the remaining two were not acceptable. Therefore, the first plan, to sell, had to be abandoned because there were no buyers. At this point, the task force decided to hire a consulting firm, Hardman Group Limited, whose task would include exploring the remaining options and handling any related negotiations.

The exploration of options for developing the Motherhouse land identified a myriad of problems, from the need for an access road to tunnelling under the railroad tracks to ensure proper storm drainage into the Bedford Basin. To develop the land with the goal of making a considerable profit would be very costly. To sell it without developing it would yield such a small revenue that it would not be financially wise to do so. Other complications made this a difficult option, and the process was still ongoing at the time of next chapter in 1992.

Moving out of the Motherhouse and razing the building was not so simple as it first sounded. The amount of housing that the congregation would have to build or purchase to accommodate the 140 sisters at the Motherhouse and the 70 projected to be needing health care in the future was far beyond what the congregation could afford. Building another large facility or several smaller houses would not solve the problem of providing support services and health care. The other matter of concern was that the congregation did not want to be left with property that would be difficult to sell later on. These were among the reasons this plan was dropped.

To continue to live in the Motherhouse for the next fifteen to twenty years while consolidating the space within did not present the kinds of obstacles as the other options. The existing healthcare facilities were not at capacity and would be able to accommodate the growing number of sisters who would require health care. On May 1, 1991, a report came from the Health Care Feasibility Study, conducted by Peat Marwick Stevenson and Kellogg, offering the following information:

> The health care space presently occupied by the sisters is more than adequate, surpasses most facilities in the city, and can continue to meet our needs for the foreseeable future. The Mother Berchmans Centre space is underutilized and probably will continue to be so as we encourage a policy of 'aging in place.' It is unlikely that expansion of health care facilities is an answer to space utilization in the Motherhouse. There is not a recognized need for licensing more health care beds in the Halifax area.

Further minutes record the depths of uncertainty involved in the Motherhouse question. This fourth option remained open.

The possibility of sharing the building with other users seemed a hopeful option, but it, too, had its own set of problems. Mount Saint Vincent University had been renting dormitory space and was interested in occupying the north wing (auditorium/gym, corridors) on a permanent basis, but government regulations for funding were making that difficult. Several groups interested in using the building as a nursing home or other healthcare facility showed interest. When they visited, they realized that the space occupied 350,000 square feet, was 34 years old, and was not in conformity with the 1989 building code because the corridors were one to two feet too narrow. While impressed by the structure and the good condition of the building, none of those initially interested parties submitted bids. The Hardman group explored the idea of using one wing for apartments. Another idea was to have a section zoned for senior citizen apartments. Many avenues were pursued, leaving this option open to further study.

Finally, if, after consolidating the space needed for the sisters, there were no interested buyers or tenants for the remaining areas of the Motherhouse, the committee proposed that those vacant sections be mothballed. The Plenary Council, with assistance from the Hardman group and the Motherhouse Task Force, would continue to search for the most effective use of the building.

When Sister Louise Bray was interviewed in 2008 and asked about her time as superior general, she recalled,

> One of the mandates for us was to sell the Motherhouse. That was a big one, and we took it very seriously. To give you a little background, the economy and the housing market were not favorable. We had construction people, we had developers, we had everybody coming in looking around at that time. They would all tell us how clean the building was and how wonderful the building was, but they had no interest in it because it was too big, and they couldn't do anything with it, and there was no money available. That's what we were faced with, and we had to come up with other ways that we could continue to live there and still have enough money to support the sisters and keep up the building.

In her second term, Sister Louise and the council of Sisters Mary Louise Brink, Helen Danahy, Patricia Mullins, and Phyllis Giroux would continue to work on this project.

In 1988, the Motherhouse was made up of three units: health care, the vice province, and sisters of the Halifax Province – a diverse grouping – and it seemed that restructuring was in order. To that end, in October of 1990, the Plenary Council established the Motherhouse Restructuring Committee. One sub group explored whatever changes were necessary in Mother Berchmans Centre and also considered the effects that a separation of Mother Berchmans Centre from the Halifax Province would have. A second sub group was aimed at developing ways that would enable the more active sisters in the Motherhouse to live their lives in a full and enriching manner. The conclusion of the first group was to separate Mother Berchmans Centre from the Halifax Vice Province. As a result, Berchmans Community came into being on September 1, 1991. Sister Doris Schoner, who administered Mother Berchmans Centre, was named superior. Thus, the most senior sisters were the first ones to be plunged into the new restructuring and refounding plan, blazing the trail for the many changes that would follow. Berchmans Community was in effect for four years, after which time the sisters once again became part of the Halifax Vice Province. This was the first of many adjustments that the Motherhouse would experience during the 1988 to 1996 period and beyond.

During the four years of study on the future of the Motherhouse, seven established community houses closed: in Nova Scotia, Seton House (Saint Anthony) in Glace Bay, Saint Anselm in West Chezzetcook, and Sacred Heart in Metaghan; in Massachusetts, Saint Kevin in Dorchester, Saint Peter in Dorchester, and Saint Mary in Randolph; and in Quebec, Saint Patrick Convent.

Although the issue of the Motherhouse took a great deal of attention, other issues also demanded care. It is significant that the 1992 Chapter was the first chapter of full participation. An enactment from the Sixteenth General Chapter read, "That the membership of the Seventeenth General Chapter be determined by the Plenary Council in consultation with the members of the congregation taking into consideration the experience of the 1988 Chapter." For many years, only elected representatives attended chapters, and only they had voting power. Because membership was representational, the attendance was not large. The unusual participation of 400 sisters in the first phase of the 1988 Chapter was very successful and had met with much support. This fact added impetus to the Plenary Council's desire to have the widest participation possible in the next chapter. At their February 1990 meeting, they established a subcommittee of Sisters Mary Louise Brink, Anne Harvey, and Maria

Sutherland who set about researching how to make this happen. They weighed with the Council the pros and cons of an open chapter, studied the *Constitutions*, consulted canon lawyers and charted several possible courses of action. At the Plenary Council meeting in May of 1990, they made two recommendations: "1. Whatever type of chapter we have, we must use it as a vehicle to continue our learning about communal decision making. 2. Whatever type of chapter we have, the direction for the chapter should be a continuing focus on the elements of our Plenary Council vision which are timely, motivational and would probably be welcomed by all." In June, the committee reported on the possibility of an open chapter, having particular concern for the prescriptions of Canon Law and of the *Constitutions*. In November of 1990, they prepared a packet, which they sent to each sister along with a letter from the Plenary Council. At that time, they asked the sisters for their input about a chapter of full participation. Over 87% of the sisters participated in the survey and of those, more than two-thirds, voted to engage in a chapter of full participation.

After much committee work, consultation with experts and, most importantly, input from the sisters, the Plenary Council, in a letter of February 22, 1991, invited each member to full participation in the 1992 Chapter. All the members of the Plenary Council signed it, and, acknowledging the concerns some had about the possible large numbers, they encouraged the "maximal participation of the congregation." Sister Maryanne Fitzgerald would be the coordinator of the Chapter Planning Committee. Sisters Barbara Thomas and Donna Kenney, both Nazareth Sisters of Charity, would be facilitators. Regarding her role, Sister Maryanne recalled, "One of the best things that happened in terms of getting the work done was the use of the FAX machine. They were just coming into being, and it helped so much to get things back and forth to Halifax. It seems silly now, but in those days, it was a great help." She further reflected, "It was a wonderful experience of the congregation working together. Committee members really reverenced each other, respected differences and worked as a team. It was an experience, for me, of us at our best!"

As for levels of participation at chapter, there were necessarily different modes. The Report to the Seventeenth Chapter reads,

> As of September 1991, four hundred fifty-two sisters opted to be supporting participants, committing themselves to prayer for the chapter and any reading and participation they might be able to do. One hundred seventy-one collaborating participants had promised to participate in chapter preparation and follow-up, to read materials distributed to the congregation, and to pray for the chapter. Two hundred sixty sisters, including fourteen *ex-officio* delegates, will be attending participants/delegates at the Seventeenth General Chapter. (56)

So, while not all could be physically present, all supported the chapter's endeavours and prayed for a successful outcome.

Prior to the chapter, the sisters engaged in theological reflection, a prayerful way of reflecting on life experiences and bringing them into the realm of faith. This connection between faith and life is consistent with Saint Vincent de Paul's tradition of seeking the opinion of each sister at his conferences. This joining of a theological perspective with one's experience calls for new action in mission. The tangible product of such reflection in the assembled chapter would be a directional statement, giving a clear direction of intent and/or action for the next number of years.

One of the many messages Saint Vincent de Paul gave his daughters was, "Do not worry yourself overmuch … Grace has its moments. Let us abandon ourselves to the providence of God and be very careful not to run ahead of it." This seemed like good advice across the centuries, as the financial state of the Sisters of Charity was tenuous at best. The Sisters of Charity were called to serve the poor and, whatever the challenge, that call must be met. Members of the Plenary Council were exploring ways to increase income. In fact, one proposed route under consideration was to pool funds with other religious congregations to allow the congregation's funds to continue working on projects for the poor. An excerpt from the October 1989 Plenary Council report reads, "As to the poor, it was noted that care for the poor is not a 'preferential option' for the Sisters of Charity. The poor are our inheritance, and it is to bring the Word of God to the poor that we are challenged and called and given a vision." These are difficult words when you are faced with depleting income and growing costs, and that was the situation at hand at that time in their history. It was challenging to search for ways to deal with this situation.

One way was to continue involvement with the Interfaith Center for Corporate Responsibility (ICCR), based in New York, and the Taskforce on the Churches for Corporate Responsibility (TCCR), based in Toronto. The ICCR, begun in 1971, was a coalition of Protestant, Catholic, and Jewish institutional investors committed to merging social and environmental values with investment decisions, based on the shared belief that long-term investors must achieve more than an acceptable financial return. Through the lens of faith, ICCR strove to build a more just and sustainable world by being responsible stewards, by working to change unjust or harmful corporate policies, and by striving for peace, economic justice, and stewardship of the Earth. The TCCR was an ecumenical coalition of the major churches in Canada. As a research-action program, the task force assisted member organizations in promoting social and environmental responsibility of Canadian-based corporations and financial institutions.

These connections, with representation by Sisters Mary Elizabeth Finn and Therese Moore, had begun in the previous administration. Through these ecumenical coalitions, the representatives gathered information that enabled the congregation to use their shareholder rights as investors in accordance with their heritage as Sisters of Charity. Consistently, they paid particular attention to our focus on peace, the poor, and women.

Some of the issues addressed in these discussion were third-world debt reduction, apartheid, environmental pollution, shareholders' rights to a secret ballot, adherence to the UN code regarding infant formula especially in third-world countries, health and safety standards, and living wages for workers. Through such alertness and involvement in social justice, the Sisters of Charity, despite their internal financial concerns, were able to continue being sensitive to the needs of the world. However, the financial situation of the congregation continued to be a challenge for the council, as evidenced in this excerpt from the General Treasurer's report: "It was pointed out that in comparison with the half-yearly report for the same period last year (ending February 28, 1989) the total income increased by .45% and the total expenses increased by 8.93%. There is need to control expenses to the extent possible." (PCM June 1990). Adhering to the congregation's responsibility to look to the needs of the world, the same set of minutes reflected regret that they were not able to make a donation at that time to the International Commission for the Coordination of Solidarity Among Sugar Workers, but they pledged to do so in September 1990. The minutes of that September indicate that the donation was made.

The increasing expenses and decreasing income were among matters that led the council to engage the financial expertise of Samson Belair/Deloitte & Touche. This organization would examine the community's expenses and income, then project, according to their findings, what the financial situation might be in 2015. The council hoped this future-oriented picture would provide guidance on steps the community might take to improve its financial status and thus enable the congregation to continue its ministries and care for its increasingly aging population. Sister Patricia Mullins gave a brief update on the progress made towards implementing the long-term financial projection to be undertaken by the external firm, as approved by Plenary Council in June of 1991.

The June 1992 minutes of the Plenary Council report that two representatives from Samson Belair/Deloitte & Touche Management Consultants presented to the council an explanation of the summary of the financial report to be presented to the Chapter. Their financial actuarial study indicated that because of the increasing number of aging sisters and the diminishing amount of revenue from sisters' salaries, the congregation was not able to continue the present pattern of expenses. However, the minutes of the meeting indicate that "After presenting their recommendations and conclusions, the gentlemen concluded their narration by stating that there should not be a sense of discouragement but a sense of challenge to react to the knowledge gleaned from the report and to adjust." It was decided that prior to the Chapter, the Provincials would distribute to the sisters of the congregation the recommendations and conclusions of the report, along with a letter from the General Treasurer.

The report made several recommendations among which were to review all costs, particularly those related to health care; to continue to monitor the use of land with a view to selling what was not needed in order to free up capital; to encourage sisters to remain in paying jobs for as long as possible; and to keep the members aware of the financial status of the congregation so that they might have a more informed input. The congregation took these recommendations very seriously and through the years was able to see appreciable results because of them. The end of the Samson Belair report that was presented at the 1992 Chapter stated, "Although most of our recommendations may seem to be the responsibility of administration, we feel that it is important that the whole membership be aware that the sum of small actions will have as large an impact as major interventions of financial results." It was the hard work and collaboration of everyone concerned, particularly Sister Patricia Mullins, that almost completely turned around the financial situation. The General Council had led the congregation through yet another "transformation."

While Sister Patricia Mullins worked tirelessly on the congregation's finances, Sister Mary Louise assumed responsibility for many undertakings, including being liaison for the Elizabeth Seton Federation. The federation, an organization of groups of women religious connected by varying degrees to Saint Elizabeth Seton or Saint Vincent de Paul, sponsored several programs. One of them, which originated in St. Louis in 1988, was Charity Connections. Seven sisters, including Sister Mary Louise Brink, met twice yearly and wrote articles for reflection, basing the topics on some common theme of interest, such as mission and spirituality, the virtues of simplicity, humility and charity, poverty, and the place of work in Vincentian and Setonian spirituality. These thought-provoking newsletters provided readers with material for reflection and discussion. The Plenary Council Minutes of February 1989 included a copy of a recent *Charity Connections* newsletter that contained this definition of Mission Spirituality: "The principal characteristic of the mission spirituality of the Charity tradition is its outward thrust. Mission spirituality sees the arena of the search for and the discovery of God to be the world, the daily engagement with and on behalf of God's people, most especially the poor and those others the world passes by."

Charity: A Shared Vision, a formation program that originated in St. Louis in 1988, provided an opportunity to explore the mission and spirituality of the Sisters of Charity and the possible effect that women religious could have on the future of the church. St. Louis hosted the first program in 1988, followed by events at Mount Saint Vincent Motherhouse, Halifax in 1989, Convent Station, New Jersey in 1990, and Cincinnati in 1991. Several Sisters of Charity of Halifax attended each gathering. The Plenary Council minutes of June 1989 expressed gratitude to Sister Maryanne Fitzgerald for her contributions toward organizing this program.

The Roots program, begun in 1985, made it possible for new members to share in joint novitiate experiences sponsored by six federation congregations. This provided an opportunity for sisters to study areas common to all, such as the charisms of Saint Elizabeth Seton and Saint Vincent de Paul, and to dream ideas for the future. In 1989, Sisters Nancy Brown and Mildred Crowley planned and hosted a program in Halifax which 26 people attended. A benefit of this connection was the sharing of personnel. In 1988, twenty-five formation directors from nine congregations of the Federation met in Cincinnati. This paved the way toward the establishment of a collaborative novitiate in Fort Lee, New Jersey, in 1991.

In 1988, the Plenary Council established a program called Third World Connections. Its function was to connect sisters to the missionary field by providing them with first-hand experience in Sisters of Charity foundations in either Peru or the Dominican Republic. The congregation mailed a letter of welcome to the program, signed by all the sisters in Peru. Representative sisters from every province had the opportunity to experience the culture, worship, and everyday life of people in third-world regions. In turn, the hosting sisters provided hospitality and assistance in language and a general understanding of the lifestyle of the people. Some sisters acquired similar experiences through other agencies and programs. When asked what they found helpful about the experiences, those who took part responded with a range of comments such as, "Greater awareness of contrast between desperate poverty in Peru and absolute wealth of North America," "Understanding more of the isolation and hardships of missionary life," and "Gratitude to the congregation for having the vision to connect the north and the south." In their evaluations, all the participants were enthusiastic about their time living with the poor in culturally different circumstances, and through the years have remarked on the profound and lasting impact the opportunity afforded them.

Formation, the ongoing training and preparation of novices and newly professed sisters, underwent changes as the numbers of new members diminished. Because of the shrinking numbers, fewer formation personnel were needed, and a new, more collaborative approach was pursued. At a meeting in October of 1988, representatives from local communities met with formation personnel to discuss the theme "Exploring Formation Communities – Issues and Problems." This lead to a focus for the next four years of identifying what refounding really meant and planning for the future. The following year, Sister Gertrude Foley, SC, facilitated the group and helped them "to learn and to deepen our understanding of the emerging world view; to look at the interactive system in relation to religious life values and structures both past and present; to begin identifying resulting implications, issues, and questions for our future" (GCR 1992).

Changes in formation occurred at the local level. The Canadian Novitiate Board was dissolved and replaced by the Canadian Formation Council, which was made up of the four Canadian provincials and three resource persons. Their focus was "to support, initiate, and coordinate action that will enhance and advance the formation goals of the Canadian Provinces as expressed in the Formation Manual" (CFC August 1990). In 1991, the American Formation Council, comprised of the Boston and New York provincials, personnel directors, and formation personnel, decided to share a director of novices and other formation personnel. In 1992, the American Formation Council participated in the collaborative novitiate in Fort Lee, New Jersey.

An unusual and sad event took place in August 1990, in relation to Sister Katherine O'Toole, superior general from 1972 to 1980. When her mother became ill, Katherine returned to Boston to be near her mother and family. She secured the position of Vicar of Religious for the Archdiocese of Boston. However, in 1989, she was diagnosed with cancer. With her typical industriousness, Katherine forged ahead with her duties and tried not to let her handicap interfere with her everyday activities. In August of the following year, while Katherine was being treated with chemotherapy in the hope that the cancer might be arrested, a frightening error occurred. The wrong drug was administered to her, and the doctor told her that she had a very short time left before she would lapse into a permanent unconscious state. Her reaction to this horrendous mistake was swift and deliberate. In addition to thanking her gathered family and friends for all they had done for her, she also made a request that no lawsuit be pursued. "It was," she said, "an honest mistake." As predicted, she lost consciousness that afternoon and died twelve days later, on August 20, 1990, at the age of fifty-five. Sister Katherine's willingness to forgive a grave error that ended her life so unexpectedly and suddenly touched those who knew her. Those who did not know her were amazed and inspired.

The sisters in the provinces and vice-provinces throughout the congregation were seeking ways to be part of the refounding process. They met among themselves, discussed topics such as the environment, reconciliation, social justice, and the teachings of Elizabeth Seton and Vincent de Paul. Together they sought ways to embody the words of the chapter statement. In Antigonish, some sisters gathered for an intercongregational experience, "Revitalizing Religious Life," and the sharing of Michael Crosby's *Transforming Religious Life.* Conscious that they were in the province with the highest median age, they made efforts to establish smaller intentional communities, even as they closed larger ones. In this dual process, they saw the need for structural change. They listened to Paula Gonzales, who challenged them to be caretakers, not destroyers, of the earth and her resources and to be aware of the interconnected and interdependent nature of everything in the world. They were involved in many different ministries including work with chemically dependent women, leadership training of the laity, and collaborating with Seton Foundation (Houses for People) and with the broader-based Amnesty International.

At their Provincial Chapter, the Boston sisters set as their theme "Creating the Future." In the ensuing years, they celebrated their common heritage by re-examining membership and leadership. This led to the question, "How can we express, in a timely way, what it means to be a Sister of Charity in the world of today?" This was a question closely akin to that of the General Chapter's question, "How can we embody charity?" They touched on issues such as the ecological perspective of the charism of charity, and ways of dealing with the aging process that emphasised quality of life. These discussions led to the theme "One in Charity," which was illustrated in a picture that contained the names of all of the Boston Province sisters wound around a spiral with the congregational symbol in the centre. The image represented a group of women rooted in their charism of charity, making efforts to spread it throughout the world.

The Central Province (Bathurst, NB to Windsor, ON) focused on their provincial enactment, in which they were moved "to address the growing violence in our society, a violence that affects all aspects of life, that touches every human person, that is especially pressing on women, children, and the elderly." They set up a task force to prepare a study/reflection tool that would help them understand and address the ways in which the misuse of power can foster unhealthy and perhaps "violent" relationships among people, institutions, and structures. They felt that over time, this process affected the quality of their listening and

interaction. Communally, they were using and celebrating their "power to embody charity."

At the 1988 Halifax Provincial Chapter, the sisters chose three words as a focus: celebration, participation, and reconciliation. In addition to gathering yearly for the renewal of vows and for the Christmas celebration, the highlight for the sisters that year was a bus trip in May to Elizabeth Seton's shrine in Emmitsburg, Maryland. A significant point during that adventure was an overnight stop at Mount Saint Vincent, Wellesley, where the Massachusetts sisters greeted them warmly, renewed bonds from years past, and gave the pilgrims a glimmer of Elizabeth Seton's convivial spirit.

Sisters in the Halifax Province formed two objectives based on the 1988–1990 Halifax assemblies: "to increase our understanding of communal discernment and to develop our habit of personal and communal reflection on our lives and ministries." Several workshops helped the sisters integrate the provincial goals into their daily living. One presentation on World Connections centred the day on the exploration of issues of environment, health, aging, and family life in their own world and in developing countries.

In the Western Province, the move was toward interdependence, bonding as they journeyed together, and enabling one another to make free choices in the embodiment of charity. As the years unfolded, they aimed to create a climate conducive to active listening and gifted presence, responding freely and generously to the challenges facing religious women, listening to the earth as a dynamic part of their journey, and keeping in mind that God was in charge! A statement from one of their provincial chapters was closely aligned to the chapter statement on refounding: "We choose to commit ourselves to refounding by taking into account the disintegrating and diminishing factors we have had the courage to name together. In the faithful risk-taking spirit of Vincent and Elizabeth we commit ourselves to a self-help process so that revitalization and refounding will begin."

A question on refounding that struck at the heart of the matter and evoked a variety of answers over a series of meetings in the New York

Province was, "What are the poor teaching us about refounding and our identity as Sisters of Charity?" The sisters acknowledged that the question inspired them to approach the present and future as people who have a lot to learn. After some input from speakers, and chances to share insights on local and provincial levels, another question, simple yet profound, arose, "Why do you do what you do when you do it?" While sisters explored at the local level ways of embodying charity in daily living, the Provincial Council committed itself to engaging in a communal action that would militate against social injustice. A study of Gerald Arbuckle's book, *Strategies for Growth in Religious Life,* challenged the sisters to realize they had within themselves, individually and corporately, the capacity to bring about their own change and radical conversion.

The first associate of the congregation, Susan McMahon, made her commitment in New York in 1990, opening the door to this structure for alternative belonging. Working with the Elizabeth Seton Federation in New York by sharing insights about the future, as well as speakers and facilitators, was another form of collaboration that was in line with the concept of refounding.

Along with the sisters in North America, refounding was also occurring in the missionary regions as well. There were ten sisters living in four communities in the Dominican Republic and Peru. Vast geographical distances lay between them; yet all of the sisters in each country met three times a year, and every two years all ten met in one of the countries. At these meetings, they reflected on issues that affected their lives as Sisters of Charity and shared their missionary experiences. In Peru, political unrest and violence were so prevalent that religious groups were advised to weigh their decisions to stay or leave. The Shining Path movement looked upon anyone affiliated with the Church as the enemy and created an atmosphere of fear. Undaunted, the people held onto hope as the sisters there tried to model a non-violent mode of living. The closing in 1993 of their original mission in Chiclayo, La Victoria, brought both a sense of gratitude for the well-established lay group there, as well as sadness in leaving. At the present writing, Sister Martha Loo continues to minister where she feels God calls her, serving the needs of the poor in Latin America.

The sisters in the Halifax Vice Province felt that their response to the chapter statement would necessarily be limited by the circumstances of age and frailty. However, the realization that with age comes wisdom gave them the confidence based on knowing how to put first things first. They were involved in workshops on the psalms, on the sacraments, and on communication and they took advantage of many offerings. They had to endure many changes, one of which was the separation of Mother Berchmans Centre from the Halifax Vice Province in September of 1991. Living out of their sense of dedication was how they dealt with the effects and inconveniences of the restructuring of the Motherhouse. They cooperated fully and graciously with the directions to relocate and sought to allay one another's fears and concerns. They attended meetings with the General Council on the future of the Motherhouse with its attendant disruptions and felt comforted and encouraged by what they heard. They hardly realized how well they were living the ideal of abandonment to Divine Providence.

In 1992, the Wellesley Vice Province had 130 members, 83 in the self-care communities of Mount Saint Vincent and 47 in communities associated with the Elizabeth Seton Residence healthcare facility. The sisters had a strong belief that one does not retire from the mission of being a Sister of Charity. Each contributed to the extent that her health and energy allowed. They attended workshops on aging and on self-knowledge. Many became involved in projects sponsored by their own Social Justice Committee. They worked on behalf of Amnesty International. They wrote letters to politicians at the state and national levels urging compassion when voting on issues related to the poor and other matters of social justice. They made crafts and sponsored used clothing sales, all in an effort to share their resources with the poor.

Sometimes provinces joined one with another for initiatives or events. In September of 1991, the Halifax and Antigonish Provinces gathered in what they called The Causeway Connection "to join midway to celebrate our rootedness in the gospel, *Constitutions* and charism, and to explore our continuing response in ministry" (GCR 1992). They met for prayer, conversation and for the purpose of being together, focusing on the question, "What are my dreams for the future?" They found the experience of bonding and sharing one of social value and deepening of faith.

In 1989, 1990, and 1991, the New York and Boston Provinces met in Connecticut to listen to speakers like Liz Vermaelen, SC, Gertrude Foley, SC, and Barbara Fiand, SND. Good discussions followed and timely conversations about how refounding takes place only if there is a deep sense of mission, and that regardless of where we live, the purpose of Sisters of Charity is to embody charity.

The General Chapter of 1992, because it was attended by so many, was a historical event. The facilitators, Sisters Donna Kenney and Barbara Thomas, both Sisters of Charity of Nazareth, congratulated the assembly for being the first congregation of that size to hold a chapter of such wide participation. The sisters on the General Chapter Planning Committee made a great effort to communicate with those unable to be present. Each evening, telephone newscasts were available for those sisters who wanted to hear about the proceedings of the day. On July 6, the message said, "The missionary sisters gave an audio-visual presentation showing slides of Peru and Bani. Sister Martha Loo addressed the present violent situation in Peru. The missionary sisters declared their desire to remain in Peru."

A July 7 message contained questions for theological reflection: "How does what you have read in the report to the General Chapter, and what you have heard about the report, relate to the three issues of community, identity, and diversity that we chose as the focus for the General Chapter? What is our 'peculiarity' as Sisters of Charity? What is the gift of Elizabeth and Vincent that is begging for a new translation as we stand at the threshold of the 21st century? How can we break through to that new reality?" These daily phone messages kept all of the sisters informed and connected during the chapter.

The minutes recount that on the first day, after Sister Patricia Wilson called the assembly of 230 delegates to prayer, the three sisters who comprised the team for the study of authentic belonging made their presentations. Using the format of an imaginary letter from Mother Basilia McCann, Sister Joan Holmberg drew parallels between the congregation's early and recent history; Sister Donna Geernaert based her talk on the inclusiveness of the Trinity's relationship and its connection to relationship and community, and spoke of the role of prophecy in the covenant community; Sister Mary Manning dealt with community, identity, and mission by setting a broader perspective for discussion through the ecological underpinnings of our cosmic reality, cracking open for many a new and deeper awareness of ecology that would reverberate in years to come.

In her report to the Chapter, Sister Louise Bray outlined some issues that had surfaced in comments and questions sent before the Chapter began: finances, leadership, forms of association, models of collaboration, identity in the Church, focus on God's presence, and development of think tanks. She identified five trends in the Church and in society that had had an important impact on the congregation in the past four years: conservatism, violence, economic decline, a growing respect for the earth, and a yearning for bonding and community.

The day that the team from Samson Belair/Deloitte & Touche presented their findings, referred to above, Sister Patricia Mullins and Mr. Gregory Walsh, Director of Finance for the congregation, joined the consultants for the question period. Sisters expressed appreciation for the clear explanation of the present fiscal situation. The team's analysis of the future trends raised the sisters' awareness of expenses, costs, and individual responsibility. Generally, the sisters received this report with gratitude and expressed the desire to continue to be informed of the congregation's financial state on an annual basis.

Sister Donna Kenney outlined the guidelines of theological reflection to be used after every input session. This reflective thread was woven throughout the Chapter. Sister Donna reminded the delegates that theological reflection assists a group to make connections between faith and life and helps them to move in a common direction. The goal was that by the end of the Chapter, the sisters would have found a statement that would become a direction and vision for the next four years. The feedback from small discussion groups during the Chapter was collated and commonalities noted. The syntheses of these findings created a common statement to be worked on and refined as the days progressed. This process culminated in the articulation of a statement in which all could take ownership. As the process unfolded, a number of topics arose including the function of leadership and structural changes. Finally, by a show of hands, sisters affirmed the key concepts: solidarity with the poor, participative leadership, and stewardship. Five sisters, Sisters Barbara Buxton, Donna Geernaert, Anne Harvey, Joan Holmberg. and Margaret Molloy, formed a writing committee to put into words the spirit and substance of these deliberations:

> Called to a contemplative stance
> through which we are transformed and empowered
> to live in love,
> we commit ourselves to
> making the love of God visible in today's world.
> As prophetic witnesses, we
> stand on the side of the poor,
> embrace a simple lifestyle,
> respect our global interconnectedness,
> collaborate and network with others,
> promote inclusive community,
> honour the diversity among us,
> commit our resources to what we value,
> find and implement solutions to our financial reality,
> develop life-giving structures based on mutuality.
> By joyful fidelity to these commitments,
> we release charity into our imperiled world
> with a passion that cannot be contained.

After the assembled group signalled their affirmation, the entire body sang the *Magnificat*. The telephone message for that day reflected the value of theological reflection and the work of the Spirit:

> Since the beginning of Chapter, we have been describing for you our involvement in the process of theological reflection. As we mentioned, the goal of this process is to formulate a directional statement for mission for at least the next four years. At times there were difficulties to be surmounted. There were joys and insights to be shared. We learned to listen to the spirit speaking in each of us. Today our goal was achieved.

Sister Theresa Corcoran, the Congregational Secretary, read the canonical requirements for the elections, and presided at the election of the General Superior. The sisters voted for Sister Louise Bray to continue her term of office for another four years. Sister Louise accepted the election and Sister Theresa Corcoran formally declared her as General Superior. Sister Mary Louise was elected as General Assistant/Vicar, Sister Helen Danahy, General Assistant, Sister Phyllis Giroux, General Assistant/Secretary and Sister Patricia Mullins, General Assistant/ Treasurer (GCM 1992).

These would prove to be years of challenges and accomplishments for the congregation – a reflection of what was happening in the world. Between 1992 and 1996, William Jefferson Clinton was the first Democratic president to be re-elected since Franklin Delano Roosevelt. Kim Campbell became the first female Canadian Prime Minister, succeeding Brian Mulroney and preceding Jean Chrétien. Madeleine Albright became the first woman to be appointed United States Secretary of State. South Africa held its first multi-racial elections and Nelson Mandela became its first black president. The Irish Republican Army declared a cease fire, announcing "a complete cessation of military operations." Yitzhak Rabin and Yasser Arafat signed a peace accord and Rabin was assassinated less than two years later. People of the province of Quebec defeated by less than one percent a referendum on Quebec independence. The World Trade Organization came into being. Halifax, Nova Scotia, hosted the G7 Conference. In New York, the vulnerability of the United States was starkly exposed with the bombing of the World

Trade Center, during which six lives were lost. At the beginning of this four-year term, the Academy Award-winning song was "A Whole New World."

With the election of the new leadership team began the task of implementing the most recent chapter directional statement of the Sisters of Charity, Halifax. The importance of the insight that our lives are rooted in a contemplative stance is underlined in a letter included in the Report to the Eighteenth General Chapter (1996) that Sister Louise Bray wrote to the sisters as she completed her term in office. In the opening paragraph, she makes reference to the first line of the directional statement, which refers to the contemplative stance, the underpinning and motivating force of the statement:

> The opening sentence of the directional statement calls us to a contemplative stance, to a continual inner conversion toward a consciousness of God's presence in our lives and in our decisions. It is this contemplative stance that empowers us and transforms us to live in love and to make that love visible to all around us.
>
> As a congregation, we have eagerly and sincerely turned toward a contemplative stance. Almost all of our meetings – plenary and general councils, provincial forums, the assemblies last summer, and even smaller groupings – have begun with reflective prayer and sometimes personal sharing, allowing space for quality listening to each other. Often readings were sent out from general or provincial offices so that others might share in the reflections. In some provinces groups were formed on the topics of contemplative stance and reflective prayer … It is by continually growing in this contemplative stance that we ourselves become transformed and are empowered to love in the world about us.

While Sister Louise distilled the heart of the matter, she shared with the rest of the Plenary Council the realization that a contemplative stance needed to support action for the mission of the Sisters of Charity.

As the new directional statement was so packed with challenges, the new team set about to plumb its depths, to analyse it, and to pray for direction on how to begin the broad task of understanding and implementing it. The Plenary Council Report of December 1992 described the seriousness of the Council's approach when they met in October of that year in Edmonton, Alberta. The minutes recorded that "the prayer asked that we welcome the new, see our possibilities, accept our limits, and begin living in such a way as to 'release charity into our imperiled world'." The Plenary Council members felt that in reflecting on the chapter experience, they should not deny either the joy or the pain they experienced. They agreed that both experiences reflect who the Sisters of Charity are and both can lead to improved self-understanding and growth. Two probing questions helped direct them: What is it that unites us? What is at the root of our frailty? They concluded that they would strive to strengthen their fundamental bond – the love of God and the sense of mission.

Because each chapter's directional statement guides the congregation for the following four years, it is a helpful framework for examining the internal and external life of the congregation. The opening line, "Called to a contemplative stance," provides the context for the entire statement. The provincials' comments indicated that the sisters placed an emphasis on personal and communal reflection. Interestingly, the activities at many provincial chapters bore a strong resemblance to those of the general chapter. Some sisters were studying the directional statement in small groups, others were using it as the basis for their retreat. A common bond was the strong attraction many sisters had to a contemplative stance. Throughout the congregation, sisters were praying about the chapter directional statement and seeking ways to own it "committing themselves to making the love of God visible in today's world."

In the phrase "prophetic witnesses" the sisters recognized a call to view their reality from a new perspective. The Plenary Council had hoped that Donna Kenney, SCN, one of the facilitators of the July chapter, would be able to facilitate their post-chapter goal setting. Because she was not able to do this, Sisters Mary Louise Brink, Anne Harvey, and Catherine O'Leary volunteered to lead the process. This team offered a question that would help the council focus: "Reflecting on the Directional Statement and on what you consider the grace given in the chapter assembly that invites us into the future, through what one or two elements of the statement do you sense that we, as Plenary Council, are called to express leadership now?" (PCM December 1992). This was a very difficult question, as the Council members agreed that every aspect of the directional statement was important. However, they agreed that narrowing the focus would help the congregation to embrace it in more depth. They concurred that the essence of the first and third sections of the directional statement – the call to a contemplative stance and the releasing of charity – should inform each step of making the statement a reality in their lives. Because each strand of the statement was potent and meaningful, it was difficult to narrow the focus down to these two elements, but the council finally agreed that developing life-giving structures based on mutuality and finding solutions to our financial reality were imperative goals. Therefore, these two facets of the directional statement were emphasised during their term of office. The Council recalled the sense of solidarity that was evident when the financial report was shared at the Chapter. Some remarked that this piece was closely linked to committing our resources to what we value, to standing on the side of the poor, and to embracing a simple life style.

Having taken this first step, the Council set out to plan how all the sisters would be involved in the implementation of these two goals. The Council established two task forces to focus on these topics and met with those sisters in June of 1992. The liaison person for the life-giving structures task force was Sister Mary Louise Brink, and for the finance task force, Sister Patricia Mullins. With that decision, the work of the new Council was underway.

Standing on the side of the poor was not a new position for the Sisters of Charity. The General Council minutes of November, 1993 recount that a decision had been made that "all meetings will focus in some way on the question: How shall what we are doing here affect or involve the poor?" An article by Bishop Kenneth Untener, "How Should We Think About the Poor?" (1992), was a source of inspiration for council members. In a Lenten reflection booklet, sisters reflected on how they met the face of the poor in their daily lives. Their accounts, so varied in the different types of ministry they reflected, had a common bond of compassionate love for the poor. Due to the enthusiasm with which the booklet was received, the Council suggested that the project should be repeated the following year.

Awareness of the poor influenced the choice of political causes that the sisters embraced through lobbying and letter-writing; for example, they advocated for the repeal of the death penalty, cutbacks in social programs, and changes in welfare policies. Standing on the side of the poor influenced their approach to the sale of property, and encouraged collaboration with others in projects that were in keeping with our congregational care for the poor. That included extending the concept of the poor to include our earth as a living organism that also requires sensitivity and attention. One example of an action on behalf of the poor was the Plenary Council's response in the fall of 1994 to an article in *Scarboro Missions Magazine* about the effect the World Bank and International Monetary Fund were having on the poor. As suggested, the Plenary Council sent letters to four individuals in key Canadian positions expressing their concern and then circulated the letter to their Provincial Councils.

Embracing a simple lifestyle is an ideal to which the Sisters of Charity have always aspired. During the 1992 Chapter, as reported in the Eighteenth General Chapter report, the Sisters of Charity "corporately articulated that a simple lifestyle, or 'living with less,' is a basic, fundamental constituent of who they are, and who they will become." They expanded this to mean "radical non-possessiveness of things: our material possessions, our institutions, our internal structures, our finances, and our resources." They broke this down further to mean "non-possessiveness of time; sharing with the world what truly belongs to it; being respectful of the earth; holding personal ideas more loosely by dialoging, sharing opinions, and being open to the views of others; receiving everything as gift, sharing, using everything moderately; being aware of the narrow confines of individualism in order to experience community." The sisters considered all of these values to be very important in their lives.

At a Plenary Council meeting in February of 1993, simplicity was the theme of the opening prayer. Sister Anne Harvey presented dictionary meanings that spoke of the word simple as being uncomplicated, unpretentious, single-hearted, and straightforward. Simplicity was described as a state of being without guile, characterized by naturalness, candour, clarity, and sincerity. The Plenary Council Report recorded, "We know which definitions are the ones we must aim for in living out our charism of simplicity." Also mentioned were some quotations from the conferences of Saint Vincent de Paul who offers many messages promoting the value of simplicity. After reflecting on this exercise, the Council members noted that simplicity was not a virtue that was mentioned very often, but was nevertheless essential.

Visible expressions of "*respect[ing] our global interconnectedness*" included the celebration of two very special silver jubilees. The missions in Peru and the Dominican Republic marked their twenty-fifth anniversary in 1993 and 1995, respectively. Sisters who served there gathered to celebrate in joy the years of sharing with the people of God in these missions. Between 1992 and 1996, through Global Connections, several sisters had the opportunity to visit Peru, the Dominican Republic, Mexico, and India. Two sisters were able to participate in the United Nations Fourth World Conference in Beijing, China.

Closer to home, sisters connected with other parts of the global community from their respective geographical areas. In New York, sisters made a significant contribution to the Africa: A Crisis of Opportunity campaign sponsored by Bread for the World. The sisters of Antigonish assisted in a similar manner a religious community in Brazil. They also helped with the production of a Mi'kmaq Hieroglyphic Prayer Book. Several provinces used materials from the Ten Days Program for

Development and Peace. Sisters sent reading materials to political leaders in Mexico, Chile, and Bosnia voicing concern for injustices perpetrated in these countries. Several sisters participated in projects associated with Amnesty International. A sister from Halifax participated in a settlement project in Guatemala. Halifax sisters made contributions to Gambia. The Plenary Council wrote a letter to the president of Guatemala regarding the assassination of a labour leader. Many sisters participated in various types of intercultural celebrations, all of which kept them globally connected.

Refugees inspired a global connection. The Global Justice Focus Group in New York was instrumental in informally gathering people to be educated around issues of immigration and the plight of refugees. The ministries foundation in Halifax, once used to provide ministry education for the laity, redirected its funds to refugees. Sisters in Halifax and at Mount Saint Vincent, Wellesley, taught English as a Second Language (ESL) to those who wished to learn. The Elizabeth Seton Asian Center in Lawrence, Massachusetts and the Maura Clark-Ita Ford Center in Brooklyn also attended to the needs of immigrants.

Another aspect of the growing recognition of our global interconnectedness was our growing ecological awareness. The Western Province organized a two-year program about the cosmos and learning to view our earth as a living organism. This new understanding of the human relationship with the cosmos lead to a different understanding of God's presence. The Boston Province took as one of its focus areas "revisioning the vowed life." This was a means of acknowledging that religious life needed to be expressed in the context of the new cosmology, holding on to the awareness that all creation is united. Many provinces read about, practiced, and promoted various ways of recycling, expressing a growing awareness of this trend.

An important facet of respecting global connectedness was the continuing involvement in socially responsible investments. The Plenary Council minutes of February 1994 relate that over the previous decade, the congregation had been actively urging large international companies in which we had stock to be aware of their social responsibilities in their pursuit of profit. As members of the Taskforce for the Churches and Corporate Responsibility (TCCR) based in Toronto, and the ICCR in New York, we used our voice to change policies by, with others, filing shareholder resolutions.

From 1992 to 1996, the Sisters of Charity filed shareholder resolutions on the following issues: they asked American Telephone and Telegraph, General Motors, and Johnson & Johnson to improve the working and living conditions and wages in the *maquiladoras* (small plants operated by North American corporations predominantly in Mexico, but in other Central American countries as well); General Electric and Westinghouse to convert weapons plants to peacetime uses and withdraw from the nuclear weapons business; IBM to withhold sales and services to South Africa until apartheid ended; GTE, Mobil, and Texaco to work for equal employment opportunities and affirmative action; Bristol-Myers Squibb to implement the International code of Marketing for Breast-Milk Substitutes; Johnson & Johnson to adopt a drug pricing policy; Pepsico to protect the environment by adopting shareholder resolutions on recycling; Noranda to withdraw from mining on Native American land; and MacMillan Bloedel to produce an annual environmental report. Along with these efforts, council members also sent letters to the Chemical Bank about restructuring the Peru debt; to Pepsico about human rights abuses in Guatemala and Myanmar; to 3M Corporation to endorse the Code of Conduct for Businesses Operating in South Africa; and to the Securities and Exchange Commission (SEC) asking the commission to defend the right of shareholders to submit proposals to corporations (GCR 1996). These were some of the efforts the Sisters of Charity made toward respecting their global interconnectedness, bearing out their resolve to keep before them the question the General Council posed early on in their term: How shall what we are doing here affect or involve the poor?

Collaborating and networking with others, according to the Plenary Council, embraced five areas: formation, leadership, federation, social justice, and mission/ministry.

Formation personnel met regularly, well aware that the evolution of religious life had a strong bearing on the dramatic changes in formation. They attended to the coordination of initial formation at the congregational level and reviewed what formation activities had occurred in various provinces. They sponsored vocation awareness workshops so that sisters could be more aware of their part in this ministry. In a brochure called "Rooted in Charity," they included brief biographies of Saints Elizabeth Seton, Vincent de Paul, and Louise de Marillac. The Canadian and American Formation Councils, while working separately for the most part, were eager to share ideas and information. They had a joint meeting in July of 1995 to do some first-hand sharing. The New York and Boston Provinces, who played a role in the establishment of the Sisters of Charity Collaborative Novitiate, continued to support that venture. In preparation for the twentieth anniversary of the canonization of Saint Elizabeth Seton, the group planned on having articles commemorating that milestone in local newspapers and bulletins.

Sisters of Charity continued to serve on the task forces, planning committees, and administrative offices of national and international leadership organizations, including the International Union of General Superiors (UISG), Canadian Religious Conference (CRC), and Leadership Conference of Women Religious (LCWR). One of the groups to which Sister Louise Bray belonged was the UISG. At a meeting of the English-speaking superiors of Canada that she attended in Toronto in 1992, the members expressed concern that there was no plan for the representation of women religious at the upcoming Synod on Consecrated Life. At the same time, Sister Anne Harvey, vice-president of the CRC, reported that they, too, were hoping for the participation of women religious at the Synod and that they were planning "quietly and resolutely" to effect that end. In June of 1993, the Plenary Council reported, "The final outcome is that twenty women will be elected from the various regions worldwide to go to the synod. One will represent Canada and one the U.S. These women will take part in everything but the voting" (PCM June 1993).

The Synod on Consecrated Life took place in Rome in October 1994. A record 348 people attended and, according to Pope John Paul

II, the Synod occurred at a time when "religious life is experiencing a particularly significant moment in its history, because of the vast and demanding renewal imposed by new socio-cultural conditions, on the eve of the third millennium of the Christian era" (Vatican Synod Secretary 1994, 99). The issues presented at the Synod were of interest to the Sisters of Charity who lived through the transitions, the changes, the experimentation, and the refounding encouraged by Vatican II. The bishops who addressed the Synod touched on many issues from the role of women in the Church to exasperation and concern over the dubious direction the changes in religious life were taking. The universality of the event was reflected in the comments of bishops from all over the globe. The Archbishop of Kingston, Ontario, Francis J. Spence, speaking on behalf of Canadian bishops, thanked members of religious life and suggested that, in addition to gratitude, "it seems to us to be the duty of bishops to show solidarity with the difficulties as well as with the efforts in renewal which consecrated life is attempting in order to be a witness of the Gospel in the church and for the world" (Spence, 1994, 19).

Archbishop William Keeler of Baltimore, Maryland, President of the United States Conference of Catholic Bishops, reminded participants that ten years earlier, in 1984, Pope John Paul II observed that the number of vocations was beginning to decline among young women. At that time, the Pope struck a commission with Archbishop John Quinn and two other bishops to prepare a pastoral service for religious in the various dioceses. The bishops collaborated closely with the two national conferences of major superiors and developed the "Essential Elements of Religious Life" as a diocesan level tool for discussion. After the dialogues, lists of positive and negative factors regarding the post-Vatican II experience were reported. In response, Pope John Paul wrote to the bishops asking that they teach a theology of religious life and continue to dialogue with the major superiors (Keeler 1994, 346).

Despite the scant representation of women religious at the Synod, several bishops made reference to the role of women. Archbishop Maurice Couture of Ottawa said, "There are many obstacles to establishing egalitarian ways of life when masculine domination is so profoundly

rooted in customs, culture, work and relationship." He added, "Does the organization of ecclesial life adequately reflect both the Church's affirmations of the equality of persons, and its awareness of a significant evolution in the situation of women?" He further asked, "Given that more than three quarters of the world's religious are women – the percentage is even higher in Canada – can we as Church be satisfied with the existing ecclesiastical structures for the consecrated life of women?" (Couture 1994, p. 358). Cardinal George Basil Hume of England, the Synod's recording secretary, said, "Consecrated life is meant to be a presence of God in the world and in society, since its witness has meaning not only for the church, but for contemporary society." Hume noted the call made repeatedly by bishops and observers at the Synod that consecrated women be given greater roles in the church, especially in decisions that affect their lives, and that their contribution to the advancement of women in society be recognized (Commentary on Keeler 1994, 347).

Some bishops expressed other concerns. In a widely disseminated address to the Synod of Bishops in Rome in 1994, Bishop James Timlin of Scranton, PA pleaded that "The time of uncertainty and lack of direction must now come to an end ... We must be determined to chart a clear course for consecrated life ... We have dialogued enough. We have experimented enough. Some would say too much. The era of experimentation, or whatever we want to call it, has not been all that successful, and we should honestly and humbly admit it."

The charism of Vincentian Father Robert Maloney, CM, so reflective of the charism of the Sisters of Charity, came through in his address to the Synod: "Simplicity of life will enable us to share our goods generously with the poor and to stand in greater solidarity with them. The ultimate purpose of all created goods is their social use ... Saint Vincent de Paul said this of simplicity, 'It is the virtue I love most. I call it my gospel.'" (Maloney 1994, 323). The many views expressed at the Synod were a reflection of the variety of approaches to collaboration within the church.

The Elizabeth Seton Federation allowed for collaboration and networking on many levels. On September 27, 1992, several sisters in the New York area joined other Sisters of Charity in Saint Patrick's

Cathedral to commemorate the one hundred seventy-fifth anniversary of the arrival of Mother Seton's Sisters of Charity in New York. In 1994, the Plenary Council hosted the Federation meeting in Halifax, where the group developed a Federation Vision Statement: "Claiming our future as women of faith, we are bonded by the charism of charity; impelled to respond to the needs of our day, especially among the poor; committed to collaboration." This collaboration continued to be manifest in the sisters' participation in Federation programs such as Charity: A Shared Vision, contributions to the Charity Connections papers and the Federation's newsletter *Connectives*, and in providing speakers, writers, and committee members for a variety of joint programs. Another program, Seton Legacy, consisted of gatherings in different locations including Halifax, Nova Scotia, Albuquerque, New Mexico, and Louisville, Kentucky, at which sisters delivered papers, which were later published, on the spirituality of Elizabeth Seton. The Federation agreed to apply for status as a non-governmental organization (NGO) in order to have a permanent representative at the United Nations. The name was changed from the Elizabeth Seton Federation to the Sisters of Charity Federation in the Vincentian-Setonian Tradition (GCR 1996).

The Sisters of Charity also worked with other religious congregations and lay organizations supporting social justice endeavours, serving in small or large capacities, eager to make contributions to good and just causes. The Antigonish Province participated in STAFF (Sisters Taking Action for Fairness), a collaborative effort seeking more effective networking, greater concerted action, and the building of strong coalitions. The sisters in Wellesley worked for better healthcare benefits for citizens by taking part in telephone campaigns to legislators. In a commitment to non-violence, members of the Boston Province, carrying a banner that read "Sisters of Charity for non-violence," marched with the Sisters of Saint Joseph in the Jane Doe Inc.'s Annual Walk against Domestic Violence. There were also many examples of collaboration and networking in the ministry. Sisters from all over the congregation worked with groups and individuals who were eager to bring the message of the Gospel to God's people. Some served on diocesan committees and

Sisters' Senates and in educational and ecumenical organizations, while others provided workshops as the need arose.

Promoting inclusive community is a goal with broad applications. Some of the projects implementing this goal were the addition to Mount Saint Vincent Motherhouse of the Elizabeth Ann Seton Apartments and the creation of the DePaul Centre, which offered overnight accommodations for people who had relatives staying in local hospitals; the Spirituality Centre, established in 1972, which continued to provide spiritual programs; and the Motherhouse Advanced Education Team, a GED program specifically designed to help poor single women.

Many opportunities presented themselves for sisters, laity, and priests to share in a spiritual environment and in some facets of daily religious living. The General Council Report of 1996 summarized such experiences of inclusivity. Throughout the congregation, sisters invited people to share prayer and ministry concerns with them. Sisters explored new models of belonging. The Associate program invited interested people to share the charism of charity as exhibited in the lives of Saints Elizabeth Seton, Vincent de Paul, and Louise de Marillac. By 1996, there were approximately forty members involved in the associate movement with prospects for an even larger membership. In Peru, there were also *Vicentinas*, groups of women who met regularly and sought to find how the charity charism could affect their lives. The sisters also tried to become more inclusive interculturally and tried to raise their own awareness of the diversity of the milieu in which they ministered and lived. They sought to be more aware of extending their respect and embracing the broadness and variety of God's people.

Honouring diversity, which Pierre Teilhard de Chardin refers to as the fundamental law of the universe that underlies its growth and regeneration, was an underlying value of these four years. Many provinces included the theme of diversity in local communities, assemblies, and provincial chapters. The Council minutes reflect the discussions on this topic, comparing healthy diversity with individualistic behaviour. These conversations led to the identification of five non-negotiable aspects of the life of a Sister of Charity: a personal commitment in response to a call from God; the framework of a vowed life; the context of church; community connectedness; and contribution to the mission (GCR 1996). Flowing from that conversation, the topic became the vowed life, and from that came this unanimously supported articulation:

> We live in a time of transition. Our life can no longer be defined in terms of the vows of poverty, chastity, and obedience as traditionally presented, although values we have found in them continue to need contemporary expression. What is essential is a public permanent commitment to God, a commitment to living the baptismal call together. This requires celibacy, and urges us to humility, simplicity, and charity. This also requires mutuality, accountability, and discernment in decision-making, leading to communion (PCM June 1995).

In considering *committing resources to what they value,* the Sisters of Charity realized that it is not finances, but their members, that comprise their greatest and most valuable resource for providing assistance to God's people. The *Constitutions* advise that they be "open to ways in which the Spirit may lead us and strive to respond with courage and generosity" (*C.* 45). The resources of energy, ability, time, and interest come into play in their ministries. Throughout their history, sisters became educated to enhance their positions in education, social work, health care, and other new ministries that opened up. They learned about non-violence, aging, caring for the earth, and other topics relevant to current concerns. They served in whatever capacity they could and did not stop when their career days waned. Those not involved in active ministry volunteered to do a myriad of helpful works like writing letters in support of programs for children, the poor, the aged, and the sick. Groups and individuals participated in programs that are sensitive to the poor and had membership and interest in groups like Amnesty International, Development and Peace, Pax Christ, Network, and other organizations. They sought education on topics such as holistic health, aging, dealing with substance abuse, and healing the earth. At local, provincial, and congregational levels, the sisters studied requests for finances and attempted to respond to those who seemed most in need. They were aware of investing with an eye to the poor, and tried to divest themselves of any surplus real estate. All of the giving and planning of budgets was done in light of common values that reflect justice and the needs of the poor (GCR 1996).

The sisters' ongoing work gave them a common bond. Sisters in the New York Province involved themselves in social justice causes. They took part in a Pax Christi sponsored grape boycott, participated in a candlelight procession for the slain Jesuits in El Salvador, sent letters to Governor Pataki about the death penalty, and, touching on the work of the ICCR, wrote to President Clinton urging peaceful means of intervention in crisis situations. In the four areas of Whitehorse, Kelowna, Edmonton, and Vancouver in the Western Province, sisters chose a two-year focus of respecting our global interconnectedness. They spoke in their gatherings of having respect for the preservation of earth, air, water, and soil – a global ethic. In the Central Province, the sisters posed to one another some key questions: How is what we are doing here going to affect the poor? What is the Good News that we proclaim with our lives? How are we allowing the poor, our masters, to affect us? In the Wellesley Vice Province, plans were developing to establish Mount Saint Vincent Assisted Living, Inc. The retired sisters there were swept up into the spirit of the congregation's directional statement. They took small steps to reduce expenses, being careful of the use of water, gas, electricity, and heat. They participated in preparing for Christmas bazaars, making and then purchasing items, the proceeds of which went to the poor. The resale of old items provided additional funds that the sisters were happy to see directed to needy causes. In Halifax, the Spirituality Centre, a haven against hopelessness and violence, moved from the Motherhouse to Terence Bay, allowing the continuation of a needed ministry in the area.

Meanwhile, sisters were involved in writing letters to the Premier and Minister of Social Services to express concern regarding pending cutbacks that would affect the poor. They volunteered with a refugee program at the Motherhouse, and assisted with educational needs in Gambia. The sisters in the Antigonish Province, with the backdrop of the directional statement, posed such questions as: What is the reality of our situation to which we must bring the critique of the gospel? How do we bring hope to people involved in mining, fisheries, etc.? In addition to being attuned to the needs of the people around them, they took part in workshops on both non-violence and addiction. In the Missionary Region, the sisters reflected on standing on the side of the poor and searched for ways that the poor would feel comfortable with them. They shared Vincentian spirituality as they strove to share themselves. The retired sisters in the Halifax Vice Province were involved in workshops on the use of media, health care for the aging, and the spirituality of Elizabeth Seton. They actively participated in preparing for the presentations on finance and restructuring. They dealt with their own restructuring during the separation of Berchmans Community from their province. As they made efforts to cut back expenses, they donated to causes like the Archbishop's annual appeal and sponsored the walk for AIDS. In Boston, work continued in the inner-city and in adult literacy programs at WAITT House.

A plan put forward by the Plenary Council was the establishment of a "Ministry Development Fund," another vehicle for committing our resources to what we value. This necessitated the reorganizing of the well-established Needs of the World Fund. A subcommittee comprising Sisters Mary Louise Brink, Helen Danahy, Patricia Mullins, and Rose McNeil recommended that the Ministry Development Fund would use one half of the Needs of the World Fund for ministry development; the sisters would use the funds to respond to the emerging needs of the global community. The goal was to encourage and enable sisters to enter the new ministries to the poor that the times required. Any part of the funds not used in a given year would revert back to the Needs of the World Fund. The council appointed a small committee whose responsibility would be to administer the fund, to establish criteria for the allocation of monies, and to plan and facilitate a yearly process whereby applications would be received and evaluated. According to the Plenary Council

Minutes of October 1994, the work of the Ministry Development Fund Committee and the overall effectiveness of the fund would be evaluated every two years. The subcommittee also put forth the idea of having the congregation initiate an Alternative Investment Fund. This Fund would have a policy modelled on those of other Federation congregations, and it would be publicized to the congregation and to interested organizations. Loans from this fund would enable some small agencies serving the poor to get other loans and it would be a way of working toward changing the root causes of poverty and injustice.

At the time of the 1996 Chapter, there were 864 Sisters of Charity; 101 had died since the previous chapter. The majority of the 501 involved in mission and ministry worked in education and pastoral ministries. Between 1988 and 1996, over a dozen established convents and houses closed: Saint Mary (Cranbrook), Saint Helen (Burnaby), and Seton House of Prayer (Kelowna) in British Columbia; Saint Paul (Wellesley) in Massachusetts; Saint Vincent (Edmonton) and Immaculata Hospital (Westlock) in Alberta; Saint Mary (Port Hawkesbury), Saint Vincent (Glace Bay), Saint Paul (Herring Cove), Saint Andrew (Eastern Passage), and Marian Provincial Residence (North Sydney) in Nova Scotia; Hermanas de la Caridad (Chiclayo) in Peru; Saint Sylvester (Brooklyn) in New York; and Saint Veronica (Dorval) in Quebec.

The congregation continued its efforts to *find and implement solutions to its financial reality.* Searching for ways to confront and change the financial picture of the congregation was one of the two issues that the council agreed would be a focus of their term of office, the second being developing life-giving structures based on mutuality. On September 8, 1992, Sister Louise Bray sent a letter to the congregation with words that reaffirmed the current financial challenges: "In our world, the cry 'to bring the good news to the poor' is now deafening. Injustices abound. Creation groans because of our abuse and misuse. Violence has become a way of life. As Sisters of Charity, how do we make the love of God visible in today's world?" One answer was to get the congregation's finances in order so that sisters could continue to carry out their mission. Thus, in February 1993, the Council named six sisters to be part of a Finance Task

Force: Sisters Joan Butler, Margaret Mary Fitzpatrick, Margaret Griffin, Mary Ellen Loar, and Maureen Pitts, with Patricia Mullins as the liaison. Their mandate, which was the same as the mandate for the task force on developing life-giving structures, included the following: to explore a wide range of possibilities; to research which of these possibilities were viable for the congregation (and as a registered charity, in the case of finance) and were in accordance with our charism; and to make recommendations to the Plenary Council and the congregation. Both groups were to prepare a tentative plan, to motivate local, provincial and congregational participation, and to elicit suggestions and ideas. Using the materials presented in *Seeding a Future Rooted in Charity,* the Finance Task Force at the June 1993 meeting of the Plenary Council identified the following issues to be considered: the present/future model of being a religious congregation, common values, and finances at a personal and organizational level.

Realizing that the participation of all the sisters would render the Council's work more effective, the council members planned a program, which they called "Solutions: Committing Our Resources to What We Value," which consisted of group meetings and provincial financial assemblies that would culminate in a congregational assembly. The goals of the process were education, reflection, and decision making. There were five sessions and each was designed to provide financial management information, an opportunity for discussion and reflection, and to generate solutions. The task force succeeded in engaging 484 sisters who agreed to take part either by reading the educational materials provided or by joining a focus group. All of the participants received factual information and questions for discussion and reflection. As time went on, task force members encouraged sisters to submit suggestions and solutions that would be part of the agenda for the July 1995 finance assembly. When the input was collated, there were 115 solutions from 324 sisters. Twenty-one proposed solutions were presented at the two-and-a-half-day financial assembly attended by 252 sisters.

The first solution proposed at the finance assembly in July of 1995 was that the Plenary Council and Board of Advisors of Mount Saint

Vincent Motherhouse continue to explore the transfer of ownership of the Motherhouse, planning the method, timing, and manner of transfer so as to ensure health care for members. The proposed year for the transfer was 2010. The second matter voted on was to develop long- and short-term plans to utilize Mother Berchmans Centre to its fullest, to consider engaging in partnerships with other groups, to transfer administration and or ownership, and to continue pursuing licensing.

Another facility discussed was the Elizabeth Seton Residence in Wellesley, Massachusetts. At the finance assembly, it was recommended that the institution work toward maximum utilization and to plan to be self-sufficient by 1998. One of the resolutions passed at the Finance Assembly called for the Plenary Council to appoint a Finance Committee in August 1995. The assembly determined that this committee would, with the offices of the general treasurer and provincial treasurers, develop and coordinate the Common Values Zero-Based Budgeting Process, which is a budgeting process that is based on reviewing the needs of the activity under consideration rather than building on the previous year's figures. The finance assembly passed another resolution to expand the Congregational Financial Advisory Board so that six to ten members from both Canada and the United States would serve on it. Their role would be to monitor financial practices on a regular basis, to make recommendations regarding congregational deficit reduction and increased revenue, and to research alternative strategies for financial health. They would prepare an annual report for the members. Another proposal mandated that the Plenary Council set up a Development Office Exploration Committee, and those appointed to this ad hoc committee would explore the possibility of establishing a Development Office to seek external funding. The council would also set in place a 150th Anniversary Fund Committee to be in place by February 1997.

The assembly also approved other resolutions: simplifying accounting within the framework of new structures, setting up an ad hoc telecommunications task force to try to minimize travel expenses, maximizing use of space in convents and community-owned houses, and regularly including prayer solutions to the financial situation. The recommendations of the Samson Belair report of 1991 found a strong echo in the conclusions arrived at during the finance assembly. The findings of that report, and the desire of the sisters to implement them for the good of all, were further instances of the transformation that marked the era of this Plenary Council.

The work of the finance committee was not over at the end of the finance assembly. Months later, on January 3, 1996, they wrote a letter to the sisters expressing appreciation for their participation:

> We are truly grateful to you for the time and effort that you spent in responding to our recent mailing re: budget priorities. A total of five hundred eighty-seven sisters participated in the process, which is an excellent response, considering all the pressures that most people experience during this festive season. It is also indicative of the genuine concern and desire on the part of all of you to assume responsibility for the finances of the congregation … We ask for your continued cooperation, patience and prayers.

In the meantime, sisters made efforts to economize in different ways. Sisters in the United States provinces who were eligible enrolled in Medicaid programs, which helped reduce healthcare costs. Some provinces took part in fleet programs for the purchase and repair of cars. Reuse of furniture and books was commonplace. Members worked at tighter budgeting and recycling to reduce costs and raise ecological consciousness. Using the computer for provincial accounts increased efficiency. A unique, though sometimes circuitous, internal mail delivery system was used to defray postal costs. Sisters felt they saved a fair amount on that "free mail" plan! Furthermore, boards of advisors volunteered to lend support by monitoring invested funds and researching fundraising opportunities. They also assisted in seeking licensing and helping to restructure the healthcare centres in Halifax and Wellesley.

Developing life-giving structures based on mutuality was the second focus of the Plenary Council. Some background on this may be

helpful. Restructuring was not a new idea. It began at the Fifteenth General Chapter in 1984 with a proposal submitted by one of the Canadian provinces recommending that the Canadian provinces look at a restructuring plan. From this proposal flowed a variety of insights, among which was a proposal to include all the provinces in this study of restructuring and to do so in the context of fidelity to their mission as Sisters of Charity. The initial proposal was revised to suggest that the Plenary Council initiate a study to explore appropriate structures for the future of the congregation. This would be a creative approach to shaping the future with a plan to look at the congregation as a whole rather than a composite made up of individual provinces. The resulting proposal was "[t]hat the Plenary Council initiate and coordinate a collaborative study of the provinces to explore possibilities for future restructuring within the congregation," and this became an enactment of the Fifteenth General Chapter (Weavers, Background Folder).

For the next four years, the Plenary Council worked in collaboration with the provinces on questionnaires regarding new structures. They collected data and gathered and shared statistical information. The result was that the Plenary Council submitted a proposal to the Sixteenth General Chapter of 1988 that included the following points: that restructuring be gradual, that provinces look at ways of sharing resources and personnel, and that the aim be to strengthen their spirit and mission, to foster bonding and communication, and to lead to a change of structures.

The Sixteenth General Chapter in 1988 took place in two phases. During the first week, all who wished to participate did so; however, only the delegates attended the second week. It was during the discussions in the first week that key ideas surfaced; specifically that the concept of restructuring be broader than geography, that it flow from mission, and that the structure be life-giving and reflect the communal dimension of the sisters' lives and their corporate identity. It was then that the term "refounding" was offered as a substitute for restructuring. The resulting enactment of the Sixteenth General Chapter was as follows: "Called to a radical refounding of our life as Sisters of Charity, we will continue to explore, creatively and responsibly, ways of bonding and restructuring that will strengthen community and the living of our spirit and mission." Refounding became a strong theme after 1988. A short time later, concerns about structures surfaced in *Seeding a Future Rooted in Charity: Report of the Commission on Models of Authentic Belonging* (1991). At the Seventeenth General Chapter in 1992, reflection and discussion on the findings of that project led to the inclusion in the directional statement to "develop life-giving structures based on mutuality."

In October of 1992, the Plenary Council established a task force to explore restructuring for the Eighteenth General Chapter of 1996. Members were Sisters Marjory Gallagher, Esther Plefka, Mary Beth Moore, Virginia Turner, and Maryanne Fitzgerald with Mary Louise Brink as liaison. They called themselves "The Weavers" and set about the task of continuing to lay the groundwork for implementing this key piece of the directional statement, weaving strands of the past with threads of the future. Before delving into their task, they set guidelines that were published in the Plenary Council Minutes of June 1993. Realizing that in the reflective process they designed, they would be engaged in constant communication with the sisters over a long period of time, gathering and receiving information, they determined that their manner of communication would be clear, jargon free, to the point, and invitational. Further, they expressed their desire for an emphasis on collaboration and mutuality.

In proposing a convening of the members of the congregation in the summer of 1995, the Weavers stated that this gathering would not take precedence over the general chapter, but would allow time to reflect on issues to be brought to the 1996 General Chapter. At its October 1993 meeting, the Council endorsed this plan, agreeing that two distinct assemblies would be held within a seven-day period in early July 1995. As changes in structures would have an impact on finance, the Plenary Council agreed that the Weavers assembly would precede the one on finance.

One of the tasks of the Weavers was to elicit from the sisters their ideas on how to explore and present possible structures that would lead

to a unifying and life-giving model of government. The discussions on life-giving structures recognized that such structures should facilitate mission; respond to the needs of all members; facilitate congregational connectedness; and that there be a realization that creating new structures would require openness to change.

The Weavers extended an invitation to all to design, create, or suggest a model or an image for the congregational structures that would be supportive of them in their personal lives, their communal life, and the mission of the congregation. From the input of the sisters, the values that surfaced for life-giving structures based on mutuality were dignity of the person, diversity, mutuality, subsidiarity, and unity, thus confirming the values expressed in the *Constitutions* under "Spirit of Government."

There was a broad consensus that structures have life to the extent that they arise from common values and that they provide a way for the community to live these common values. At the heart of any discussion would be the community's mission and a deep desire for this mission to continue and flourish. According to the material that the Weavers published in their folder, the criteria for the new structure included a focus on continuing the mission of the congregation with widespread participation and mutual accountability; respect for financial realities and diversity; provision of internal networks among individuals, local units, and regions throughout the congregation; opportunities for collaboration with other individuals and groups external to the congregation; and simplicity and flexibility.

The Weavers felt that since the 1996 Chapter would bring about a change in structures, it might be advisable to start experimenting beforehand. As three provinces were due to hold elections soon, they recommended that those provinces be given the flexibility to choose the structure that would be most effective for them. Each of the provinces involved endeavoured to establish participative procedures and encourage mutual responsibility (PCM October 1993).

In January 1992, Sisters Louise Bray, Mary Louise Brink, and Marjory Gallagher met with Father Frank Morrissey, OMI, to discuss the canonical ramifications of changing the government structures. They learned that many other religious congregations were looking into similar changes (PCM February 1994). By June of 1994, the congregation engaged Joy Barton and Sister Mary Jo Moran, HM as facilitators and consultants for the 1995 assembly. At this time, the Weavers reviewed the models for life-giving structures suggested by the sisters and prepared to send the results in booklet form to the congregation by July 1994, a year before the assembly. At that point, 257 sisters had already registered for the assembly. Because the work of the Weavers was so closely connected with the upcoming chapter, they developed a tool that would elicit from the sisters their ideas on the most appropriate style for the 1996 Chapter as well as their thoughts on leadership. They also explored the question of whether to elect or appoint the General Secretary and Treasurer (PCM October 1994). The Weavers assembly of July 1995 was a significant turning point in the history of the Sisters of Charity.

After the numerous exchanges of information and ideas between the sisters at large and the Weavers, the model of governance selected at the 1995 assembly and voted upon at the 1996 General Chapter was that of a central congregational administration with the sisters living in local communities and gathering voluntarily in clusters. In adopting a new structure, several topics needed to be dealt with: the formation of clusters, assemblies, congregational leadership, adjustments to the *Constitutions*, and pertinent matters related to finance.

Clusters are groups of sisters formed to support each other in engaging in mission, participating in the congregational agenda, bonding with other Sisters of Charity, and living the religious life. This structure was set up to be flexible and with the understanding that no two clusters would function in the same way. At the time, there was some dissatisfaction with the choice of the word "cluster," but no other term was found to describe as effectively the different configurations that might take shape. According to the *Constitutions,* the local community is the "basic unit of our life and mission as Sisters of Charity"(*C.*109). Clusters, groups of about twelve to twenty, did not replace the role of the local community, but provided opportunities for additional support and bonding. The sisters in the retirement centres in Halifax and Wellesley were invited to participate in clusters in ways that were possible and life giving for them. In this new structure, the purpose of assemblies would be to promote the charism and mission of the congregation, to foster bonding with other Sisters of Charity, and to strengthen a sense of congregational identity. Ordinarily, each sister would also attend an annual assembly.

The proposed structure for new congregational leadership was that nine sisters serve as full-time leaders for the congregation, one as congregational leader/general superior, one as first assistant (vicar), one as general treasurer, one as general secretary, and five as additional congregational assistants. These elected leaders would be responsible for the ongoing life and mission of the congregation. For the most part, their responsibilities would be consistent with those of past administrations: to challenge the congregation to live its vision for the future; to support the ongoing mission of the congregation and to encourage the ministries of the sisters; to ensure quality of life for sisters in retirement and nursing care centres; and to exercise responsible stewardship for the financial resources of the congregation. Their newer responsibilities included encouraging the development of an associate program and representing the congregation in conversations with local, national, and international groups. Also, as one purpose of these new structures was to increase participation, congregational leadership would have resource teams of sisters to assist them in fulfilling their responsibility for various areas of congregational life.

These changes meant that some portions of the *Constitutions* needed to be changed. References to provinces, provincial superiors, and the interval between chapters needed to be removed. The new congregational leadership set up a process to revise the *Constitutions*, with the goal of presenting the adjusted form at the 2002 General Chapter. Another issue, the expenses relating to the clusters, would be included in the congregational budget.

A dramatic shift on this scale had many ramifications. Once the General Chapter affirmed the proposal for the new government structure, all of the provinces and their related structures such as provincials and provincial boards would be dissolved. The Plenary Council, with its composition of General Council members and provincials, would be no more, forcing the congregation to consider what would replace these groups. Bishops in dioceses where the sisters ministered had to be informed. Provinces held rituals at fall assemblies at which they expressed both thanks for their history and prayer for a peaceful transition to this new step on their congregational journey. The official closing date for all provinces and vice provinces was July 14, 1996. That was also the date on which the new leadership team would be installed.

Joyful fidelity to our commitments is a phrase both welcoming and challenging. At the first meeting of the Plenary Council in December 1992, the ongoing pursuit of a license for the Mother Berchmans Centre was part of the agenda. In an effort to be in compliance with the fire marshal's requirements, Sister Margaret Molloy arranged for the relocation of some groups of sisters to other parts of the Motherhouse that she was able to make available. This allowed workers to remove asbestos, install a sprinkler and water system, and set up firewalls and smoke detectors. In another attempt to seek licensing, Sister Louise Bray and Sister Patricia Mullins met with Premier Donald Cameron on April 7, 1993, to tell him of the congregation's financial difficulties and to appeal to him for assistance with licensing and funding for the care of their ill and infirm sisters. They told of their previous efforts and showed him the audited statement for Mother Berchmans Centre with its astounding healthcare expenses which, with the exception of a few donations, were borne by the congregation. To their delight, Premier Cameron agreed that the government had an obligation to assist these women who spent their lives serving so many in need. He assured the sisters that they need not reapply for licensing and that he would speak to the Deputy Minister about the situation. The resulting joy was dashed when Premier Cameron and his party were voted out the next month. Disappointed but undaunted, Sister Louise began planning for a meeting with the newly elected Premier John Savage (PCM June 1993). In January, 1994, Sisters Louise Bray and Patricia Mullins met with Premier John Savage, Dr. Ron Smith, Minister of Health, and Dr. James Smith, Minister of

Community Services, to address the issues of licensing and funding for the residents of the Mother Berchmans Centre, Ltd. The meeting went well. Sister Louise sent a follow up letter to Premier Savage.

The Mother Berchmans Centre Board continued to keep licensing as a top priority. On August 24, 1995, Sister Doris Schoner sent the application for licensure, along with the required documents, to Sheila Ross, Regional Director, Department of Health. In her letter, Sister Doris recounted that the request for licensing had previously been presented to Premier John Savage, Honourable Ronald Stewart, Minister of Health, and Honourable James Smith, Minister of Community Service, all of whom would receive notice that the application process had begun. According to the Plenary Council Minutes of October 1995, Sheila Ross responded promptly and requested a meeting and a tour of the facility. Three Department of Health staff members came and asked many questions such as how many sisters might utilize the facility in the future, how many were from Nova Scotia or had established residency in Nova Scotia for at least one year, how long the congregation would be able to sustain subsidizing the sisters, and how the deficit was presently being met. On January 26, 1996, Mr. Bob Fowler, Director of Policy and Planning, assured Sister Louise Bray that his office was making great efforts toward the licensing and that he was preparing a status report that would be presented the next month. It was two months before the end of Sister Louise Bray's term, and sadly, in spite of many efforts on its behalf, the Mother Berchmans Centre still was not licensed at that time (PCM February 1996).

In December 1992, the Plenary Council set up a Planning Committee for Elizabeth Seton Residence/Mount Saint Vincent (ESR/MSV), Wellesley. Their mandate was to explore creative options relating to the present and future use of MSV Wellesley and ESR with particular focus on quality of life, financial feasibility, creative housing options, and future use of the facilities. The committee proposed a new model of responsibility and accountability for the administration, the provincial, and the various departments of MSV Wellesley that included the new position of pastoral care coordinator. In a continuing effort toward making ESR solvent, they recommended that ESR receive applications from lay persons, in addition to the parents of some sisters who were already residents (PCM June, 1990). Sister Blanche LaRose, who assumed the office of Administrator July 1, 1993, successfully implemented many changes that culminated in ESR's receiving deficiency-free evaluations from Massachusetts state inspectors in 1995 and 1996. The housing subcommittee of the Planning Committee proposed that the congregation look into initiating a unit for Assisted Daily Living in MSV. They would ask Sister Blanche LaRose to assist in setting it up.

The building at Mount Saint Vincent, Wellesley, while physically attached to Elizabeth Seton Residence, was a separate entity. In December 1994, the Joint Commission for Accreditation of Healthcare Organizations approved Mount Saint Vincent Assisted Living Program, allowing the partial reimbursement for sisters' personal care costs. Later that year, renovations began, including improved lighting and the installation of an elevator.

Structural problems at the Mount Saint Vincent Motherhouse, Halifax and the question of how to best utilize the Motherhouse space were waiting for the ingenuity and creativity of this Plenary Council. February of 1993 brought with it the disturbing discovery that severe leaks had critically affected the stone facing on the building. This was not a matter for a band-aid solution, but rather a crisis that had to be handled at once. In fact, the projected cost of the estimated fifteen-year project was between 3.5 and 4 million dollars. The familiar options of mothballing or demolishing part of the north wing were again raised. While the use of space was being addressed, Sister Helen Danahy presented the idea of using available space for refugees and volunteered to look into that matter (PCM February 1993).

Consultants had recommended during a study of extra space at the Motherhouse that the meeting centre be expanded because the cost of renting rooms and providing meals was not expensive. Sister Elizabeth McGrath took on that challenge as director and did so very successfully. The centre grew to such an extent that the income paid for a salary and the cost of rent. Groups also rented the auditorium and gym. Plenary

Council minutes report that about 3,500 people used the centre in 1994 and 1995.

In 1993, in an attempt to consolidate space and make the living areas as liveable as possible for the sisters over the next several years, the Plenary Council began the process of renovating the Motherhouse. To draw on the creativity of as many people as possible while pursuing the reconfiguration of the building, the Council established a team of sisters from Halifax and the Halifax Vice Province who would brainstorm, research, and recommend creative ways to use the Motherhouse space. The goal was to provide some outreach to the poor without incurring costs. The sisters who were part of this called themselves the Dreamers and Doers, a name reminiscent of the Nova Scotia tourist group, the Doers and Dreamers. These sisters let their creative juices bubble and stir and, in time, eagerly presented their ideas to the Plenary Council. Some suggestions that flowed from them were to create living units for seniors on fixed incomes as well as for retired priests, to provide hospitality to families of hospital patients, to accommodate refugees and students, and to have a daycare or learning centre. Plans for the apartments went forward, and there was hope that the rent received would balance the expenditures. Seven apartments were occupied by March 1, 1996 (PCM June 1993).

With grants, Sister Martha Westwater began to offer literacy classes in the Motherhouse, and in 1994 the Motherhouse opened its doors to patients and their families who came to Halifax for medical care and who otherwise would have had to find accommodations in motels in the area. Initially, the DePaul Centre was started by Sister Marie McPherson in response to an appeal by the Victoria General's Liver Transplant team. The program grew to include any medical conditions that required patients and family members to stay in Halifax for a short or even lengthy duration. Sisters Patricia Theriault and Marcella Gouthro joined Sister Marie on the team and they received help from many volunteers. It was a low cost and peaceful haven for those burdened with the anxiety of illness. People from all ten provinces in Canada, as well as from the

United States and other countries, were able to avail themselves of the services and hospitality of DePaul Centre.

In another area, a dramatic change took place with Immaculata Hospital in Westlock, Alberta. The Catholic Health Association of Alberta was pursuing a legal process with Alberta Health to ensure that all Catholic hospitals would receive their full equity (GCR 1996). After much thought, the congregation transferred the new hospital to the government of Alberta through the Ministry of Health.

The area of *communications and technology for mission* saw transformative changes that supported community living and enabled ministry. Sister Phyllis Giroux led the Congregational Communications Committee which, after eliciting ideas from the sisters, made several suggestions: improve the congregational newsletter; change the format of the obituaries; send a monthly fax bulletin with time sensitive information; and create a one volume alphabetized congregational directory. The other major change was to restructure the congregational database and upgrade and update the congregation's computer system. The door to cyberspace was beginning to open (PCR February 1994).

The focus for the 1996 General Chapter was Mission. In weighing the input from the sisters, the committee found that the topics of greatest interest were two that had been emphasised in the past: the poor and social justice. Two new ones were added in 1996: to combat violence and alleviate hopelessness. With these four topics in mind, the co-chairs of the General Chapter Planning Committee, Sisters Evelyn Williams and Marie Sorenson with Sister Anne Fahey as the liaison, forged ahead with their preparatory tasks (PCM February 1996).

The two assemblies (on structure and finance) and the 1996 Eighteenth General Chapter were all significant events in the history of the Sisters of Charity. It was unusual that all three were for a time on parallel courses. With the usual high level of organization and intelligent direction and participation, all three projects travelled speedily and with diligence toward their respective goals.

The 1996 General Chapter saw the affirmation of what was decided at the previous year's assemblies and the many months of work leading up to that point. Some of the agenda items of the 1996 Chapter were as follows: mission, life-giving structures of government, Office of Advancement Potential, and the Telecommunications Task Force. Discussions of mission during the Chapter identified three areas, affirmed by the delegates as the focus for mission for the next six years: commitment to the poor; commitment to justice; and joyful witness to love in a world wounded by violence and emptied of hope. They also agreed to entrust the new leadership with carrying forward the congregation's desire to be in mission with vowed members, associates, and those who would be connected in less formal ways.

After study of the mission brochure prepared for the Chapter, and pre-Chapter discussion, the delegates affirmed the following values as being especially significant: respect for the dignity of the human person; the virtues of humility, simplicity and charity; the commitment to cherish one another; service in solidarity with the poor; the desire to serve and live from a contemplative stance; and collaboration with others. A unanimous show of hands reaffirmed these values (General Chapter Minutes).

An anticipated proposal was brought forward by Sister Elizabeth Bickar: "Be it proposed that the Eighteenth General Chapter dissolve all present provinces and vice provinces." The sisters indicated their unanimous acceptance with a sense of courage, excitement, some apprehension, and a realization that congregational history was being made. They also discussed and voted on other points attended to during the previous year's assemblies referred to earlier in this chapter.

Key questions called for committed answers during the course of the Chapter. The first questions asked by Sister Louise Bray was "Can you, personally, affirm our commitment to the poor and our commitment to justice?" After a period of reflection, she asked, "Sisters, do you recommit yourselves to the values of the Gospel? Do you recommit yourselves to live the Charism of Charity?" Her final question linked the twentieth century with the twenty-first: "As we look to keeping charity alive for the twenty-first century, to what do we commit ourselves?" (Chapter Minutes).

Elections were held during the chapter and the installation of the new team took place in Halifax on July 14, 1996. Thus ended Sister Louise Bray's two terms of office, a time of transformation that witnessed a genuine effort towards the refounding of the Sisters of Charity. In 1996, as the new administration prepared to assume the leadership of the congregation, the Grammy winning song was "Change the World."

General Council (1988 - 1992).
Sisters Louise Bray, Helen Danahy, Theresa Corcoran,
Patricia Mullins, and Mary Louise Brink.

Project North, Cape Breton, NS.
Sisters Christene Forbes, Agnes Morley, Margie Gillis, and Agnes Burrows.

General Administration (1992 - 1996).
Sisters Helen Danahy, Phyllis Giroux, Louise Bray,
Mary Louise Brink, and Patricia Mullins.

Plenary Council (1992 - 1996).

Reception of Associates at Our Lady of Angels
Convent in Brooklyn, NY (April 1993).

Sister Louise Bray after receiving Honourary Degree of Doctor of Humane
Letters from St. Francis Xavier University, Antigonish, NS (1994).

Sister Maureen Wild with Daisy Girl Scouts from Our Lady of Angels School in Brooklyn, NY at Genesis Farm, NJ (1995).

Cluster meeting at Elizabeth Seton Centre, Quebec City, QC. Sisters Georgina Christie, Maureen Kane, Joan Cassidy, Marcia McQuaid, Miriam McKenzie, Evelyn Claire Quinlan, Margaret Murphy, and Joan White.

Father Greg Campbell, Sister Louise Bray, and Father John Captsick display the mural they received at the 20th anniversary celebration of Seton Foundation.

Selected Sources

Primary Documents

1-8-33 Enactments - 16th General Chapter. Office of the Congregational Secretary fonds. Sisters of Charity, Halifax Congregational Archives.

1-8-44 Plenary Council Minutes with supporting documents and reports, September 1988. Office of the Congregational Secretary fonds. Sisters of Charity, Halifax Congregational Archives.

1-8-45 Plenary Council Minutes with supporting documents and reports, February 1989. Office of the Congregational Secretary fonds. Sisters of Charity, Halifax Congregational Archives.

1-8-47 Plenary Council Minutes with supporting documents and reports, October 1989. Office of the Congregational Secretary fonds. Sisters of Charity, Halifax Congregational Archives.

1-8-48 Plenary Council Minutes with supporting documents and reports, February 1990. Office of the Congregational Secretary fonds. Sisters of Charity, Halifax Congregational Archives.

1-8-49 Plenary Council Minutes with supporting documents and reports, June 1990. Office of the Congregational Secretary fonds. Sisters of Charity, Halifax Congregational Archives.

1-8-51 Plenary Council Minutes with supporting documents and reports, February 1991. Office of the Congregational Secretary fonds. Sisters of Charity, Halifax Congregational Archives.

1-8-52 Plenary Council Minutes with supporting documents and reports, June 1991. Office of the Congregational Secretary fonds. Sisters of Charity, Halifax Congregational Archives.

1-8-53 Plenary Council Minutes with supporting documents and reports, October, 1991. Office of the Congregational Secretary fonds. Sisters of Charity, Halifax Congregational Archives.

1-8-54(4) General Council Meetings, Official Minutes, September 1989 - April 1990. Office of the Congregational Secretary fonds. Sisters of Charity, Halifax Congregational Archives.

1-10-3 17th General Chapter Minutes, July 5 - July 14, 1992. Office of the Congregational Secretary fonds. Sisters of Charity, Halifax Congregational Archives.

1-10-5(1) Report to the 17th General Chapter. Office of the Congregational Secretary fonds. Sisters of Charity, Halifax Congregational Archives.

1-10-20 Plenary Council Minutes with supporting documents and reports, February and June, 1992. Office of the Congregational Secretary fonds. Sisters of Charity, Halifax Congregational Archives.

1-10-22 Plenary Council Minutes with supporting documents and reports, February 1993. Office of the Congregational Secretary fonds. Sisters of Charity, Halifax Congregational Archives.

1-10-23 Plenary Council Minutes with supporting documents and reports, June 1993. Office of the Congregational Secretary fonds. Sisters of Charity, Halifax Congregational Archives.

1-10-24 Plenary Council Minutes with supporting documents and reports, October 1993. Office of the Congregational Secretary fonds. Sisters of Charity, Halifax Congregational Archives.

1-10-25 Plenary Council Minutes with supporting documents and reports, February 1994. Office of the Congregational Secretary fonds. Sisters of Charity, Halifax Congregational Archives.

1-10-27 Plenary Council Minutes with supporting documents and reports, October 1994. Office of the Congregational Secretary fonds. Sisters of Charity, Halifax Congregational Archives.

1-10-29 Plenary Council Minutes with supporting documents and reports, June 1995. Office of the Congregational Secretary fonds. Sisters of Charity, Halifax, Congregational Archives.

1-10-32 Plenary Council Minutes with supporting documents and reports, February 1996. Office of the Congregational Secretary fonds. Sisters of Charity, Halifax Congregational Archives.

1-10-35(3) General Council Meetings, Official Minutes, April 1993 - January 1994. Office of the Congregational Secretary fonds. Sisters of Charity, Halifax Congregational Archives.

Seeding a Future Rooted in Charity: Report of the Commission on Models of Authentic Belonging. Sisters of Charity of St. Vincent de Paul, Halifax. November 1991. Sisters of Charity, Halifax Congregational Archives.

Constitutions, 1985 version. Sisters of Charity, Halifax Congregational Archives.

Report to Chapter, 1996. Office of the Congregational Secretary fonds. Sisters of Charity, Halifax Congregational Archives.

Plenary Council Report, December 1992. Office of the Congregational Secretary fonds. Sisters of Charity, Halifax Congregational Archives.

Plenary Council Report, February 1993. Office of the Congregational Secretary fonds. Sisters of Charity, Halifax Congregational Archives.

Plenary Council Report, October 1989. Office of the Congregational Secretary fonds. Sisters of Charity, Halifax Congregational Archives.

Plenary Council Report, June 1993. Office of the Congregational Secretary fonds. Sisters of Charity, Halifax Congregational Archives.

Plenary Council Report, February 1994. Office of the Congregational Secretary fonds. Sisters of Charity, Halifax Congregational Archives.

Booklets and response sheets, 1993 - July 1994. Weavers fond. Sisters of Charity, Halifax Congregational Archives.

Background, 1996. Weavers fond. Sisters of Charity, Halifax Congregational Archives.

Correspondence, 1988. Sister Louise Bray fonds. Sisters of Charity, Halifax Congregational Archives.

18th General Chapter Minutes, 1996. Office of the Congregational Secretary fonds. Sisters of Charity, Halifax Congregational Archives.

Published Sources

Arbuckle, Gerald. 1987. *Strategies for Growth in Religious Life* Staten Island NY: Alba House.

Boff, Leonardo. 1977. *Ecclesiogenesis: The Base Communities Reinvent the Church.* Maryknoll, NY: Orbis.

Boulding, Kenneth. 1956. *The Image: Knowledge in Life and Society* Ann Arbor, MI: University of Michigan Press.

Couture, Archbishop Maurice. 1994. "Consecrated Women: Equality in the Church." *Origins* Vol. 24 No. 21.

Keeler, Archbishop William. 1994. "Voices of Religious: Themes of Pain, Tension, and Promise." *Origins* Vol. 24, No. 20.

Kung, Hans. 1989. "Kung: Church not so much Roman as Global," *National Catholic Reporter* 26 No. 1.

Maloney, Father Robert CM. 1994, "Say to Us, 'Live a Simple Lifestyle.'" *Origins* Vol. 24, No. 19.

Rahner, Karl. 1979. "Towards a Fundamental Interpretation of Vatican II" *Theological Studies* Vol. 40.

Schneiders, Sandra. "New Skins: A Legacy for the Third Millennium," *Delta Epsilon Sigma Journal* Vol. 31.

Spence, Archbishop Francis J. 1994. "Canadian bishops look for deeper ties with the country's religious." *Prairie Messenger*. Vol. 72, No. 13.

Vatican Synod Secretary. "The Consecrated Life and Its Role in the Church and in the World: Working Paper for October 1994 World Synod of Bishops." *Origins* Vol. 24, No. 7.

Whitehead, James D., and Whitehead, Evelyn Eaton. 1988. *The Emerging Laity:Returning Leadership to the Community of Faith*. New York: Doubleday.

Interviews by Author

Interview with Sister Louise Bray by the author, 2008.

4

Living into New Structures, Moving into a New Millennium: 1996–2002

Julia Heslin, SC and Mary Sweeney, SC

The Eighteenth General Chapter of the Sisters of Charity took place at Mount Saint Vincent Motherhouse from April 10 to April 17, 1996. To accommodate the 308 sisters participating, the large dining room was converted into the Chapter Hall. Those sisters who did not participate were able to keep informed of each day's events by calling an 800 telephone number to hear a recorded message. Assisted by facilitators Joy Barton and Sister Mary Jo Moran, HM, the delegates moved through the agenda and into a time of prayer for the elections. In a break with the previous 24 years of congregational history, the sisters elected for this administration would serve a term of six years instead of four years. On April 15, Sister Mary Louise Brink was elected General Superior/ Congregational Leader on the second ballot. The delegates then elected Sister Maureen Pitts as General Assistant/Congregational Treasurer and Sister Joan Verner as General Assistant/Congregational Secretary. The delegates also elected Sisters Elizabeth Bellefontaine, Joan Holmberg, Judith Park, Esther Plefka, Marcella Ryan, and Patricia Wilson as General Assistants/Congregational Councillors. The installation of the new leadership took place on July 16, 1996.

Sister Mary Louise Brink was born in the Bronx and grew up in Babylon, New York. Following her first profession as a Sister of Charity in 1958, she began her ministry as an educator and served as teacher and administrator in Catholic schools in New York, including her alma mater, Seton Hall, in Patchogue. Following the close of Seton Hall in 1974, Mary Louise turned her attention to theology, earning a Master of Arts degree at Boston College. As the Church had turned toward the laity and the cultivation of their gifts for ministry, Mary Louise served as Associate Director and designer of the Training for Ministry program for lay ministers in the Archdiocese of Brooklyn, a position that gave her scope to express her creativity.

Sister Mary Louise's intelligence and forward-thinking, as well as her commitment to the life of the congregation, were evident in her ministry and in her involvement in provincial activities in New York. In 1988, she was elected – and re-elected in 1992 – as First Assistant/Vicar to General Superior Sister Louise Bray. This congregational experience, in addition to her former administrative work and her doctorate in systematic theology from Fordham University, prepared her well for her role as congregational leader at a time of significant change.

In another break with congregational history, the women elected to leadership at the Eighteenth General Chapter were called to function as a team. To their new roles, they brought a host of gifts. They were women of great faith and education who had varied experience in administration in diocesan, parish, educational, and community service contexts. They had roots in Massachusetts, New York, and Nova Scotia, including Cape Breton, and they had experience from farther afield, including Western Canada, Michigan, New Hampshire, and Bermuda, providing them, collectively, with a broad congregational background. They brought with them gifts of creativity, financial acumen, music, counselling skills, and insights from theology and the social sciences. For the first time in the congregation, four of the team were formed outside the traditional Halifax formation program, three in Wellesley and one in Halifax. During their time in office, these sisters would face significant challenges within the congregation and, along with the rest of the sisters, would witness an array of national and international events that evoked joy, grief, hope, and frustration.

As ever, it seemed that human progress was uneven. In December of 1996, the Peruvian revolutionary group Túpac Amaru staged a takeover of the Japanese embassy, seizing hundreds of hostages. Although they released some, they kept others for more than four months. Tensions were building in the Middle East around a new issue: the threat of weapons of mass destruction in the hands of Iraq. The Balkans, too, saw upheaval, as religious and ethnic tensions in Kosovo led to attempts at ethnic cleansing. In addition, Afghanistan was dealing with the presence of Al Qaeda, extremists whose interpretation of Islam's scriptures led to violence not only in Muslim countries but also in the West, and would eventually lead to deaths of many in the United States. There was much to lament. Still, progress was slowly being made: tensions were reduced in Northern Ireland when, on Good Friday in 1998, an agreement was reached; in Rwanda the search for justice for the victims of attempted genocide in 1995 went on; and in South Africa Nelson Mandela was serving as President after the defeat of apartheid.

With the world population reaching 5,840,000,000, progress was essential for the health not only of humans but also of the planet. Advances in science, technology, and medicine were rapid. The sheep Dolly was the first mammal cloned successfully. Google was founded and the number of mobile phones increased, signalling the advent of more and more sophisticated means of communication. There was some progress in the fight against AIDS. Concerns about the environment were growing, but damage to the earth's ozone layer was increasing, making life on the planet less hospitable. As awareness of sexual orientation issues increased, there were mixed responses. In some cases there was violence; in others, the loosening of laws that had limited life choices.

The world was saddened in 1997 by the deaths of Princess Diana and Mother Teresa, two women with vastly different backgrounds who had come together as they worked to alleviate suffering. That same year, J. K. Rowling's first Harry Potter book cultivated young readers and brought joy to many, regardless of age. Despite fears about Y2K, the new year/ new millennium of 2000 dawned with few technological glitches.

In Canada, Jean Chrétien of the Liberal Party served as Prime Minister from 1993–2003. The Province of Quebec was living with the fact that a move toward sovereignty had been narrowly rejected by voters in 1995, and the newest territory, Nunavut, whose population was majority Inuit, was established in 1999 in the northernmost area of the country. The eight-mile Confederation Bridge linking Prince Edward Island to New Brunswick was completed on May 31, 1997 at a cost of $1.3 billion.

Of growing concern was the recognition of the harm that had been done to Indigenous peoples and to their cultures in the residential schools that had been established by the government and run by various churches. This story would unfold over the years with the retelling of the former students' experiences, and the religious groups who had staffed the schools would be called to face their own stories.

Closer to the centre of the congregation, the tragedy of Swissair Flight 111 touched many in coastal Nova Scotia when, on September 2, 1998 the flight went down off Peggy's Cove. The noise from the crash shook homes and woke many residents in the scenic seaside town and nearby Blandford. Dozens of fishermen from the towns headed out in their boats to rescue survivors. Two hundred fifteen passengers died in the crash.

In the United States presidential election of 1996, William (Bill) Jefferson Clinton was re-elected for a second term. It was marked by the scandal over his relationship with a young White House intern, Monica Lewinsky. Impeached by the United States Congress, he was acquitted by the Senate but cited for contempt of court in his failure to speak the truth. During his term as President, Clinton appointed the first women to hold positions as Secretary of State and Attorney General. He also named the first Asian American cabinet secretary. For the first time since 1969, the 1998 federal budget projected a surplus, an accomplishment repeated in 1999, 2000, and 2001.

Amid controversy over ballots, George W. Bush became the

forty-third President of the United States in November 2000. Within his first year, he faced the enormity of the September 11, 2001 attacks on the World Trade Center and the Pentagon, as well as a second failed attack on Washington, D.C. in which airline passengers overwhelemed hijackers, resulting in the plane's crashing in Shanksville, Pennsylvania. With the loss of nearly 3,000 lives and with 6,000 people injured, the shock and grief of those events spread over much of the globe. Terrorist attacks around the world increased, though none on such a scale, and targeted nations sought to respond with increased surveillance and security measures. Like most of the nation, Bostonians were still feeling the pain from the September 11 attacks when, on January 6, 2002, *The Boston Sunday Globe*, in its Spotlight investigative series, published news of the sexual abuse of numerous children by priests and of the cover-up by those in authority. As the accounts unfolded, more and more victims gained the courage to speak up. The institutional Church struggled to respond. These stories alienated many Catholics from the Church and set the stage for other investigations around the world. The effects were both deeply personal and universal.

The papacy of John Paul II would continue until 2005. A relatively young pope at the time of his election in 1978, he travelled the globe, finding special joy in the World Youth Days. He fostered relationships with world leaders and influenced political movements. His outreach extended to leaders of other religions, and in 1999 Roman Catholics and Lutherans signed the Joint Declaration on the Doctrine of Justification, a significant step in ecumenical relationships. In 2001, it was confirmed that the Pope had been diagnosed with Parkinson's disease. This, coupled with the after effects of two attempts on his life, led to a diminished schedule. As the news of sexual abuse by priests increased, the Pope's poor health limited the response of the Institutional Church to the abuse claims, although he did issue an apology in 2001.

While these events captured international headlines, it was a tragic car accident that registered on a deeply personal level in the congregation. The deaths of Sisters Elizabeth Bellefontaine and Agatha Vienneau and the serious injury of Sister Martha Westwater brought shock and grief.

The accident occurred in New Brunswick on October 9, 1998 when, like a number of sisters that holiday weekend, they were enroute to a cluster meeting. Many people expressed their sympathy for the loss of Sisters Agatha and Elizabeth and support for Sister Martha who would require months of rehabilitation. All the members of the Leadership Team, numerous sisters, family members, friends, and colleagues participated in the funeral liturgies that were celebrated in Bathurst, NB at Sacred Heart Cathedral for Agatha and in Halifax at Mount Saint Vincent Motherhouse Chapel for Elizabeth. In a moving show of solidarity, the Sisters of St. Joseph of Toronto invited other women religious in that area to a liturgy at their Motherhouse in Morrow Park to pray for the Sisters of Charity. Four hundred women from sixteen congregations joined in what *Charity Alive* described as a "visible, overwhelming sign of solidarity and support."[9]

In addition to their sense of personal loss, the Leadership Team faced the reality that their number had decreased. Sister Elizabeth had served as Vicar General in the administration, and, according to Canon Law, that position had to be filled. Mindful of the gifts and the trust that they had for one another and the effort that had gone into creating a sense of a trusting community among them, the team members decided that they would rotate the office of Vicar among the other team members, and no one would be elected to fill that role of councillor.

As the world moved from one millennium into the next, these were the events that characterized the times in which the new leadership fulfilled their role. These women accepted their new ministry gracefully and proceeded to implement the enactments of the Eighteenth General Chapter in a consistent, dedicated manner. As they assumed their roles, the Leadership Team recognized that they would face new challenges – and opportunities – in serving the sisters, and so they planned to make the best use of the resources offered to them. They were more than a group of individuals who took on the responsibility of leading the

[9] Unpublished materials discussed in this chapter are from the Sisters of Charity, Halifax Congregational Archives or from interviews conducted by the author. For more detailed information see the Selected Sources.

congregation. They worked at being a team, with all that this entailed. They participated in the Myers-Briggs Personality Type Inventory, the Work Style Inventory, and the Leadership Team Profile exercise. As one team member wrote at the time, "Each tool has revealed different dimensions of team working, and has been valuable in assisting us to identify our skills." With the help of Mary Jo Moran, HM, they created a Mission Statement for themselves and shared that in *New Fire,* the new leadership newsletter.

Interviews with members of the team make it clear that among their strongest graces was the plan that each Congregational Leadership Team meeting would begin in the context of prayer in fidelity to the Chapter call to act out of a contemplative stance. Every September, Sister Mary Jo facilitated the opening meeting. In addition, in November 1996, the team began their first meeting with a retreat at Madison, CT, led by Sister Regina Bechtle, SC, Assistant to the President of the Sisters of Charity, New York. Sister Regina's reflections on leadership gave the new team much to ponder: "Leadership is not essentially about skills but about the call to go more deeply into the mystery of formation." Sister Regina outlined three aspects of the leaders' role: tell the story; tend the body; and let go of the future. "Every time we tap into the collective well of our communal story, we touch into a movement that is bigger than we are, and we are propelled by its dynamic of which we are an integral part. Every time we retell our congregational story, we reshape it according to who we are. The disciples did this as they spread the good news of Jesus. In this way, we all carry the story forward." Sister Regina suggested that the role of the leader is "to invite us all to find our places in our story." Perhaps as you read this, you can find your place in the story of this chapter. Where were you then? Where are you now?

In this retrospective look at the 1996 to 2002 period in the life of the congregation, the primary lens will be the enactments of the Eighteenth General Chapter. Of great significance among these enactments were the topics of mission, the move to life-giving structures, the resolution of issues related to the Motherhouse Project, and the development of an Office of Advancement. The spirit of that chapter may be found in the statement that was written by Sisters Barbara Gorham and Miriam Patrice McKeon during the chapter process. It was also used as part of the closing prayer for the event. Following the Chapter, it was frequently recalled as sisters drew inspiration from its phrases:

> We affirm our commitment
> to a contemplative stance that
> gives joyful witness to love,
> stands on the side of the poor,
> addresses unjust structures.
> Empowered by the Spirit of God,
> enriched by the lives of one another,
> we will stand
> in the fire of gospel values
> and respond to
> a world wounded by violence
> and stripped of hope.
> In humility, simplicity and charity
> we will go forth-
> cherishing one another,
> energized and empowered
> to abide in the Fire.

The internal developments of these years were numerous and significant, but they occurred against the ongoing background of *mission,* which had been a major agenda item of the Eighteenth General Chapter, a chapter whose theme was "Charity Alive for the 21st Century." The new Chapter highlighted values, virtues, and practices that sisters brought to their ministries: respect for the dignity of the human person, a phrase that echoed the *Covenant of Renewal*; the Vincentian virtues of humility, simplicity, and charity; and a spirit of solidarity with the poor and a desire to collaborate with others – all cultivated by serving and living out of a contemplative stance. The Chapter affirmed a three-pronged thrust for mission for the following six years: "Commitment to the poor; commitment to justice; joyful witness to love in a world wounded by violence and emptied of hope." The idea of collaboration was present in the Chapter's Summary Booklet statement: "It was agreed that the new leadership would carry forward our desire to be in mission with others as vowed members, associates and those who would be connected in less formal ways."

Many sisters continued the missions and ministries in which they had been involved – some for decades – yet others faced changes that were put upon them by the closing of the institutions where they had laboured or by age or health issues. Others felt the call to something new. During these years, the congregation faced the closing of more convents, local communities, and schools. Names such as Our Lady Help of Christians, Brooklyn, Saint Margaret's, Dorchester, Convoy Avenue, Halifax, St. Brigid's, Quebec, Saint Vincent's, Edmonton, O'Connor Drive in Toronto, and St. Nicholas of Tolentine in Queens would bring back memories of all that had happened, of all who had lived there over the years, and of the ministry that had been carried on.

While some things were ending, others were beginning. Sisters responded to a variety of needs, some in full-time ministry, some in part-time positions or volunteer roles in their retirement. A random sample gives an idea of the range of activities: after completing studies, Sister Alice Mailman began her work with St. Joseph's Deaf Community in Ottawa; in New York, Sister Ann Woodford took on the role of director of Amethyst House, a residence for women battling alcohol abuse; and Sister Melda Comeau responded to a call to Peru to teach Reflexology there for two weeks. During these years, Sister Sadie Henneberry succeeded Sister Agnes Pickup in the role of director for the senior citizens' group, Aging Gracefully, in New Waterford where Sister Margie Gillis was involved in community organizing; Therese O'Malley worked with senior citizens in a group named SHELL (Sharing the Healing Effects of Love) in Windsor, Ontario, thanks to a congregational grant; Sister Maureen Wild pursued her dream of developing a program for Earth Literacy in British Columbia; in the Dominican Republic, Sister Roberta Mullin joined the community and Sister Catherine McGowan responded to the needs of the people of Bani by opening a daycare centre for young children; at the Motherhouse, sisters assumed the role of hospitality as they welcomed refugee families from Kosovo whose papers were being processed by Canadian immigration; they also welcomed travellers whose plans collapsed in the aftermath of September 11. In Vancouver, Sister Nancy Brown began her ministry at Covenant House, serving as a pastoral counsellor for young people who were on the streets, sometimes abused, addicted, or trafficked. Sister Elana Killilea took on the role of director for the Elizabeth Seton Asian Center in Lawrence, MA. At the retirement centres, sisters found new calls as they were relocated within their buildings in response to renovation needs, and Seton Spirituality Centre, which had been housed at the Motherhouse, moved to Terence Bay.

In reviewing the various congregational newsletters of these years, it is easy to see how the sisters responded to the needs of the times. In addition to the traditional work of the congregation such as health care, social services, and education, there were new concerns about the environment, refugees, and addiction. There were concerns for the imprisoned and the children of the streets. Sisters learned about micro-loans and demonstrated against the proliferation and use of nuclear weapons. Senior sisters at Mount Saint Vincent, Halifax and Mount Saint Vincent, Wellesley made sandwiches for the hungry; others collected cans for recycling and with the refunds purchased materials to create toys for children with AIDS. Some sisters participated in demonstrations at the School of the Americas in Georgia to protest the involvement of the United States in training military for Central America. Others joined in the World March for Women and the March for Life.

The congregation continued to voice its opposition to corporate injustices through letter writing and statements from shareholders, and in 2000, as the Nova Scotia legislature considered the reduction of social assistance benefits to more than 38,000, a letter from the congregation was read aloud in the legislature. The Church had called for efforts to bring about social justice, and the sisters had responded, educating and encouraging one another, and joining with others of like mind to "stand on the side of the poor." They also handed on that spirit by providing experiences for a younger generation, experiences such as the Seton Way Program at Archbishop MacDonald High School in Edmonton and through service programs at St. Francis Prep in New York and Monsignor Ryan Memorial High School in Boston.

And behind all of this was the affirmation of a "commitment to a contemplative stance." Sisters cultivated their prayer, participated in retreats, broadened their experiences of spirituality, and celebrated their commitments as vowed religious at professions, jubilees, and days of renewal. They read a host of authors, including Patricia Wittberg, Barbara Fiand, Elizabeth Johnson, Macrina Wiederkehr, and Joyce Rupp. They appreciated Cardinal Bernadin's own story of facing his death. Numerous retreats were planned to renew the spirit of Vincent de Paul and Elizabeth Seton.

As sisters continued their varied ministries, leadership and members faced the ramifications of the Chapter enactment that called for *life-giving structures.* Months, even years, of discussion and deliberation had preceded the chapter statements on *government structures.* The chief movers of these discussions were the members of the task force named The Weavers: Sisters Maryanne Fitzgerald, Marjory Gallagher, Mary Beth Moore, Esther Plefka, Virginia Turner, and Mary Louise Brink. Sister Mary Louise was First Assistant/Vicar to General Superior Sister Louise Bray and served as the liaison between the task force and the Plenary Council. The purpose of The Weavers was to move forward the conversation on creating life-giving structures, and in the summer of 1995 they sponsored an assembly on congregational structures and brought the sisters to a new understanding and a decision about how the congregation might be restructured. It was not an easy decision, but as the topic developed, sisters began to hope for new ways of participating in the life of the congregation, ways that superseded geographic borders. Foundational to the issue were the *Constitutions* Articles 71–76, in the section entitled "Spirit of Government." Those articles dealt with mission, the Spirit's direction, leadership/authority, relationships of mutual trust and support, the principles of respect, co-responsibility, subsidiarity, accountability, and the common good.

When the delegates assembled for the Eighteenth General Chapter the year after these discussions, they voted for a new structure that eliminated provinces and vice-provinces and provided new means for participation. The decision to eliminate provinces meant that the sisters, especially those in leadership roles, had to re-envision how the congregation would function structurally. This refiguring of the government structure would affect many dimensions of the sisters' lives, congregational interactions and personal living; finances; communication; legal concerns and new initiatives, such as advancement; and ongoing planning for the Motherhouse. Gradually the elements came together.

The Leadership Team members grew in their understanding of the great challenges they faced in implementing the Chapter mandate and the new congregational government structure. The provinces had first been created in 1956 when the congregation numbered more than 1,460 professed sisters. (That number peaked in 1966, with 1,645 members.) While there had been some fluidity in the number of provinces and the existence of vice-provinces, and some variations in provincial boundaries, their structure – usually consisting of a provincial superior, provincial secretary, provincial treasurer, provincial board, and personnel director – had given a measure of cohesion, focus, and even identity to sisters living in the various geographic areas of the congregation. In 1996, as members of the new administration began to assume their duties, the number of professed sisters was 860, and the entire congregation was in the process of assuming a new sense of identity. As the provinces were dissolved, each sister became a part of the whole in a new way.

According to the 1985 version of the *Constitutions* (C.131), the local community is "the basic unit of our life and mission as Sisters of Charity," and it would continue to be so under the new structure. There would be no change in the activities such as prayer and decision-making that facilitate communal daily living, but local communities were asked to decide to which Leadership Team member they would relate. In the absence of the provinces' geographic boundaries, the team members could find themselves flying across the continent or driving in unfamiliar territory, frequently alone, as they fulfilled their roles, even though some other team member might have been nearer the need. Fewer in-person meetings were possible, and so phone calls often became the primary mode of communication between sisters and team members – phone calls complicated by the sharing of personal information as well as by differences in time zones. Still, the process continued to unfold as both the team members and the sisters grew into the new structure, and came to know one another. Gradually, team members came to learn more about life and ministry in other parts of the congregation.

Local communities continued, but another element of life-giving structures was developing. Clusters are small groups of sisters who gather to deepen relationships and to support one another, to share faith, and to tend to the issues of the congregation. Although the term "cluster" was intended to be temporary, it quickly became a familiar and enduring part of the congregation's vocabulary. Nearly 600 sisters joined clusters. Sisters were free to choose their own clusters, and some chose to be part of two clusters. Members of the retirement communities were free to participate, as their health and energy allowed, and some clusters invited sisters who were not able to participate in the cluster meetings to be cluster prayer members.

For the sake of convenience, many clusters were composed of sisters who lived in the same geographic area, but others drew their membership from diverse areas, including Peru and Bermuda. In addition to gathering together, some clusters also made use of other means of communication such as teleconferencing, email, newsletters, and sharing minutes. To help identify clusters, members chose names for them, some light-hearted (Danza, Danza), some rooted in Scripture (Emmaus), and some from other spiritual traditions (Namaste). Decisions about how each cluster was composed, how it functioned, and how often it met were made by the group's membership. While prayer, discussion, and a shared meal seemed to be fairly consistent elements, clusters sometimes included trips to important sites, such as the New York shrines of Elizabeth Seton or a meeting at Genesis Farm in New Jersey where sisters furthered their education in environmental issues. Clusters served as an important

element of the new structure, inviting participation of sisters and building and strengthening the bonds of charity within the congregation.

For most clusters, preparing for annual assemblies was on the agenda, and much of the discussion during the formal part of cluster meetings centred on questions and issues related to the agenda of assemblies. In several areas, a number of clusters noted that the creativity and depth of sharing in prayer was a great gift in their coming together, and that gathering in clusters fostered relaxation and freedom. As cluster life continued, there was a growing desire for various types of cluster-to-cluster networking. Initiatives in this direction included gathering for a social event, regularly planned meetings, or occasionally inviting a different group to join a cluster for all or part of its gathering. Some clusters offered to arrange regional events such as December 8 (for renewal of vows) or January 4 (the feast of St. Elizabeth Ann Seton), and the annual remembrance of our deceased sisters-days that have traditionally brought together many sisters in an area. Without a local provincial superior, these initiatives became important. If no cluster or local community thought to plan the event, there was no one else to step in to provide leadership.

Six members of the Leadership Team became Cluster Coordinators and had the responsibility of communicating with their assigned clusters. Cluster coordinators responded to invitations to attend their assigned clusters' meetings, which were being held throughout the various regions of the congregation. Such meetings provided opportunities for dialogue on both cluster and Leadership Team concerns and events. Members of the Leadership Team found that they were energized by connecting with the clusters and joining in prayer, discussions, questions, and social events. Cluster members and Leadership Team members appreciated the diversity among the groups as well as the hope, creativity, enthusiasm, and congregational interest that the clusters generated.

Complications sometimes arose from the new structures because sisters were participating in both their local communities and their clusters, and members of the Leadership Team were relating to both clusters and local communities. It was agreed that "if two or more cluster coordinators relate to members of the same local community, a Leadership Team member may approach the local community when an issue relative to that community needs to be addressed." Any sister considering a ministry or residence change or an educational or sabbatical request would contact her cluster coordinator. If a sister did not have a cluster coordinator, she would contact any member of the Leadership Team. As sisters came to know one another, such complications would be resolved easily.

A second element of the new structures was the creation of annual assemblies. Each year, from 1997 to 2001, with the exception of 1999, there were either four or five such events that took place in various parts of Canada and the United States including Massachusetts, New Jersey, New York, Nova Scotia, and Ontario. At Mount Saint Vincent, Wellesley and Mount Saint Vincent, Halifax abbreviated versions of the assemblies were held in order to facilitate participation by senior sisters. Other sites included hotels, college campuses, and conference centres, including the labyrinthine NAVCAN in Cornwall, ON. These gatherings, which usually lasted from Thursday evening until Sunday noon, provided a mix of people from the various geographic areas of the congregation, highlighting the rich cultural diversity and unity of the congregation. Planning committees and subcommittees (dealing with issues such as welcoming, ambiance, liturgy/prayer, and entertainment) structured the assemblies and worked with the facilitators and hotels/conference centres to organize and manage the events. They worked with care and creativity. The evaluations which the sisters completed helped to build the theme for the following year's assembly.

In addition to addressing whatever theme had been chosen, agenda items included the annual report from leadership as well as the annual report on the financial health of the congregation. A key contributor to the financial reports was Mr. Gregory Walsh, Director of Finance, who worked with Sister Maureen Pitts. Greg served the congregation for many years in that capacity, earning confidence and respect. He was a welcome presence at the assemblies with his patient response to questions and his knowledgeable overview of the congregation's finances.

The assembly that took place in July 1999 was a special Homecoming Assembly to mark the sesquicentennial of the congregation's beginnings in Halifax; the theme was "Standing in the Fire: Preparing for the New Millennium." The four original sisters had arrived in Halifax in May 1849. In recognition of this, the congregation marked the event with a special liturgy at St. Mary's Basilica in May 1999. The celebration continued in July when sisters gathered from across the congregation for the assembly and sesquicentennial celebrations. After the work of the assembly, the sisters gathered at Pier 22 for the closing festive dinner to which associates and former members were invited. Many spoke about this event as a healing time for them as they renewed their gratitude for friends in the congregation.

A third element of the new structure was congregational resource teams. These proved to be another opportunity for sisters to collaborate with one another regardless of geographic regions and to deal with topics of import to the whole congregation. The number of sisters in each group usually varied from six to twelve. As with the clusters, the Leadership Team members served as liaisons between the groups and Congregational Leadership. Team meetings usually took place on weekends in a variety of settings, such as the retirement centres in Wellesley and Halifax, retreat houses, and congregational vacation houses. Members might find themselves crossing several time zones to participate, but they bore the inconveniences because of the value they placed on the work they did.

The Global Concerns Resource Team was instrumental in raising awareness of the needs of the world. Its purpose was to share a vision which centred on four themes: enhancing human-earth relationships; eliminating global poverty; participating in decisions shaping all of life; and forming prophetic partnerships. The team agreed to focus its energy on engaging in transformational experiences, inserting global concerns into the congregational agenda, redesigning collaborative projects, and carrying the team's vision beyond the congregation. The influence of this team was felt within the congregation in a host of ways, and they made a decision that along with presenting a report at the next chapter in 2002, they would provide materials and resources in a resource room for delegates to visit. The prayer and ritual space at the Chapter focused on global concerns such as peace, the Earth Charter, and violence against women. In many instances, their efforts served as catalysts for action on behalf of justice.

The Theological Education Resource Team was instrumental in providing numerous materials for theological readings, reflection, and prayer. One of the team's early projects was making resources on world religions available to the congregation. Perhaps one of the most unusual initiatives of the Theological Resource Team was its distribution of $25 to each sister. The funds, the result of a grant received from the Koch Foundation, were to be used for theological updating and spiritual renewal. Some sisters used the funding for books, lecture fees, hermitage days, and videos; others pooled their funds to provide lectures.

The Charism Promotion Team formed because of the members' enthusiastic belief in the value of the charism of charity. Their discussions covered a wide range of topics, including volunteers, associates, mission effectiveness, incorporation, vocation awareness, and ongoing religious development. The team invited sisters to consider ministry in vocation work and helped to create positions to oversee charism promotion/ vocation awareness. Because of the importance of these areas, the Congregational Leadership Team appointed Sisters Susan Dean and Maryanne Ruzzo to full-time ministry in that area. As the number of applicants to the congregation decreased, some sisters questioned the need for these positions, but Susan and Maryanne pursued their new ministries, reaching out to women who expressed interest and participating in numerous vocation events and in World Youth Day in Toronto in 2002, among other events.

Clusters, assemblies, and resource teams: each element of the new structure brought a new dimension to the life of the congregation. For some sisters, the transition was easy, but many agreed that the new structure was not perfect. Issues had to be addressed as they arose, and the members of the Leadership Team and sisters throughout the congregation learned to deal with or compensate for whatever was lacking. In 2000, a survey was distributed to the sisters and one question related to the idea of creating regional coordinating committees which would address local issues such as organizing for local events and other concerns. When the survey was completed, more than 250 sisters had voiced their opinion: by a margin of three to two, they vetoed the idea of adding another body to the structure.

In addition to the three major resource teams, the leadership established other teams and committees to assist the congregation during their term, including the Congregational Structures Committee, the Pastoral Resource Team, and the Constitutions Committee. These resource teams were active elements of the new structure, providing materials for reflection and education, and raising awareness of new issues for the sisters. Drawing on membership from various parts of the congregation, they became an important part of the new reality that the congregation was living.

The Congregational Structures Committee developed a working paper based on the review of evaluative data related to the congregation's structure. The material was gathered from sections of the 1998 Leadership Conference of Women Religious Self-Study, the 1999 regional meetings, and the 2000 and 2001 assemblies and focus groups that met throughout the congregation. As a result of the research, the Committee sent out a reflection/discussion booklet, a response sheet, and a bibliography for the congregation. In the responses, Sisters made a number of suggestions: that the Leadership Team should relate to the communities; that there should be a method of electing/appointing the vicar; that the secretary and treasurer should be elected; that clusters should be optional; that the roles of councillors should be specified before elections take place; and that the number of councillors should remain at the current number. These response clearly show that the new structure of the congregation had not been completely satisfying to all members, and, like so many changes, would take time, discussion, and some adjustments to be more completely accepted.

The Pastoral Resource Team responded to the needs of some individuals and communities for education in certain issues, such as depression, addiction, stress management, and losses of various kinds, or for support or guidance in particularly difficult times. Sisters who had training in various fields and who would be willing to give some of their time to respond to requests for information or assistance would be part of this team. The team distributed two publications, one on making end-of-life decisions, and the other, an explanation of therapy and suggestions for coping strategies for difficult issues. Members of the team also wrote pertinent articles in the newsletters. The team received positive feedback on these materials.

The Constitutions Committee was a response to the Eighteenth General Chapter's mandate that leadership establish a process to revise the *Constitutions* so that they included the new congregational structures. The new committee worked to establish changes in terminology that were consistent with that used since 1996 and to delete the articles dealing with provinces. The committee presented to the congregation decisions that had already been approved by Rome in the draft copy along with proposed omissions. Committee members set a timeline from September 2001 to April 2002 for congregational leadership review, for congregational review/feedback, and revision, if warranted, with the goal of having a final draft at the Nineteenth General Chapter.

The retirement centres in Halifax and Wellesley also faced restructuring. In the 1970s, they had been designated as vice-provinces and had evolved over the intervening years. Now they too experienced changes in their organization structures. Although there were similarities, each centre brought its own physical reality, its own history, and its own needs to the conversations. The 1996 Chapter had determined that the congregational Leadership Team would meet with the community leaders of the Retirement Centres in Halifax and Wellesley at least twice a year. These meetings would provide opportunities for the exchange of information, for support, and for considering how the congregational decision concerning structure might impact life in the retirement centres.

To provide new leadership at Mount Saint Vincent, Wellesley, the Congregational Leadership Team issued an invitation for active sisters to consider whether they might be called to that ministry. In May 1997, a group of twelve sisters who had responded to the invitation gathered at

Campion Renewal Center in Weston, MA with several members of the Leadership Team. Their purpose was to spend time in discussion, prayer, and discernment around a team approach to leadership at Mount Saint Vincent, Wellesley. Sister Blanche LaRose, who was administrator of Elizabeth Seton Residence, and Sister Kathleen Casey, who had served as Vice Provincial there, participated in part of the day, offering insights from their experience and expertise. The day came to a close with the participants expressing a need for time to pray and to consider what they had heard. By mid-May each one was to indicate if she desired to continue in the discernment process. For those who chose to stay in the process, an additional discernment day took place at Mount Saint Vincent, Wellesley on June 1. As the process drew to a close, Sisters Ann Marie Barry, Elizabeth Groome, and Ann Regan agreed to form a team, a new way of providing leadership for the sisters in Wellesley. On September 5, 1997, these three sisters at Saint Vincent, Wellesley began their ministries to senior sisters. In Halifax, Sister Mary Jean Burns continued her term as community leader for the sisters at Mount Saint Vincent, Halifax.

Like the team approach to congregational leadership, the team approach in Wellesley was a learning experience as the three sisters worked in complementary roles to serve the residents. During this period, another life-giving structure was put into place: the Mount Saint Vincent, Wellesley Coordinating Committee, which fostered ongoing collaboration and sharing. Four members of the congregational leadership (Sisters Mary Louise Brink, Joan Holmberg, Maureen Pitts, and Esther Plefka) and the three members of the Wellesley Leadership Teams, together with the administrator of Mount Saint Vincent (Barbara Heavey), and the administrator of Elizabeth Seton Residence (Lori Ferrante), sought to provide the sisters with the many kinds of care that were needed, making sure that the elimination of the vice-province structure did not have a negative impact on these sisters.

A major accomplishment in Wellesley was the licensing of 94 beds that took place on November 19, 1999. The process had taken two years and involved numerous projects related to the health, care, and safety of residents such as sprinkler system updates, handicap access, room renovations, hiring of required staff (including an activities director), the installation of call bells, and approval by the Department of Health. The state required the formation of a Board of Directors and the submission of an annual report. To facilitate the work, the residents had to move to other areas of the building. In all, the project required a great deal of advanced planning, adaptability, and many generous sisters who helped the senior sisters move. Following the wishes of the residents, the renovated area was named Marillac Residence, and the dedication on March 12, 2000, was a joyful occasion.

In the spring of 2001, the Wellesley Leadership Team met with congregational leadership to discuss some of their concerns regarding the number of empty rooms at Marillac Residence. Massachusetts had licensed 94 beds in Marillac, the front section of Mount Saint Vincent that was officially referred to as a rest home facility. As such, it was eligible for Religious Level IV reimbursement. On average about 85 sisters resided there at any one time, resulting in a 90% occupancy rate. This could have a negative financial impact on the *per diem* rate, which the congregation received. This research led to the decision to invite retired members from other religious congregations of women to live there. The Religious of Jesus and Mary responded to the invitation as did the Marist Sisters. When these sisters arrived, they moved into available rooms in the existing small communities in the building, creating grassroots examples of collaboration and community, with members finding similarities and differences, friendships as well as new stories!

Like the topic of restructuring, what came to be known as The Motherhouse Project had a history of concern, of thought, of discussion and care. For those who were familiar with the Motherhouse, it is easy to conjure up a mental image of the structure. For readers who are not familiar with it, some specifics will help. The building measured 350,000 square feet, and covered a ground area of two and one-third acres with 1.7 miles of corridors. Over the years, it had served many populations related to the congregation: general administration; infirm and senior sisters; postulants; novices; junior professed sisters; and professed sisters.

In addition, it had housed an academy for girls and provided some housing for students from Mount Saint Vincent University down the hill. However, by the Sixteenth General Chapter in 1988, it was clear that new plans were needed to care for sisters who resided at the Motherhouse. As healthcare costs for the sisters had grown, the financial strain was difficult. In addition, the building, which had opened in 1959, no longer matched the needs of the congregation's declining membership. Given the ongoing repair (particularly to the exterior of the building) and upkeep costs, it was time to consider an alternative. Several options surfaced: sell the building and land; develop the Motherhouse land; raze the building and construct a separate new healthcare centre and residence; continue to occupy the building and consolidate the space occupied; rent or sell the surplus space to other tenants; or "mothball" the surplus space. Whatever option was chosen, it was clear that a major change was unavoidable. Near the conclusion of the 1988 Chapter, the delegates were invited to join in prayer in front of the building. They recognized the role that the Motherhouse had played in the life of the congregation and they anticipated a time when it would no longer be the centre of congregational life. Little did the congregation anticipate just how long this would take to come to a resolution.

Over the years, the congregation had sought to have the Mother Berchmans Centre, that part of the Motherhouse where sisters who needed nursing care resided, become a licensed facility according to the criteria of the Province of Nova Scotia. This licencing would ease the financial burden that the congregation carried. More than once, as renovations were made to meet these standards, the provincial government established new standards or changed political parties, thus delaying the approval and frustrating the congregation; finally, in September 2000, the provincial government did grant a preliminary fifteen-bed license.

The previous April, the Mother Berchmans Centre Board of Directors had met to develop a strategic plan for the Centre based on its mission. Three resulting goals focused on the expansion of current services, the provision of a leading-edge program for care delivery, and the commitment to build upon the Centre's organizational strengths, philosophy, values, and heritage. At the May Congregational Leadership Team meeting, Sister Elizabeth Vermaelen, a Sister of Charity from the New York congregation, facilitated a planning day on the future use of the Mount Saint Vincent Motherhouse. This prayerful discernment continued over the next few months with ongoing review of data that would impact the decision-making process.

At their February 2001 meeting, the Congregational Leadership Team received a variety of reports that related to Mother Berchmans Centre. Community leaders Sisters Marguerite Hagarty and Patricia Campbell spoke of the increasing age and frailty of the residents and of the related needs for their care. Sister Evelyn Pollard, Administrator, and Ms. Anne Highet, Director of Nursing, reported a smooth transition to the use of the newly licensed beds. That same month, the team gathered a group of people in a 'think tank' session related to a plan of action for the Motherhouse. The group included Sisters Evelyn Pollard and Marguerite Hagarty, Pat Whitman, Administrator of Mount Saint Vincent Motherhouse, Barbara Voye, Director of Advancement, and members of the advisory boards for the Motherhouse and Mother Berchmans Centre, who brought expertise in public relations and development. At this gathering, the group agreed that before a specific plan could be formed, there were several things that needed to be established: exact needs; cost estimates; time lines and dates; an organizational structure that would serve to underpin the project; and a project manager for the entire project who understood the local culture and the Sisters of Charity, and who would research local and global markets. This group recognized the need to establish a core/steering committee, including Sisters of Charity and others with the expertise to direct the process while keeping it integrated, moving forward, and insuring continuity through the 2002 change in congregational leadership.

In March, the Leadership Team gathered with the sisters in various parts of the congregation to discuss again the future of the Motherhouse. While sisters were grateful for the review of the history of the decision-making process, they understood that this was a difficult move to make.

For the most part, there was strong support of the decision to leave the present building and to create something more suitable to meet the needs of the sisters.

While so many committees were meeting and conversations were being held, the work of caring for the sisters at the Motherhouse continued. New activities were planned, new sisters were welcomed, just as the deaths of others were marked by liturgies and words of warmth – and sometimes humour – as sisters recalled the years spent living together in community where gifts, as well as foibles, were recognized. In late winter of 1997, sisters marked the opening of The Vienna Room, a space set aside in the Motherhouse for music therapy. Another development in 2000 was the creation of the Seton Serenity Garden, an enclosed area with a gazebo, benches, and non-toxic plants, where sisters with memory difficulties or limited physical stamina would be able to relax and enjoy the outdoors. Such creativity revealed the ongoing care for the sisters.

Still, meetings continued. The Mount Saint Vincent Motherhouse Executive Committee, composed of Sisters Mary Louise Brink, Patricia Campbell, Marguerite Hagarty, Maureen Pitts, Evelyn Pollard, Joan Verner, Patricia Wilson, and administrator Pat Whitman, reviewed the information gathered at the 'think tank' meeting held in Halifax in February 2001 as well as a role description and process for hiring a project manager. The team made every effort to keep the sisters informed through Leadership Team News Notes in *New Fire* as well as the publication *Motherhouse Project Updates,* starting with Update 1 (April 2001) and concluding with Update 5 (January 2002). The sisters in Bermuda, Bani, Ilo, and Lima received booklets of the presentation slides and copies of the script and prayer services used in presentations about the project. The team sent copies of each of these resources to each regional office. The Leadership Team continued to keep the congregation informed through consistent communication.

The Congregational Leadership Team met again in September 2001 in Madison, CT. Possible options for future use of the Motherhouse were still being carefully researched and reviewed. The Leadership Team forwarded a more comprehensive update on the Motherhouse to sisters in a separate mailing. As conversations continued, another option had been presented: The Shannex Corporation was planning to open a facility for long-term health care, Parkstone Enhanced Care, located about a ten minute drive from the Motherhouse. Parkstone Place, or as it was usually called Parkstone, could accommodate the needs of the sisters of Mother Berchmans Centre and was supported by government funding. With a limited time-frame, the leadership of the congregation met in December to make the most significant decision of their term. Recognizing the needs of the sisters, the future needs of the congregation, as well as the condition of the Motherhouse structure itself, the Leadership Team made the decision to relocate the sisters from Mother Berchmans Centre to Parkstone. It was not an easy decision, and Sister Mary Louise and the team met with strong opposition from some quarters outside the Motherhouse communities, but they recognized the intersection of congregational need and opportunity. They presented their decision to the sisters at a meeting in Halifax and sent communications to those in other parts of the congregation.

The sisters who resided at Mother Berchmans Centre recognized the need for the decision and, with the help of sisters and staff, began preparations for the move. At the next Congregational Leadership Team meeting in February 2002 in Halifax the words by Margaret Wheatley set the tone for the theological reflection: "The challenge is to see beyond the innumerable fragments to the whole, stepping back far enough to appreciate how things move and change as a coherent entity."

When the Company of Mother Berchmans Centre met that same month, time was scheduled so that Congregational Leadership Team members could meet individually with sisters to discuss the upcoming move. One member recalled, "This gave us the opportunity to hear their concerns, fears and hopes. We had good heart-to-heart talks with those sisters who were still able to communicate." The scheduled dates for moving were April 29, April 30, and May 1, 2002. The Nova Scotia Department of Health would spend much of February 2002 conducting medical and financial assessments of the sisters at Mother Berchmans Centre. The move from the Motherhouse required a great deal of planning and the help of many hands. On the Parkstone end, as well, great preparation took place and the management did much to accommodate the needs of the sisters before they arrived. Sister Doris Schoner, who had served as administrator and community leader of Mother Berchmans Centre, recalls previewing a model room for the sisters at Parkstone and making specific recommendations which the management accepted. Having their own floor there, with telephones in their rooms, ensuite bathrooms, and all new furnishings, the sisters felt welcomed. Shannex Corporation did much to make the transition for the sisters as easy as possible. A chapel, complete with a stained glass version of the congregational symbol, and a caring staff provided great comfort.

Still, there were questions about the Motherhouse. On January 16, 2001, 50 representatives from approximately 20 different firms attended the January 16, 2002 information session hosted by the Mount Saint Vincent Motherhouse Project Coordinating Committee. This was a valuable first step to involve interested developers. The next step was to have several local firms submit proposals related to project management. Subcommittees ascertained congregational administrative space requirements, managed internal and external communications, and prepared the building property. An information paper was sent out in response to the many questions that surfaced throughout the congregation regarding the sisters' move to Parkstone. The question-and-answer format was meant to help clarify what was taking place. Also included in the mailing was a Census by Level of Care and a Census by Ten-Year age groups for the next fifteen years. In addition, *Motherhouse Update 5* and a letter from Sisters Marguerite Hagarty and Patricia Campbell were distributed. The team members agreed that some of them would meet with sisters in the various areas of the congregation to discuss options, explain or clarify concerns, and engage in conversations regarding the future of the Motherhouse Project.

At the March 2002 meeting, once again the congregational leaders reviewed what had taken place with regard to the Motherhouse Project. With the move to Parkstone scheduled, they turned their attention to the options which existed for sisters who would benefit from daily assistance but who were not yet ready for nursing care. A section of Parkstone was available that could accommodate all those sisters who needed assisted care services. On March 16, the team met with the sisters in the Retirement Centre and, later the same day, with the sisters in the Halifax area to present the option. This was not a topic to be resolved immediately, but rather one for additional discussion and prayer. It would not be resolved until the next congregational administration was in office.

The closing of Mother Berchmans Centre was a significant event not just for the residents and the congregation, but also for the staff who worked there. A Celebration of Life Ceremony ritualized a significant event in the life of the congregation; it provided an opportunity for thanksgiving, grief, and the recognition that new life would arise. At the closing ceremony, Sister Mary Louise and the team took the opportunity to recognize the spirit, faith, and generosity of everyone living and working there. In reflecting on the role that Mother Berchmans Centre had played in the life of so many sisters and staff members, Sister Mary Louise noted,

> [W]e realize that nothing will be able to replace it in our hearts. The spirit that exists here is unique. It is made up of the faith life, the energy, the dedication, the generosity of everyone who lives and works here … [W]e cannot but realize that what exists here will soon be no more. In a few weeks, for all of us, the life that we have shared will be changed forever.
>
> Addressing the staff, she added,
>
> Thank you so much for all the countless acts of service you have performed here in this building, especially in caring for our most frail sisters. You have gifted us with your energy, your loving spirits, your sense of humor, your professionalism, your reliability. What would we

> ever have done without you? And so, we ask you to remember the good things that you have experienced here, and to spread the same atmosphere of love and commitment wherever you will be working in the future.

In the midst of the leadership's efforts to accomplish the work of the Eighteenth General Chapter, the congregation began preparations for the next chapter of 2002. The co-chairs, Sisters Doris Schoner and Ann Woodford, were appointed, a committee was assembled and gradually the preliminary pieces were set in place. Articles about the chapter and about leadership began to appear in *Charity Alive*, and soon the Committee had chosen a theme: "Love Changes Everything," based on the title of a song by Andrew Lloyd Webber from his musical *Aspects of Love*. The logo was a spiral with the word for love in several languages intertwined with it. The facilitator would be Marge Dennis. Before the delegates assembled for that chapter, which was scheduled for July 3 to July 10, 2002 at the Motherhouse, much would be accomplished.

In addition to cultivating the spirit of mission, building new life-giving structures, and dealing with the Motherhouse Project, the leadership also facilitated the growth of other elements of congregational life. One such element was the associate program. Although associates are not an official part of the congregation, they have brought new life and a sharing of the charism to the congregation. Members of the Charism Promotion Resource Team served as liaisons to the groups of associates, but many sisters accompanied them.

In its Handbook of Associates, the North American Conference of Associates and Religious (NACAR) defines the relationship of associates to religious congregations in these words:

> The Associate relationship is a way in which adults outside of the vowed membership can share in the mission and goals of a religious congregation … The relationship is intended to foster a creative mutuality which can enrich, support, and challenge both

> Associates and vowed members in their response to the gospel. The essential element of association is to widen and strengthen bonds with others who affirm the goals and mission of a religious congregation and who wish to live these from within their own lifestyle.

Congregational guidelines define associates as "men and women who share the charism of the Sisters of Charity, Halifax, and are called by the Spirit of God to recognize this charism of charity in themselves." The Charism Promotion Resource Team designated the associate movement as an integral dimension of the congregation and encouraged the development of the associate program throughout the congregation. The Congregational Leadership Team supported the expansion of the associate program in Bermuda, Boston, Cape Breton, Dorval, Edmonton, Halifax, Kelowna, Vancouver, and New York and the growth of the *Vicentinas* in Peru.

Additionally, sisters who were interested in journeying with associates gathered for two weekend meetings to share resources and to revise congregational guidelines and procedures for associates. These associates, both women and men, attended various gatherings and celebrations throughout the congregation, including the sesquicentennial celebrations, and gradually developed their own assemblies. Sisters and associates planned associates' commitment ceremonies throughout the congregation, and many sisters attended events whenever possible. A process was established for keeping official records of associates as part of our congregational history. Increasingly, associates became very involved in the mission of the congregation as parish pastoral associates, religious education directors, liturgy directors, ministers of the Eucharist, youth directors, sacristans, members of Parish Councils, ministers of music, and support staff for retreats for people with HIV/AIDS, to name a few activities. Many associates facilitate prayer groups, set up scripture study groups, and speak in various settings about the charism of charity. Sisters and associates find great mutual support and inspiration as they journey together.

Another area of growth was that of communications. Based on the work of the Telecommunications Task Force, the Eighteenth General Chapter had made several recommendations, included in the Chapter's Summary Booklet, regarding emerging communications technologies. These recommendations would lead to a more effective carrying out of the mission and promote more empowerment of individual sisters to participate fully in the life of the congregation. They would also lead to a more effective use of the congregation's financial and human resources. Furthermore, the recommendations urged that the new technology should be appropriate to the specific purpose of a communication situation and there should be comparison of costs and benefits of available options.

Due to the newness of the technology, in addition to recommending that all sisters should deepen their understanding of it, there was hope that some members would become resource people and technological advisors. The task force urged the use of audio conferencing and, for large-group meetings, video conferencing. The recommendations also urged local communities to make use of fax machines and answering machines. Email and fax numbers could then be included in the congregational directory. In order to have a congregational presence online, the recommendation was made that a cost/benefit analysis be done regarding a congregational webpage to provide accurate, useful, and appropriate information about the congregation to the general public and to those interested in the Sisters of Charity. Thanks to the efforts of the people who worked in communications, the congregation's website, including a private side, was unveiled in 2000. Another aspect of telecommunications that was especially practical was the development of the Caritas list, the listserv for email within the congregation. As we look back on these recommendations, we may smile, but they were significant steps on the way to the technological developments of the twenty-first century.

These many years later, we can see the benefits of these intentional efforts to move the sisters ahead technologically, using the latest means available to keep the congregation united, to assist in the internal work of communication, to assist in ministry, and to keep the congregation visible online. These developments in technology, along with the later proliferation of computers and laptops and other advanced devices, have surely contributed to the ways in which members have built and strengthened bonds in the new structures and updated the tools available for ministry.

While telecommunication was certainly an important development, the care given to print communications was also important. In 1997, Susan Corning was named Director of Communications and soon established a new newsletter, *Charity Alive,* to replace *Changing Times.* This newsletter, published four times a year, contained pieces submitted by individual sisters about their involvements in ministry, general announcements, updates from clusters and resource teams, calendars, and book reviews. The leadership also determined that they should have their own form of communication, a newsletter for the congregation, and so *New Fire* was created. In addition, the Leadership Team approved a new logo, debuted in January 2000, for printed materials.

From Wellesley, the Congregational Leadership Team received reports that activities flourished, with sisters learning new computer skills, thanks to a generous donor who arranged for the purchase and installation of several computers. Day trips to the beach house in Falmouth as well as various performances and social gatherings were events to which the sisters looked forward. The hiring of an activities director also afforded many new opportunities. On the administrative side, the congregational leadership established an Executive Committee of the Board of Directors of Elizabeth Seton Residence to provide more effective stewardship of the Wellesley complex. The team also related to the Board of Advisors of Elizabeth Seton Residence, receiving from them the administrative annual reports and departmental reviews, as well as budgets. They recognized the work of Sister Maureen Pitts, her staff in the Treasurer's Office, and the branch office treasurers who contributed to the financial health of the corporations not only of Elizabeth Seton Residence, Inc., but also of the Sisters of Charity (Halifax) Corporate Mission, Inc., and Sisters of Charity (Halifax) Supporting Corporation. The Congregational Leadership Team members were grateful to board members for their gifts of time and expertise which enabled Elizabeth Seton Residence to achieve stable and commendable operational and financial performance.

Recognizing the importance of maintaining the good health of sisters who lived outside Wellesley, the leadership sought a means to encourage sisters in the Boston-New York areas in that endeavour. In conjunction with Healthcare Management Associates of Lynnfield, MA, a Needs Study was created which included interviews and focus groups. To implement a program to "age in place," the congregation sought the assistance of qualified healthcare professionals to serve on a part-time basis in a wellness program. The congregational leadership hired two women, both trained as nurses: Barbara Heavey, who coordinated the New York program, and Arlene Ryan, R.N., who coordinated the Boston program. They assumed their duties in 1997. In 2001, when Barbara Heavey was appointed Administrator of Marillac Residence, Rosanne Holtzman succeeded her as Health and Wellness Consultant in New York. In so many endeavours, from health to finance to communications and beyond, the congregation was blessed by the assistance of a host of men and women, some in paid positions, others in roles as volunteers, who seemed to catch the spirit of the congregation and who enabled the work of charity to continue.

As the members of the congregation committed themselves to mission and to continuing a contemplative stance toward life, they knew well that there were fundamental, concrete necessities that made their commitments to prayer and mission possible. Among those things were the realities of finance. Following up on the recommendations of the previous summer's Assembly on Finance, the Chapter faced the issue of finance squarely, with the local communities acknowledging their responsibilities to make a realistic yearly budget, to strive to live within it, and "to contribute as much as possible of its income to meet the collective needs of the congregation." In personal interviews with the former Leadership Team, several commented on the importance of Sister Maureen Pitts's financial guidance throughout their term.

Given the aging population of the congregation, there were

significant questions about the financial implications of retirement. To that end, the congregation established a committee to study the topic. The committee was composed of representatives from both Canada and the United States. One topic they addressed was the procedures for retirement from full-time ministry. After consideration, they issued the following guideline: "Ordinarily, a sister has the option to move from full-time to part-time or to volunteer ministry somewhere between the ages of 65–70." As a means of addressing concerns about retirement finances, the congregation established the Basilia McCann Retirement Fund to supplement the necessary income for local communities where one or more retired members resided. Another development in the area of finance was the decision to change the fiscal year to coincide with the calendar year instead of the academic year.

Also related to finance was the Chapter's acceptance of the recommendations of the Special Task Force to Assess Advancement Potential. The Task Force had its origins in New York and Boston, with the New York Financial Advisory Committee and the Boston Finance Committee, composed of sisters and friends of the congregation. With the dissolution of those committees, many of those men and women continued to assist the congregation. At the Eighteenth General Chapter they presented their recommendations: the establishment of an Advancement Office and the establishment of an Executive Search Committee to identify and recommend a professional to direct the new Advancement Office. The report to the chapter also recommended that this new director report directly to the congregational leadership and to the next chapter. The implementation of this enactment was shepherded by Sister Mary Louise and the team. Such collaboration with friends of the congregation was consistent with the congregation's tradition that invited the support of others, an attitude exemplified by both Vincent de Paul and Elizabeth Seton who relied on help from wealthy benefactors. Over the years, the sisters' work has benefited from many varied kinds of assistance, including gifts of money, skills, in-kind gifts, and the experience of people in the trades and professions. These kinds of contributions, sometimes referred to as part of an *enabling ministry* helped the sisters to see how the development of an Advancement Office could be part of the congregation's tradition.

The Halifax-based executive search firm of Robertson-Surrette conducted the search for an advancement director free of charge. After interviewing several candidates, the congregation hired Barbara Voye. By the fall of 1997, Barbara and a part-time support person had set up an office in Mount Saint Vincent Motherhouse and developed an advancement plan. The Congregational Leadership Team established regional advancement committees in Halifax, Boston/Wellesley, Central/Western Canada, and New York. These committees set about identifying top prospects for financial contributions and, in Boston and New York, they gathered names of graduates of the Sister of Charity schools. By the time of the sesquicentennial of the congregation (1998–1999), income from all sources totalled approximately $325,000.

With the approach of the sesquicentennial year, the Advancement Office sent out a fundraising brochure highlighting the celebration of 150 years of service. A second brochure focused on the renovations at Mount Saint Vincent in Wellesley. Barbara Voye also submitted grant proposals to the National Religious Retirement Office (NRRO) in the United States and to SOAR (Support our Aging Religious). The Advancement Office developed strategies for the establishment of an annual fund campaign, including a direct mailing to more than 18,000 prospective donors, the pursuit of two grants for $25,000 each, and a major gifts program which was implemented in New York. Other efforts included seeking corporate level assistance and continuing to refine our donor database.

In the fall of 1999, the New York Advancement Committee held a workshop to update sisters on the congregation's financial reality and the goals and structure of the Advancement Office. In spring of 2000, there was a similar workshop for sisters in the Boston area. Shortly afterwards, several sisters who resided in central and western Canada gathered to discuss how they might move advancement efforts in their areas. With this increased activity, it was apparent that a full-time staff person would be valuable, and in 1999, Heather MacIsaac was hired as full-time advancement associate. In 2002, she was promoted to Director of Advancement and worked out of the office at Mount Saint Vincent, Wellesley. Advancement efforts continued throughout the congregation: New York hosted its first Sisters of Charity Golf Outing and Caritas Award ceremony in August 2001. The event netted more than $60,000 in support of ministries and health care/retirement needs. Later that month, when Sisters Rita MacDonald and Francis Lillian Riley joined graduates of Our Lady Help of Christians in Brooklyn for a fiftieth reunion, guests contributed nearly $7,000 in donations to the retirement fund at an event that was not specifically a fund-raising event! Both Boston/Wellesley and New York committees continued their efforts through receptions, luncheons, dinners, and award ceremonies. The central/western Canada committee began developing ideas for advancement efforts in their region, and the Halifax region planned their Elizabeth Ann Seton Award Dinner.

In order to use congregational resources wisely in the advancement endeavour, the Congregational Leadership Team invited Susan Corning, Director of Communication, and Barbara Voye, Director of Advancement, to discuss how their offices could work together more effectively, given the increased amount of printed material that the congregation was issuing. The Advancement Office continued researching the establishment of a Sisters of Charity foundation in Canada, while the Board of Advisors of Elizabeth Seton Residence in Wellesley established the Friends of Elizabeth Seton Residence Endowment Fund.

Certainly the sisters had ministerial commitments to various populations, but the ongoing call to see the suffering people of the world and to respond to them called for new visions for ministry. In response, the previous General Superior, Sister Louise Bray, along with Sister Mary Louise Brink, at that time First Assistant/Vicar, initiated a Ministry Development/Global Concerns Fund that distributed funds annually. In October 1998, when Sisters Agatha Vienneau and Elizabeth Bellefontaine died in the car accident, people had asked about giving donations in their memory. In response, the congregation established the Sisters of Charity Ministry Fund, and assimilated the Ministry Development/

Global Concerns fund into it. The following criteria highlighted the Vincentian spirit: the sister who requested the grant must be involved in the ministry in some way, as a member of staff, administration, or board. New endeavours, particularly collaborative ones among the poor, women, and those who (quoting Vincent de Paul) "through shame would conceal their necessities." Through the selected projects, the congregation hoped to assist recipients in becoming self-sufficient.

At the festive meal that marked the Sesquicentennial Celebration at Pier 22 on Halifax's waterfront, the congregation awarded fourteen grants, totalling more than $180,000. The projects that received the grants served a variety of needs and assisted people of all ages in the fields of education, health, and social service. These grants spoke of the desire of the congregation and of our generous benefactors to keep charity alive for the twenty-first century. There were also many other dimensions to the sesquicentennial celebrations. The theme, "Thanksgiving, Healing and Hope," reminded the congregation of all that had passed over the previous 150 years. The history had included a long list of reasons to give thanks, from the women gathered in community to the works of the congregation, all based in gratitude for God's faithful love. The second aspect of the theme for the sesquicentennial encouraged healing of any broken relationships, as did the Homecoming celebrations that summer to which many former members came. Healing also took place in the relationship with the Sisters of St. Martha of Antigonish, whose origins had mingled with our story. There had been painful misunderstandings. When they celebrated their hundredth anniversary, also in 1999, the misunderstanding had been resolved, and many Sisters of Charity journeyed to Antigonish to celebrate with them. The theme of hope turned the congregation toward the future, despite limitations, relying on God's love.

The sesquicentennial also unleashed a great deal of creativity. Liturgical music was rich and full, and visual artistic expression brought joy. A tri-part banner of the earth was created to be carried into the celebration in the Basilica in Halifax, expanding the celebration beyond the congregational story and reminding participants of their home in the universe. After the Basilica celebration, the banner was used on numerous occasions when the sisters gathered. At the Motherhouse, another example was the sesquicentennial candle that burned throughout the celebrations, a reminder of the needs of the congregation and of the world. Celebrations were held throughout the congregation, and members of the Leadership Team participated in Bani (Dominican Republic), Bermuda, Boston, Cape Breton, Edmonton, Halifax, Kelowna, Lima (Peru), Montreal, New York, Quebec City, Toronto, and Vancouver – signs of the vitality within the congregation.

The sesquicentennial celebrations across the congregation were also a vivid example of how the spirit of collaboration had taken root. Sisters from many congregations and numerous colleagues, family members, and friends joined us to mark the event. As ministries in parochial schools and in congregation-sponsored hospitals had decreased with their closing or transfer of ownership, sisters sought other positions. The trend towards diversity of ministries that had begun in the 1970s had continued, and sisters brought their charism of charity and their skills to many different endeavours, working with a variety of organizations and co-workers, in secular, ecumenical, and interfaith settings. Chief among collaborators were the members of the Federation; that is, those religious congregations that traced their roots to Elizabeth Seton.

Formation became one arena in which collaboration with several members of the Federation benefited participants, notably through the establishment of a collaborative novitiate in Fort Lee, New Jersey in 1992. In addition to the Sisters of Charity, Halifax, other Federation congregations who participated were from New York, New Jersey, and Pennsylvania. Along with the full-time residential program, the staff also offered part-time programs, and these attracted other members of the Federation. When the novitiate opened, Sister Maryann Seton Lopiccolo and Sister Mary Ann Daly from the Sisters of Charity of New York assumed the role of Co-directors of Novices. In 1998 Sister Lorraine d'Entremont became director and in 2001, the program moved to Yonkers, New York. Several members of the congregation had their novitiate in that collaborative setting.

Other Federation endeavours included Seton Legacy programs, which were gatherings to foster an understanding of the heritage bestowed by Elizabeth Seton and, simultaneously, to create bonds among the members. Volunteer programs were another opportunity for collaboration with Federation members as well as with those who lived according to the spirit of Vincent de Paul. A third instance of collaboration was the program *Charity: A Shared Vision* which planned the *Charity 2000 and Beyond* events.

In 1996, the Federation became affiliated with the United Nations Department of Public Information, giving it non-governmental organization (NGO) status. This status gives the NGO access to most UN meetings, publications, government delegates and library. That same year, Sister Marie Elena Dio was appointed by the Federation, or, as it was known in that context, The Elizabeth Seton Federation, to represent its members as their NGO representative. Four years later the Federation obtained affiliation with the Economic and Social Council of the United Nations, a higher affiliation that allows the NGO representative to suggest new topics for UN consideration and to present written and oral statements on UN issues. These statements then become official UN documents. To better represent the members of the Federation, and in a manner that modelled collaboration, Sister Marie Elena gathered a committee of sisters representing all the other congregations of the Federation to focus on issues related to the charism: the elimination of poverty, the role of women, and care for women and children. Representing the Sisters of Charity, Halifax on that committee was Sister Margaret Gillis. In 1998, together with the representative of the Sisters of St Joseph and of the Dominican Sisters, our NGO organized a monthly gathering of all Catholic religious NGOs at the UN (RUN), which continues to meet to this day.

Participation in various associations of religious provided other arenas for collaboration, both nationally and internationally, and the congregation continued its membership and active participation in the CRC, the LCWR, and the UISG. These organizations brought together women religious in leadership, providing input, support, and means of observing trends. The Chapter Report to the Nineteenth General Chapter listed the names of a host of associations related to the Church, women religious, formation, finance, and social justice with whom the congregation maintained ties, often through investment.

In its action on behalf of justice through investments, the congregation continued to voice its values by communicating either directly or via shareholder status with major corporations such as Bristol-Myers, Squibb, Dun and Bradstreet, GTE, Heinz, Hewlett Packard, IHOP, Johnson & Johnson, Medtronic, Motorola, Sony and Warner-Lambert, Imperial Oil, and PetroCanada. Collaborating with members of the ICCR in the United States and the TCCR in Canada gave strength to the cry for justice.

During this period, Indigenous people in Canada began to come forward publically about the harm that had been done to them in various residential schools that had been created by the government in the nineteenth century. Residential school students were punished for speaking their language, denied access to their culture and families, and, in many cases, suffered physical, sexual, and emotional abuse. Many of the schools had been staffed by members of religious groups. The Sisters of Charity had staffed two such schools, one in Shubenacadie, Nova Scotia (1930–1967), the other in Cranbrook, British Columbia (1936–1971). Questions had been raised by a journalist about Shubenacadie as early as 1978, during Sister Katherine O'Toole's second term, but little had come of them (McKenna, 327). With the publication in 1992 of Isabelle Knockwood's book *Out of the Depths* about her experiences at the residential school in Shubenacadie, and with the subsequent newspaper articles written by former students, stories began to circulate about the treatment some students had received. These evoked both sadness and concern. As stories from other schools multiplied across Canada, the issue gathered force and organization, and by the end of this Leadership Team's term in office, the Roman Catholic hierarchy had begun to direct the responses from Catholic religious congregations.

It would take several years to create a path to reconciliation and healing, as religious groups contributed to a fund established to assist those whose lives had been touched by abuse. Members of the various religious groups also immersed themselves in listening circles with Indigenous People, attentive to the stories and the pain that came from the residential school experience of some students.

During these years, there were also several important signs of recognition of the work the sisters had done with the Mi'kmaq people: in a mark of respect, they bestowed honorary membership in the Mi'kmaq band on Sister Elizabeth Cody (who was later buried in that community) and in 1997 the Sisters of Charity were invited to St. Catherine Parish, Indian Brook Reserve in Shubenacadie to celebrate fifty years of service. The Mi'kmaq community also honoured Sister Genevieve Morrissey in 2000 as she completed ten years of service as a pastoral animator at Saint Catherine's Parish, Indian Brook (*Charity Alive*, May/June 2000).

Among the many external events that had a profound impact on the congregation were the events of 9/11, as September 11, 2001, came to be called. As the Leadership Team met at Mercy Center on the shores of Long Island Sound that day, their discussions were interrupted by the news of the attacks in New York and Washington. The sisters stood in disbelief as the television provided images of mass destruction and news of hijacked planes still aloft. Soon concern for the safety of sisters and their family members pervaded their consciousness. As they tried to make phone contact with New York, they heard over and over again, "There is an emergency situation in the area you are calling. Please try your call later." By evening they received news that none of our sisters were missing. Still, all were overwhelmed by the stories and pictures of so much death, injury, loss. In solidarity with the residents and staff of Mercy Center, they paused to pray for the people of America, the victims of the attack and their families, for peace, and for wisdom for government leaders.

Although no Sisters of Charity were direct victims that day, the September 11 attacks elicited extraordinary responses from them as the sad consequences to victims and first responders played out in families and parishes, neighbourhoods, cities, and towns primarily in the greater New York area. Sisters responded as teachers to shocked and grieving students, as chaplains to stunned and exhausted first responders, and as neighbours and friends to countless beloved ones of victims.

The events of that day shocked the world and called for new responses. One of the first decisions on the part of President George W. Bush was to order an end to all air traffic in the United States. With so many planes in the air, unable to reach their destinations, pilots suddenly found themselves landing in a variety of airports. Many trans-Atlantic flights found safe arrivals in the Maritime Provinces. The Broadway musical, *Come from Away* is based on a flight that landed at Gander, Newfoundland that day. Not surprisingly, flights also landed in Halifax. More than 7,000 passengers were stranded in Halifax and no one knew how long their delay would last. It was imperative that they find lodgings. At the Motherhouse, heads of departments met to find a way to respond. Once the decision was made to offer hospitality, the local Emergency Measures Organization was informed. Volunteer staff and sisters prepared beds and other accommodations. At 2 AM on September 12, close to 200 passengers from a Lufthansa flight destined for Boston arrived at the Motherhouse where they found a warm welcome.

The *Motherhouse News* for that September gives accounts of the responses of the sisters and staff who "were gracious hosts in making weary travelers comfortable, listening to their frustrations, overcoming language barriers, meeting their unexpected needs, arranging transportation, and even acting as tour guides." Many of those unexpected guests responded with messages of gratitude and even of hope. A passenger from Sweden wrote,

> Dear Friends,
>
> The terrible terrorist attack in New York and Washington was really a shock for the civilized world. However, all the kindness we experienced in Halifax clearly demonstrated that the civilized world stands even stronger!!

In addressing the staff and sisters of the Motherhouse in *Motherhouse News,* the Leadership Team wrote,

> We heard how you rose to the occasion with energy, determination and compassion. St. Elizabeth Ann Seton and St. Vincent de Paul smiled to see how a "joyful witness to love" was so evident in all that you did to dispel fear and offer a comforting welcome to everyone who came through the door.

At their next meeting, "with some of the numbness wearing off," the Leadership Team could begin to see the reality in ways that only time allows. "The words of our last General Chapter statement to 'respond to a world wounded by violence and stripped of hope' echoed in our hearts in even more profound ways." At that same meeting, the Leadership Team initiated a September 11th fund to provide money to be used by the sisters in the New York area to enable them to meet expenses in their ministries due to the withdrawal of funding in the aftermath of the World Trade Center tragedy. Some of this fund was used by sisters to enhance their skills in bereavement facilitation or to assist them in their own bereavement needs. It seemed appropriate that some of the funding flowed from the proceeds of the 2001 New York Golf Outing and the New York Elizabeth Seton Reception. With contributions from the congregation, the total amount was $100,000.

The congregation's multi-faceted response to 9/11 revealed the strong trait that the Leadership Team possessed: they desired to respond to global tragedies with financial help as well as with the assistance of available personnel and resources, a trait that was recognized by the membership of some congregations during those challenging days.

Although many tragic events filled the news, and the congregation sought to respond to them, there were other "in house" concerns. A cursory survey of religious congregations of women during the years 1996–2002 revealed that members were aging and few women were joining. There were exceptions, of course, such as the "Sister Moms" who, after being widowed and raising their families, sought membership. Still, it was clear that sisters on the (relatively) young end of the spectrum were facing issues that begged for conversation and planning. For the youngest member of the congregation, Sister Elaine Simard, this meant participating in an international congress of young women and men religious in Rome, but the event that engaged more of our own sisters was a gathering for sisters under 60 years of age that took place in Convent Station, New Jersey, in February 2002. Entitled "Prophets of a Future Not Our Own," the conference provided participants the opportunity to share their perspectives on current issues and to explore the future together. Franciscan Sister Nancy Schreck facilitated the event that energized many of the participants.

As the new year of 2002 unfolded, the leadership of the congregation knew that they would relinquish their roles in a few months. Preparations for the Nineteenth General Chapter were in process. For months, the congregation had been engaged in preparation, specifically by sending letters of support to those whom they considered potential candidates for leadership positions. From May 31 to June 2, those women gathered together for a discernment weekend at Mount Manresa Retreat House in Staten Island.

The delegates convened at the Motherhouse from July 3 to July 10. After completing the agenda of business, the delegates spent time in prayer. On July 8, elections took place. Sister Donna Geernaert was elected Congregational Leader on the second ballot. On that same day, delegates elected Sister Joan Butler as Treasurer and Sister Joan Verner was elected Secretary. The following day, the delegates elected the congregational councillors: Sisters Joan O'Keefe, Mary Katherine (Kati) Hamm, Mary Beth Moore, Patricia Kelly, and Sheila Moore. On August 10, 2002, they assumed office.

The sisters who served in the ministry of leadership from 1996 to 2002 – Sisters Mary Louise Brink, Maureen Pitts, Joan Verner, Joan Holmberg, Judith Park, Esther Plefka, Marcella Ryan, and Patricia Wilson – had moved the congregation through a unique period. The dissolution of provinces and the creation of new structures called forth their creativity, adaptability, and their willingness to learn. They worked together as a team and spent themselves in service to the sisters. While their decision to move sisters to Parkstone brought them some criticism, they also found grace and support from most of the congregation. The congregation grew into the new structures as members interacted across former geographic boundaries. Despite diminished numbers, the sisters carried on their ministries or devoted themselves to other concerns. Social justice issues evoked new responses.

The leadership team, the sisters, and the associates heard the call to a contemplative stance, realizing that in order to live the life of Charity, one had to be grounded in Love. While the diminishment of which Sister Katherine O'Toole had written in the 1970s was real, the sisters continued to show forth the love of God. The dissolution of some ministries seemed to lead to diversity in new ministries. No longer concentrated in specific ministry sites, the gifts that the sisters brought were now dispersed as leaven is in dough. This enabled collaboration with many men and women who also sought to show compassion to a suffering world.

The Leadership Team could look back at their six years in office, a time marked by critical world events and major changes in the congregation. But they could also take the time to look to the future as they finished their term. In the last edition of *New Fire,* they challenged the sisters:

> We are living into our future in ways we could not have imagined six years ago. We have been asked to let go in ways we could not envision ourselves able to do. Will we boldly accept the challenge to be the new face of women religious – a new face of Charity in tomorrow's world? … It is from here, from this new place, that we Sisters of Charity will move forward into the next six years to make choices with courage, daring, generosity and love – not just for our own life but for the life of the world.

The image they left to us as they finished their term, a new face of Charity in tomorrow's world, evoked excitement and depth and breadth. It was an image to inspire and guide us on the journey forward.

Congregational Leadership Team (1996 - 2002).
Sisters Marcella Ryan, Esther Plefka, Joan Verner, Patricia Wilson, Elizabeth Bellefontaine, Mary Louise Brink, Maureen Pitts, Judith Park, and Joan Holmberg.

Sister Marie Elena Dio, the first NGO Representative for the Sisters of Charity Federation at the United Nations (1996).

Sisters Paula Kelley (R), principal and Mary Anne Foster (L), vice principal, with students at St. Kevin School, Dorchester, MA (1997).

Staff of Women Helping Women at Fundraiser in Queens, NY.

Sister Mary Louise Brink

Sister Gertrude McGovern with Associates and friends in Kelowna, BC (1999).

Sister Alice Kenneally and her mother, Mrs. Alice Keneally at Mount Saint Vincent, Wellesley (1999).

Sister Nancy Brown and co-worker from Covenant House in Vancouver, BC (2000).

Sister William Noreen Reilly, Bob Crimmins and Sister Joan Holmberg at the Sisters of Charity Golf Outing in New York (2001).

Greg Walsh, Chief Financial Officer and Sister Maureen Pitts, Treasurer, Mount Saint Vincent Motherhouse (2002).

Sister Dolores Russo and students of Frederick Douglass Literacy Center in Brooklyn, NY (1999).

Sister Agnes Miriam MacSween in Serenity Garden at Mount Saint Vincent Motherhouse (1999).

Selected Sources

Primary Documents

Advancement Office Overview, 2002. Sisters of Charity, Halifax Congregational Archives.

Case for Support, Office of Advancement, Sisters of Charity, Halifax, March 1998. Sisters of Charity, Halifax Congregational Archives.

Changing Times Express Edition. Eighteenth General Chapter, April 1996. Sisters of Charity, Halifax Congregational Archives.

Charity Alive, Sisters of Charity, Halifax, January/February 1999. Sisters of Charity, Halifax Congregational Archives.

Charity Alive, Sisters of Charity, Halifax, November / December 1998. Sisters of Charity, Halifax Congregational Archives.

Constitutions. 2003. Sisters of Charity, Halifax.

Memo: Sisters of Charity Ministry Fund, Sisters of Charity, Halifax, December 1998. Sisters of Charity, Halifax Congregational Archives.

Motherhouse News, Sisters of Charity, Halifax, September 2001. Sisters of Charity, Halifax Congregational Archives.

Motherhouse Project Updates, Sisters of Charity, Halifax. Number 1 – 5, February 2001 to August 2002. Sisters of Charity, Halifax Congregational Archives.

New Fire: Leadership Team Meeting News Notes. Vol. 1.1 to 6.5, November 1996 to May 2002. Sisters of Charity, Halifax Congregational Archives.

1-10-5. Seventeenth General Chapter Report, 1998. Office of the Congregational Secretary fonds. Sisters of Charity, Halifax Congregational Archives.

Summary Booklet, Eighteenth General Chapter, 1996. Office of the Congregational Secretary fonds. Sisters of Charity, Halifax Congregational Archives.

Nineteenth General Chapter, 2002. Office of the Congregational Secretary fonds. Sisters of Charity, Halifax Congregational Archives.

Published Sources

Abbot, Walter M., SJ (Ed.). 1996. *Documents of Vatican II*. New York: Guild Press, 1996.

Anthony, Geraldine, SC. 1997. *Rebel, Reformer, Religious Extraordinaire: The Life of Sister Irene Farmer*. Alberta: University of Calgary Press.

Briggs, Kenneth. 2006. *Double Crossed: Uncovering the Catholic Church's Betrayal of American Nuns*. New York: Doubleday Press.

Chittister, Joan. 1995. *The Fire in These Ashes*. Kansas City, MO: Sheed & Ward.

Daly, Bernard M. 2003. *Beyond Secrecy: the Untold Story of Canada and the Second Vatican Council*. Toronto: Novalis.

Falka, John J. 2003, *Sisters: Catholic Nuns and the Making of America*. New York: St. Martin's Press.

Handbook of Associates, 2009. Sisters of Charity – Halifax.

Knockwood, Isabelle. 1992. *Out of the Depths: The Experiences of Mi'kmaw Children at the Indian Residential School at Shubenacadie, Nova Scotia*. Halifax: Fernwood Publishing.

McKenna, Mary Olga, SC. 1998. *Sisters of Charity of Saint Vincent de Paul, Halifax, 1950-1980*. Lanham, MD: University Press of America, Inc.

Wheatley, Margaret. 1994. *Leadership and the New Science*. Berrett-Koehler Publishers.

Interviews by Author

S. Mary Louise Brink, interviewed by author, October 17, 2008.

S. Judith Park, interviewed by author, October 18, 2008.

S. Joan Holmberg, interviewed by author, November 10, 2008.

S. Esther Plefka, interviewed by author, March 20, 2009.

S. Joan Verner, interviewed by author, April 17, 2009.

S. Marcella Ryan, interviewed by author, July 14, 2009.

S. Patricia Wilson, interviewed by author, August 27, 2009.

Afterword

Joan O'Keefe, SC

How this Book Came to Be

This book detailing the history of the Sisters of Charity, Halifax in the years following Vatican Council II was started in 2007. According to the original notes, "one purpose of the book is to replace a series of books called 'the lives of the Mothers.' Supposedly, there have been some objections to these volumes, one of which was too much emphasis on the individual community leader." For years, the religious life was idealized as being about perfection and the meaning of holiness. The "lives of the mothers" produced by this culture were small booklets, each one detailing the life of one of the congregation's mothers general and how she shaped the congregation during her tenure. The subtitles hint at the author's opinion of the subject's life and work: The Discerning Mother, The Forgotten Mother, The Well-loved Mother, and The Far-Sighted Mother. But no one's personality can be captured in a simple phrase. Nor can the history of a group be restricted to a single person's actions. For this book, a new approach to writing history was chosen.

Beginning with Vatican Council II and its emphasis on the values of subsidiarity, collegiality, and pluralism, the virtues that had defined our life together, anonymity, unquestioning obedience, and uniformity began to fall into disrepute and new life-giving patterns emerged. This book places the history of the congregation in this new framework. It examines the work of leading that was undertaken not just by the superior general, but also by the teams who were elected to assist her and by all the sisters whose obligation called them to participate in this process: "Listening attentively to the Spirit, we participate with our sisters in trying to discern God's will for ourselves and for the congregation, carrying out the decisions that are made for the common good." [C.27]

As the present day "mother," now called the congregational leader, I am happy that we worked so hard at renewal in those days. The changes discussed in this book, the divestment of properties, the diversity of ministries, and the decreasing numbers might, if considered as a corporate business model, be characterized as failures, but they actually acted as catalysts for "good" change. They helped us to become who we needed to be for the twenty-first century. Today, we are a small group of elder women, some among us even wisdom figures, who, looking back, shake our head and wonder how we managed through all the changes; we look at this day and wonder: Where is Providence leading us next?

What Happened Next

As I write, it is fifteen years since this section of our history has concluded. I would like to take this opportunity to comment on where the "characters" are now and how the ministry and mission has evolved in the years since. Of the congregational leaders, only Sister Mary Louise Brink is alive; she continues to be involved in living well with and for the community and mission. Other members of the various leadership teams mentioned in the previous chapters are alive – some are in nursing care and some still active and continuing to serve through their life of love. We hold them in our hearts and give thanks for all who served through these challenging years.

The evolution of ministry and mission since 2002. I am a Sister who made perpetual vows and was in ministry from 1972-2002. My view of those thirty years is similar to those of the authors of those chapters and yet different. As a native Bostonian who has served all her life in Nova Scotia, the latter is the culture with which I most identify. When I think of stories and music of those years, it is Mary O'Hara and Stan Rogers and their singing Stan's *Forty-five Years from Now* that comes to mind first. (I leave this paper and search for Mary O'Hara to see if she is alive. She is. I consider buying a ticket to *Stan Rogers: A Matter of the Heart* at Neptune, and I do buy a ticket for September 3, the last performance.) Next, still thinking about the music of those days, I remember Ron Hynes' *Sonny's Dream*, which we sang around campfires and in a pub in Ireland. Ron died in 2015, but right now I can hear and see Ron's fans singing *Sonny* several times one evening in Saint John's, Newfoundland. I also remember the music at the celebrations of sisters' final vows: O Happy Day, *Song of Joy*, *Witness Song* (Stand up, my sisters/ Give glory to God), *Prayer of Saint Francis*, *Of My Hands* ...

I am thinking about Martha, Julia, Elaine, and Mary and their willingness to write a history of the times they lived through. I think of Heidi, and how her initial connection to us when she was a student seemed random but was certainly the work of grace. The authors are alive and well and hope to see the book published soon! A special thank you needs to be offered to Marie Gillen, former archivist, who first called the group to work on the book. Marie now lives in our retirement residence in Wellesley, Massachusetts. Thanks are also due to Marjory Gallagher, former Congregational Secretary, who shepherded the project for many years and has gone home to God. Finally, a special thank you to Mary Flynn, our current archivist, who shared her passion for history and her research skills with us and to Kati Hamm who has a strong desire to put this history book in our hands.

As mentioned, there were many good-byes in the 1972–2002 period, with fewer sisters being professed and fewer making final vows each year. I felt as if I was always saying goodbye when I wanted to say hello and welcome.

Yet the mission continued. Ideas and hope came from the grassroots as well as the leadership. That has not changed. Many of the new ministries that started in those fertile years have been handed over to others or have ended. Some of us still continue in active ministry, but in recent years they have often been collaborative ventures. Our hearts and prayers are still with those whom Vincent de Paul would describe as people "who through shame would hide their necessity."

We are joined in our efforts by the Associates and Vicentinas, lay men and women who want to live out the charism in their own living situations. The Vicentinas live in Peru, where we now have only one Sister. Next year, they will be celebrating the 50th anniversary of our arrival in Peru. Associates in both the US and Canada are planning for their future, which includes inviting new and younger women and men to join them. Associates and other friends support our sisters through volunteering with them in service and/or caring for our frail sisters.

One example of the evolution in ministry can be seen in Saint Paul's, Herring Cove. In 1970, three sisters who had teaching positions were asked to allow their house to be used for retreats and for days and evenings of reflection. They agreed, and there was immediately a great demand. However, their space was small and the sisters were very busy in the school and in the parish; they found they were saying no to retreatants more often than yes. Halfway through the second year, they met with the Provincial Board to inquire if retreatants and those looking for individual spiritual direction could be hosted at our Motherhouse. The Board agreed to investigate this possibility if one Sister was willing to resign from teaching and become staff at a centre at the Motherhouse. After more prayer, Sister Genevieve Morrissey resigned from William King School in the summer of '72. Later the Renewal Centre at the Motherhouse became the Spirituality Centre, and eventually moved to another fishing village, Terence Bay, where it is still welcoming retreatants.

In the '70s and '80s, many sisters were energized by being able to suggest and consider new and not so new avenues of service. Nuala Kenny became a physician. Carmelita Currie, Mary Sepeck, and Marie McPherson became foster mothers. Nancy Brown went to Covenant House, Pat Murphy to L'Arche, and Mary McIntyre to the Inuit. Others went into universities, colleges, elementary, and to junior and senior high schools where we had not been before. We coordinated religious education, pastored in local churches, became campus ministers, attended to those in palliative/hospice care, lived in Northern Canada, Peru, the Dominican Republic, Minnesota, Wisconsin, Georgia, and other places. Often, we became more rooted in our outreach to those we taught and those we met in healthcare facilities. We went to prisons. We were – we are – strong advocates with and for others.

The next history book will speak of South Sudan and Kenya and of work with refugees, migrants, and survivors of human trafficking. It will show us claiming our Federation identity in works of justice. Perhaps, it will tell of the sale and transformation of the Motherhouse lands. It will definitely describe collaborative efforts to work on systemic change in areas such as racism, economic and earth justice, and attitudes toward the most vulnerable and frail elderly in society. It will be about leaving legacies to the "seventh generation," through commitment to the study, reflection, and prayer around *Laudato Si*. I believe there will be stories of other places and people we have not named yet.

Some More on Incidents Mentioned in the Book

There are memorials to the Swiss Air Disaster of 1998 in Nova Scotia. Some of the sisters and priests and others who met with family members and Swiss Air staff have died. Some are still connected.

The events of 9/11 impacted more than our New York and Motherhouse sisters. Some sisters were at the UN that day and walked for forever to get to safety far from the site of the tragedies. Some sisters ministered to people in shelters not as fine as our Motherhouse. In Halifax, people stranded by the events were taken from the Exhibition shelter (a pretty rough spot) to the Community Access Program (CAP) site and to homes in Terence Bay to use computers and phones for longer conversations with relatives/friends and to have a cup of tea. Interesting, many in the shelters would not accept an offer to stay in our small homes; they wanted to return to the Exhibition shelter to be with those with whom they spent hours on the planes on the tarmac. Before I started writing this, some of us were at *Come From Away*, a musical about 9/11 and the passengers who landed in Gander, Newfoundland and their hosts, the residents. There was something special about being in an audience with New Yorkers. We knew how wonderfully welcoming and helpful people who lived in Gander and environs were. We were moved as we relived that time. At the same time, we recognized how that act of terror drew a line of demarcation for people in North America. We had not thought of ourselves as having to worry about attacks on our own land. In response, fear and intolerance rose up and revealed themselves in hateful acts of prejudice. It reminded us that we still have work to do in non-violence and peacemaking.

Foreshadowed

Mentioned here and there in this history are the Residential Schools. The language changes: Indians, Native Peoples, First Nations, Mi'kmaq (Cree, Métis …), Aboriginals, Aboriginal people, the First people, Indigenous persons, and more recently, in Nova Scotia, we hear L'nu. The School in Shubenacadie closed in June, 1967. On my first assignment in Terence Bay that year, I lived with three sisters who taught there.

It was not until six years later that I learned from students from small communities of African Nova Scotians that the Residential School was not an ordinary boarding school and that children were forced to go there. We were discussing Africville and how residents of that community had been treated when my students said, "Mrs. Sister, Africville was not as horrible as how the Indian kids were treated." They proceeded to tell me that children were forcibly removed from their parents and were punished if they spoke their mother tongue.

After questioning Sisters, I let myself feel better: we had not established the schools and were asked to teach and care for the children. Later, I scolded myself for excusing myself from thinking about what we could have done for it to be different, and I began to pray for those who suffered and for their extended families. I rejoiced anytime our sisters were welcome in Indian Brook and was glad our sisters participated with First Nations people in conferences, workshops, and professional days. I treasured comments made about some sisters who ministered in residential schools: about Sister Bea who was at Cranbrook and who "always prepared and served food for everyone and was so calm and smiled a lot" or hearing at the Indian Brook TRC hearing, "You look and speak like a sister who taught me at Shubie. I think she liked skating and tobogganing"

Some of our sisters have read *Out of the Depths*, *We Were Not the Savages*, *I Lost My Talk*, *Indian School Road*, *Missing Nimama*, *Fatty Legs*, and more. On Aboriginal Day, 2017, we (Sisters, Associates, and staff of Sisters of Charity Centre) participated in a lovely gathering at the Wi'kuom on the MSVU campus.

When we write the next piece of SC history, there will be much about Residential Schools, Truth and Reconciliation, and efforts at righting our relationships. Sisters Donna Geernaert and Geraldine Lancaster (with KAIROS friends), as well as others, keep trying to honour the truth and be intentional about reconciliation. Although many were ignorant about the situation, and many sisters were appreciated, honoured, and held in esteem, there is no doubt that our own study, prayer, and reflection of this horrific time will help us to own our complicity, whatever that looks like, and to embrace the spirit of the Truth and Reconciliation Commission.

Conclusion

There is much more I could write, but my third deadline for myself was "before Labour Day." I have other people and situations to attend to now and so maybe this is close to the ending of the *Afterword*.

As an international congregation with approximately 170 sisters in the United States and 120 in Canada, we continue to claim this identity and the challenges it brings. We realize that though we speak the same language, we are still made up of people born in the US and Canada. We also have one sister from each of three other countries: Guatamala, Peru, and Ireland. There are Acadian sisters and one African Nova Scotian. Our individual histories, theologies, and approaches to the future vary, and yet we share the common call to mission. We believe our future will be linked to the Sister of Charity Federation, which broadens our world, as the Federation has provinces in Korea and India and sisters living in Ecuador, Africa, and Guatamala, among other countries. Our common ties to the founders, to the charism, and to the belief that the "love of Christ urges us" to continue to open paths to a vital future.

Right now, we are trying to live our reality, to not put so much energy into the story of diminishment, but rather into honouring those who have made their journey and are with God. We look to the horizon. We use words like generativity, for we believe we are like nurse logs in an old forest that provide a place for new life to take root and grow. In nature, life follows death. We, as Christian women in the twenty-first century, call this the Paschal Mystery. We do some practical, necessary things to care for our sisters today and tomorrow. We continue our mission – sharing the gift of a call to give joyful witness to love. We stand on the margins, aware of our beautiful blue planet and its future saying, "*From this place we call home, how will we live Charity today?*"

Labour Day, September 4, 2017

About the Authors

- Mary Sweeney is a Sister of Charity. Following her years as a classroom teacher and administrator, she has served as a campus minister in universities in New England. Combining the elements of her own academic background (MA in English, M.Div and D.Min), she has written and presented on themes of spirituality and ministry. Mary has also agreed to act as overall editor of this volume.

- Martha Westwater, a Sister of Charity, who was born in Boston but spent most of her life in Canada. She is a life-long educator, who has taught at the primary, secondary, and tertiary level. Most of her professional life was spent at Mount Saint Vincent University, Halifax, NS. She holds a Ph.D. in English literature and at present resides in Wellesley Hills, MA. Today, she and a sister colleague coordinate an ESL program for employees in the retirement residence where they live.

- Sister Elaine Nolan, a Sister of Charity, is originally from Boston and now lives in that area. For many years she taught in primary and secondary education in New York, Nova Scotia, Washington, British Columbia, and Massachusetts. Her teaching focused on English, art, and music. She enjoys reading, photography, and poetry, and has a deep appreciation for the beauty of nature.

- Julia Heslin is a Sister of Charity who resides in Brooklyn, New York. After many years as a teacher and administrator in Catholic Elementary Schools and Early Childhood Education, she received her Doctorate in Educational Administration. She began ministering at St. John's University, serving as Executive Director of Special and Opportunity Programs, where she assisted students with academic potential who wished to enter the University. She completed her full-time ministry there and continues to minister part-time as a consultant for grants and scholarships.

- Dr. Heidi MacDonald (University of Lethbridge, Associate Professor) is a historian of twentieth-century Canada with specializations in Atlantic Canada, the Great Depression, women religious, and youth. Her recent publications include a co-edited monograph with Rosa Bruno-Jofré and Elizabeth Smyth, *Vatican II and Beyond: The Changing Mission and Identity of Canadian Women Religious* (Toronto and Kingston: McGill-Queen's University Press, 2017). Her current project, funded by the Social Sciences and Humanities Research Council of Canada, is on Women Religious in Atlantic Canada since 1960. Heidi graciously agreed to write the introduction to this book.

- Joan O'Keefe, SC was born in Dorchester, MA but has lived in Canada her whole religious life. She has an M.A. from St. Francis Xavier University, Antigonish. She ministered in Nova Scotia in four public schools, four parishes, and the Single Parent Centre (now Chebucto Family Centre). She is a volunteer doula. Currently she serves her sisters in Congregational Administration as the Congregational Leader of the Sisters of Charity, Halifax and is Chancellor of Mount Saint Vincent University.

CPSIA information can be obtained
at www.ICGtesting.com
Printed in the USA
BVHW031409190819
556217BV00002B/231/P